SERIES

Work Out

Economics

GCSE

The titles in this series

MACMILLAN
WORK OUT
SERIES

Work Out

Economics

GCSE

R. Young

MACMILLAN
EDUCATION

First published 1987
Reprinted 1988

Published by
MACMILLAN EDUCATION LTD
Houndmills, Basingstoke, Hampshire RG21 2XS
and London
Companies and representatives
throughout the world

Typeset by TecSet Ltd, Wallington, Surrey
Printed in Great Britain by The Bath Press Ltd, Avon

British Library Cataloguing in Publication Data
Young, Richard, *1955–*
Workout economics: GCSE.—(Macmillan
work out series)
1. Economics—Examinations, questions, etc.
I. Title
330′.076   HB171.5
ISBN 0–333–43665–2 Pbk

To Susan and David—with love

Contents

Preface

This book has been primarily designed to prepare candidates for the new GCSE examination in economics. In addition it should provide a useful reference for the first year of 'A' level studies, and for examinations which contain economics.

The new system of 16+ assessment represents a radical departure from existing practice:

> The GCSE involves a shift away from the acquisition and regurgitation of knowledge towards the ability to apply it. Syllabus content is being reduced considerably and 16-year-olds will be tested on whether they understand what they have learnt.
>
> Source: *The Times*, 17 February 1986

Work Out Economics GCSE is based on a thorough analysis of all the syllabuses set by the main examining groups listed in the Acknowledgements. The major emphasis has switched to assessing how well candidates know, understand and can use economics. A number of 'O' level topics find no place in the GCSE, or require a less detailed treatment.

This book has been structured to meet the demands of the new exam. Each chapter contains a summary of the essential economics that students need to know, together with complete answers to data response and extended answer questions. Each chapter ends with a number of short questions and answers which enable students to test their knowledge and understanding of a topic.

A large number of specimen GCSE questions have been included. I am grateful for the advice and help all the examining groups have given in explaining the functions and characteristics of GCSE Economics questions. The questions I have set, and all answer guidelines, are my sole responsibility and have not been provided or approved by an examining group.

Witney, Oxfordshire, 1987   R.Y.

Acknowledgements

The author and publishers wish to thank the following boards who have kindly given permission for the use of copyright material:

East Anglian Examinations Board
London and East Anglian Group for GCSE
Northern Ireland Schools Examinations Council
Southern Examining Group
Southern Regional Examinations Board
Welsh Joint Education Committee

All the examining groups would wish to point out that worked examples included in the text are entirely the responsibility of the author and have been neither provided nor approved by the board. They may not necessarily constitute the only possible solutions.

The London and East Anglian Group accepts no responsibility whatsoever for the accuracy or method of working in the answers given.

The author and publishers also thank the following who have given permission for the use of copyright material:

Associated Newspaper Group plc
Economics Association
Express Newspapers plc
Financial Times Ltd
The Controller of Her Majesty's
    Stationery Office
Manpower Services Commission
Medway City Council
Observer Ltd
Oxfordshire County Council
Rover Group
Stock Exchange

Times Newspapers Ltd
Barnaby's Picture Library
Black & Decker Ltd
British Steel Corp
Camera Press
Cement & Concrete Assoc
East Kilbride Development Corp
Kentish Times
Mersey Docks & Harbour Co
Thorn–EMI Domestic Electric
    Appliances Ltd

Every effort has been made to trace all copyright holders but if any have inadvertently been overlooked the publishers will be pleased to make the necessary arrangements at the first opportunity.

I thank the following for their helpful comments on the likely structure of GCSE economics examination questions: Derek Hender (LEAG); Andrew Thompson (MEG); Lillian Crombie (NEA); Walter Corbett (NISEC); Peter Stanbrook (SEG); Vic Hubbard (WJEC); Steve Hodkinson (University of Manchester); and Linda Thomas (University of London). I must also thank Linda Thomas and Andrew Leake (Latymer Upper School, Hammersmith) for their invaluable comments on the manuscript.

I am grateful to the following heads of economics for their careful reading and correction of the original typescript: Clarrie Haynes, Marlborough School,

Woodstock, Oxon; Brian Sangster, Burford School, Oxon; Mark Waterson, International School of Moshi, Tanzania; Laurence Whitehouse, Farnborough College.

I also thank the many students who have painstakingly worked their way through the examples: the class of 1986 at Matthew Arnold, the girls of St Clots and the chaps at Cokethorpe. I also want to thank Judy Trego for her typing. The staff of Macmillans have given the most thoughtful support and advice.

Most of all, I am grateful to my wife, Susan, for her patience, help and enthusiasm throughout. The initial design of all the artwork is hers.

Any failings which remain are entirely my own.

Organisations Responsible for GCSE Examinations

In the United Kingdom, examinations are administered by the following organisations. Syllabuses and examination papers can be ordered from the addresses given here:

Northern Examining Association (NEA)

Joint Matriculation Board (JMB)
Publications available from:
John Sherratt & Son Ltd
78 Park Road
Altrincham
Cheshire WA14 5QQ

North Regional Examinations Board
Wheatfield Road
Westerhope
Newcastle upon Tyne NE5 5JZ

Yorkshire and Humberside Regional Examinations Board (YREB)
Scarsdale House
136 Derbyside Lane
Sheffield S8 8SE

Associated Lancashire Schools Examining Board
12 Harter Street
Manchester M1 6HL

North West Regional Examinations Board (NWREB)
Orbit House
Albert Street
Eccles
Manchester M30 0WL

Midland Examining Group (MEG)

University of Cambridge Local Examinations Syndicate (UCLES)
Syndicate Buildings
Hills Road
Cambridge CB1 2EU

Oxford and Cambridge Schools Examination Board (O & C)
10 Trumpington Street
Cambridge CB2 1QB

Southern Universities' Joint Board
  (SUJB)
Cotham Road
Bristol BS6 6DD

East Midland Regional
  Examinations Board (EMREB)
Robins Wood House
Robins Wood Road
Aspley
Nottingham NG8 3NR

West Midlands Examinations
  Board (WMEB)
Norfolk House
Smallbrook
Queensway
Birmingham B5 4NJ

London and East Anglian Group (LEAG)

University of London School
  Examinations Board (L)
University of London Publications
  Office
52 Gordon Square
London WC1E 6EE

London Regional Examining Board
  (LREB)
Lyon House
104 Wandsworth High Street
London SW18 4LF

East Anglian Examinations Board
  (EAEB)
The Lindens
Lexden Road
Colchester
Essex CO3 3RL

Southern Examining Group (SEG)

The Associated Examining Board
  (AEB)
Stag Hill House
Guildford
Surrey GU2 5XJ

University of Oxford Delegacy of
  Local Examinations (OLE)
Ewert Place
Banbury Road
Summertown
Oxford OX2 7BZ

Southern Regional Examinations Board
  (SREB)
Avondale House
33 Carlton Crescent
Southampton
Hants SO9 4YL

South-East Regional Examinations
  Board (SEREB)
Beloe House
2–10 Mount Ephraim Road
Royal Tunbridge Wells
Kent TN1 1EU

South-Western Examinations Board
   (SWExB)
23–29 Marsh Street
Bristol BS1 4BP

Scottish Examination Board (SEB)

Publications available from:
Robert Gibson and Sons (Glasgow) Ltd
17 Fitzroy Place
Glasgow G3 7SF

Welsh Joint Education Committee (WJEC)

245 Western Avenue
Cardiff CF5 2YX

Northern Ireland Schools Examinations
   Council (NISEC)

Examinations Office
Beechill House
Beechill Road
Belfast BT8 4RS

Introduction

How to Use this Book

This book has been designed to help you prepare for your General Certificate in Secondary Education (GCSE) examination in economics. You will be assessed on how well you know, understand and can use economics.

Specifically, the new GCSE assesses five different skills:

(a) knowledge of factual information;
(b) understanding the use of information;
(c) application of information;
(d) analysis of information;
(e) judgement of information.

Not more than 40 per cent of the final mark is given for showing knowledge and understanding. The remaining 60 per cent must be earned by demonstrating your ability to apply and evaluate information.

Simply buying a revision text does not guarantee examination success. However, by working from this book over the months leading up to the final examination you will improve your ability to understand and apply key economic concepts.

Work Out Economics GCSE is not intended as a textbook but as a comprehensive revision manual. If there are topics you have not covered in class, refer to a good textbook and make notes on the relevant chapter.

The book is divided into self-contained chapters each covering a major topic. At the beginning of each chapter you will find a summary of the essential economics you need to know. Make sure you become thoroughly familiar with the material in these summaries.

Each chapter contains a number of worked examples of structured questions. You will find that these questions are made up of 'steps' with each answer requiring more detail than the last. Structured questions mainly assess your ability to apply, analyse and evaluate economic information. Naturally this requires a thorough knowledge and understanding of the topic.

The solutions given for each question are not intended as 'model' answers. It is important to remember that in economics there is almost always more than one 'correct' solution to any given problem. Use the answer given as an indication of the sort of analytical skills of evaluation and judgement you should be using yourself.

Within each chapter economics terms are in *italic* type for emphasis and are clearly defined in the text.

Each chapter ends with a set of short-answer questions to assess your knowledge and understanding of a topic. Do these questions without looking at the answers provided. If you give an incorrect solution to one of the questions then refer back to the relevant section in the revision notes.

Revision

Most courses in GCSE Economics are over two years. Ideally, preparation begins six months before the final examination! You cannot hope or expect to sustain intensive concentration for twenty-six weeks. Start by obtaining the syllabus from the appropriate examining group listed in the acknowledgements. Use the syllabus to write out a study plan, listing the topics you are going to revise each week.

Check that you have completed, as well as you can, the coursework assignments set by your board. Chapter 21 will help you to plan and write any outstanding items of coursework.

Build up to a period of intensive revision during the last four weeks before the exam. Many people find it helpful to write as they revise. Make notes on one side of loose-leaf paper. Leave generous margins in case you want to add new ideas.

In particular make sure that when you have finished a topic you can:

(a) define economic terms;
(b) list key points;
(c) apply important concepts;
(d) draw relevant graphs.

It is important to be able to draw graphs quickly and accurately, and a little practice will be needed.

The number of hours you put in is far less important than what you put into those hours. Most students find they can concentrate better and learn faster if they work in bursts of forty-five minutes with regular breaks. Avoid uninterrupted three-hour slogs. Promise yourself a special 'treat' at the end of a successful revision session.

Try to review material covered shortly after you have done it and again a few days later. Use the question section of a chapter to make sure you can still recall the main points. You will soon find that your ability to remember the topic has improved beyond all measure.

Make sure your study programme is balanced and that you allow time for enjoyment and relaxation.

Work hard, do your best and look forward to the long summer holidays when you can take a well-earned break.

The Examination

You are bound to be slightly nervous on the day of the exam. So is everyone else. Relax. GCSE is designed to let you show what you know, understand and can do. If you have done your revision you may find yourself enjoying the next couple of hours!

There are three main types of question in the final examination.

(a) Short-answer Questions

Short-answer questions mainly assess knowledge and understanding. These can be of four types as follows:

(i) Open-response questions

Here you fill in a blank sentence in a question. For example:

A merger between two brewing companies is an example of .... integration.

Horizontal is the answer.

(ii) Objective-test questions

These give you three options. One or more of the options given may be correct. You select your answer from one of the following options found on the examination paper. For example:

A if 1 and 2 only are correct
B if 2 and 3 only are correct
C if 1 only is correct
D if 3 only is correct

Which of the following goods is/are free?
1 sunshine in the desert
2 your birthday present
3 lambs in a field

C is the answer.

(iii) Multiple-choice questions

To answer these you have a list of options. You select the only correct option. For example:

Which of the following is an example of a consumer good?
A a delivery van
B an office
C a factory canteen
D a child's tricycle

D is the answer.

(iv) Matched-response questions

Here you are given two lists and asked to match the correct answers. For example:

Pair each of the following

A electricity   1 fixed cost
B rent   2 variable cost
C pollution   3 social cost

A2; B1; C3 are the answers.

(b) Data Response Questions

Data response questions are based on *data* (graphs and tables), photographs or a passage. They use the information given as a stimulus for a series of structured questions which mainly assess your ability to analyse, evaluate and judge.

You will find that all boards set compulsory data response questions. However, the questions are designed to let you show what you know, understand and can do.

The data will contain some economic message. What is the graph or table supposed to tell you? Has unemployment gone up perhaps?

Each question will be given a mark. Aim your answer at the marks given. If there is one mark for defining unemployment then you should answer briefly in a couple of sentences. If there are four marks for suggesting why unemployment has gone up then make sure you give four clear, correct and different points in your answer.

(c) Extended-answer Questions

Extended-answer questions aim to assess all five skills and are set in several parts. Marks are given for each part. Again, make sure you aim your answer at the marks.

Read through the section on extended-answer questions and decide the topic covered by each question. Only answer questions on topics you have revised. Only attempt questions where you can answer every part.

Once you have decided to attempt a question, briefly plan your answer.

Begin your answer by defining important economic terms in the question. Write in clear, simple, short sentences.

Arguments are best developed by **stating** a point, **explaining** that point and then giving an **example** (S E E). For instance, suppose part of a question asked, 'Give one advantage of the division of labour.' You might write:

> The firm may find that practice makes perfect. [**Statement**] If a worker continually repeats the same job he will become expert and increase his hourly output. [**Explanation**] For example, a worker in a car factory specialising in fitting window seals eventually performs the job quickly and efficiently. [**Example**]

Once a point has been fully developed, start a new paragraph. Include graphs if they are relevant to the set question.

No marks are earned if the answer is irrelevant to the set question. What you are writing may be complex and perfectly correct but the examiner cannot give you any marks for your effort. No marks are earned by waffle or by repeating points made earlier in an answer.

Make sure you do not forget to answer one part of the question. Do not spend too much time answering one particular question.

Set out your work neatly and clearly. Use your economics. Above all, make sure that what you are writing is relevant and answers the set question.

Good luck!

1 Basic Economic Problems

1.1 Scarcity

(a) Unlimited Wants

Humans have many different types of wants and needs. Economics looks only at man's material wants and needs. These are satisfied by *consuming* (using) either *goods* (physical items such as food) or *services* (non-physical items such as heating).

There are three reasons why wants and needs are virtually unlimited:

  (i) goods eventually wear out and need to be replaced;
 (ii) new or improved products become available;
(iii) people get fed up with what they already own.

(b) Limited Resources

Commodities (goods and services) are produced by using *resources*. The resources shown in Table 1.1 are sometimes called *factors of production*.

Table 1.1   Different types of resource

Type	Description	Reward
Land	All natural resources	Rent
Labour	The physical and mental work of people	Wages
Capital	All man-made tools and machines	Interest
Enterprise	All managers and organisers	Profit

(c) Types of Commodity

A *free good* is available to everyone at no charge, for example air. An *economic good* is a commodity in limited supply. Figure 1.1 on the next page illustrates different types of economic good.

Expenditure on *producer* or *capital goods* is called *investment*.

(d) The Economic Problem

The *economic problem* refers to the *scarcity* of commodities. There is only a limited amount of resources available to produce the unlimited amount of goods and services we desire.

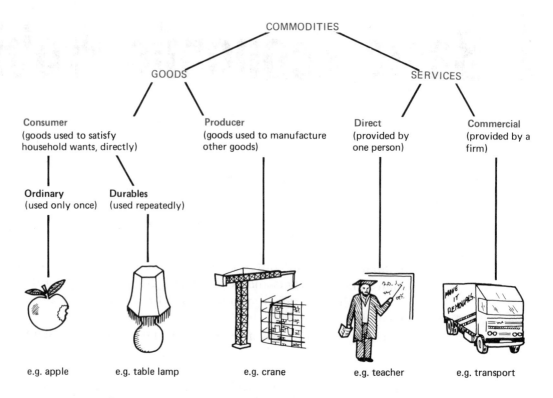

Figure 1.1 Types of good and service

Society has to decide which commodities to make. For example, do we make missiles or hospitals? We have to decide how to make those commodities. Do we employ robot arms or workers? Who is going to use the goods that are eventually made? Do we build a sports hall in Wigan or Woking?

1.2 Opportunity Cost

The *opportunity cost* principle states the cost of one good in terms of the next best alternative. For example, a gardener decides to grow carrots on his allotment. The opportunity cost of his carrot harvest is the alternative crop that might have been grown instead (e.g. potatoes). Further examples are given in Table 1.2.

Table 1.2 Examples of opportunity cost decisions

Group	Decision
Individual	Should I buy a record or a revision book?
School	Should we build a music block or tennis courts?
Country	Should we increase police pay or pensions?

1.3 Economic Systems

An *economic system* is the way a society sets about *allocating* (deciding) which goods to produce and in which quantities. Different countries have different methods of tackling the economic problem. There are three main types of economy.

(a) Market Economies

A *market or capitalist economy* is where resources are allocated by prices without government intervention. The USA and Hong Kong are examples of market economies where:

(i) Firms decide the type and quantity of goods to be made. An increase in the price of one good encourages producers to switch resources into the production of that commodity.

(ii) Consumers decide the type and quantity of goods to be bought. A decrease in the price of one good encourages consumers to switch to buying that commodity. People on high incomes are able to buy more goods and services than are the less well off.

(b) Command Economies

In a *command-planned* or *socialist* economy the government owns most resources and decides on the type and quantity of a good to be made. The USSR and North Korea are examples of command economies. The government sets output targets for each district and factory and allocates the necessary resources. Incomes are often more evenly spread out than in other types of economy.

(c) Mixed Economies

In a *mixed economy* privately owned firms generally produce non-essential goods while the government organises the manufacture of essential goods and services such as education and health care. The United Kingdom is an example of a mixed economy.

1.4 Worked Examples

Example 1.1

Study the drawings on the next page and answer the questions which follow.
(a) Use the drawings to give one example of each of the following.

    (i) free goods;   **(1 mark)**
    (ii) economic goods;   **(1 mark)**
    (iii) consumer goods;   **(1 mark)**
    (iv) producer goods.   **(1 mark)**

(b) Explain why you think one of the drawings is a free good.   **(2 marks)**
(c) Explain why you think one of the goods is an economic good.   **(2 marks)**
(d) Using the drawings, briefly explain the main differences between a consumer good and a producer good.   **(3 marks)**
(e) Select one of the economic goods shown in the drawings and describe the type of resources used in its manufacture.   **(5 marks)**

Solution 1.1

(a) (i) Sunshine in the desert; (ii) a television (or van, tricycle or crane); (iii) a child's tricycle; (iv) a delivery van.

(b) A free good is any item which is not scarce and is available to everyone without any payment. Two free goods shown in the diagram are sun and sand in the desert. These are available to anyone in the location at zero cost.

(c) An economic good is any item in limited supply. In fact, all the items shown are economic goods except the sunshine and sand in the desert. Therefore two examples are the television and crane.

(d) A consumer good is an item used to satisfy household wants and needs, i.e. the television and child's tricycle. A producer good is an item used to help manufacture other goods. The delivery van and crane are not useful in themselves but are useful because they are used to move goods. Therefore they are producer goods.

(e) Goods are produced using the four resources of land, labour, capital and enterprise. A tricycle is made mainly from the natural resource of iron. Iron ore has to be dug out of the ground and then smelted down into iron. At the steelworks the iron is processed and then drawn into steel tubes.

The tricycle factory uses labour and machines to turn raw materials into finished products. Usually, each worker concentrates on one task with the tricycle moving down a conveyor belt. Machines can be used to weld the metal and paint the finished frame.

Labour is involved directly on the shop floor in production and indirectly in management. Managers organise the production, distribution (i.e. transportation) and sale of the finished good.

Example 1.2

(a) Consumer durables are items used to satisfy household wants over many years. Give three examples of consumer durables shown in the picture. **(2 marks)**
(b) Why is a consumer durable eventually replaced? **(3 marks)**
(c) Write down two examples of the type of consumer durables you would expect to be owned by:

(i) an elderly person living on her pension; **(1 mark)**
(iii) a successful pop star. **(1 mark)**

(d) Why is the pop star likely to own more consumer durables? **(1 mark)**
(e) Explain two major factors which determine the amount of goods bought each week by the pensioner. **(2 marks)**
(f) How can the production of consumer goods be increased? **(2 marks)**
(g) What are the difficulties facing a country which wants more capital goods?
(4 marks)

Solution 1.2

(a) A fridge, toaster and glasses are examples of consumer durables.

(b) Even though a consumer durable can be used again and again there comes a point when it becomes worn out and needs to be replaced. Some people buy a new consumer durable before the old one is completely worn out because the product has been improved or because they would like a change.

(c) A pensioner is likely to own an inexpensive radio and a black-and-white television. A pop star is likely to own luxury goods such as an expensive car and a swimming pool.

(d) The pop star owns more consumer durables because he receives a much higher income than the pensioner.

(e) The size of the state pension received by the elderly person and the price of goods will determine the amount bought. High prices and a small pension will allow only a few goods to be bought each week.

(f) The production of goods and services requires resources. An increase in the quantity of resources or the better use of existing resources can be used to increase the production of consumer goods.

(g) Producing more capital goods is called investment. The manufacture of more capital goods requires the initial sacrifice of some consumer goods. A country has to switch resources out of the production of, say, private motor cars. These resources are then used to manufacture more machines. In the short run there will be fewer cars available to satisfy consumers' wants and needs. However, once the extra machines have been built then there will be a larger number of consumer goods available.

 The long-term benefit of more capital goods has to be balanced against the short-term loss of the reduced current production of consumer goods.

Example 1.3

(a) From the following list give examples of (i) two goods and (ii) two services: retailing; a blast furnace; a doctor; banking; a cigarette; a delivery van.

(2 marks)

(b) What is meant by the economic terms 'scarcity' and 'choice'? **(2 marks)**

(c) Using a simple example, explain the opportunity cost involved in buying a good.

(3 marks)

(d) Using a simple example, explain the opportunity cost involved in manufacturing a good. **(4 marks)**

(e) How does the UK decide on the amount of health care to be provided to the general public? **(5 marks)**

Solution 1.3

(a) A good is a tangible item used to satisfy our wants. Two examples of goods in the list are a blast furnace and a cigarette. (A third good is a delivery van.) A service is an invisible item used to satisfy our wants. Two examples of services given in the list are retailing and a doctor. (A third service is banking.)

(b) Scarcity occurs when the resources available to a country are unable to produce a sufficient quantity of commodities to meet desires. Choice occurs because resources are limited and consumers have to choose between alternatives.

(c) The opportunity cost of consuming a good is the sacrifice of the next best alternative. The decision to buy a record means giving up the opportunity of buying a jumper. Therefore the opportunity cost of consuming the record is the forgone jumper.

(d) The opportunity cost of producing a good is the next best alternative that could have been made with the same resources. The decision to build a Channel tunnel involves the use of resources that could have been used to construct £4000 million worth of new houses. Therefore the opportunity cost of producing the channel tunnel is the forgone housing.

(e) The major supplier of health care in the UK is the National Health Service (NHS), which is a government department. The government decides on the type and quantity of health care to be provided in each region of the country and then allocates a sum of money. Local health authorities then decide on the best use of limited funds. Some people have to wait until the resources needed for their treatment are available.

Health care is also provided by the private sector. Some people belong to insurance schemes such as the British United Provident Association (BUPA) which allows them to pay for immediate medical treatment whenever they are ill.

Example 1.4

Imagine you are marooned and alone on a small uninhabited desert island. Resources are anything which can be used to produce a good or a service.
(a) How would each of the following items be economically useful:

(i) a transistor radio;	**(2 marks)**
(ii) a penknife;	**(2 marks)**
(iii) a can of baked beans?	**(2 marks)**

(b) Using the headings land, labour and capital, describe the resources you have available on your desert island. **(5 marks)**
(c) What would be the opportunity cost of building a new hut? **(2 marks)**
(d) How useful would money be on your desert island? **(2 marks)**

Solution 1.4

(a) (i) A transistor radio is a consumer durable and would be useful in supplying information and entertainment until such time as the batteries run out.
(ii) A penknife is a capital good which would be economically useful in helping to produce other commodities. For example, the knife could be used to fashion a wooden spear to catch fish.
(iii) A can of baked beans is a consumer good which temporarily satisfies hunger.

(b) Land refers to all natural resources on the island. These may include fresh water, trees, plants, and animals.

Labour refers to human resources. Since you are alone on an uninhabited desert island you are the sole source of labour.

Capital refers to man-made resources. The only items of capital on the island will be any possessions you happen to have which could be used to help make other goods, e.g. a pair of scissors. After a while you may be able to manufacture some tools such as a stone axe and these will then be items of capital.

(c) The opportunity cost of building a new hut will be the next best preferred alternative you could have made instead, e.g. a canoe.

(d) Money is any asset which people are prepared to accept in exchange for goods and services. Money is useless in the absence of someone to exchange goods with. Paper money could be used to fuel a fire.

Example 1.5

Read the following passage carefully and then answer the questions below.

> All societies have to decide the best use for scarce resources. In a market economy the *allocation of resources* is decided by the price mechanism.
>
> A *glut* of a good forces producers to lower price and to think about producing some alternative commodity. A *shortage* of a good encourages consumers to pay more or to switch to buying some alternative item.
>
> In a planned economy the government allocates resources to the production of those goods most likely to be needed by consumers. Shortages and gluts occur when the government does not predict demand and supply accurately.

(a) Give briefly the meaning of the following terms:

    (i) allocation of resources;   **(2 marks)**
    (ii) shortage;   **(1 mark)**
    (iii) glut.   **(1 mark)**

(b) Who is responsible for production in:
    (i) a market economy, (ii) a planned economy?   **(2 marks)**

(c) How do producers in a market economy react to a shortage?   **(2 marks)**
(d) Why do shortages of some goods occur in a planned economy?   **(2 marks)**
(e) Using examples, explain the type of resources allocated in the UK:

    (i) by the price mechanism;   **(3 marks)**
    (ii) by the government?   **(3 marks)**

Solution 1.5

(a)   (i) The allocation of resources involves deciding the amount of land, labour and capital to be used in the production of different commodities.
    (ii) A shortage of a good occurs when the amount demanded by consumers exceeds the available supply.
    (iii) A glut of a good occurs when producers have made more of a commodity than consumers are willing to buy.

(b)   (i) In a market economy production is organised by private firms with no direct government interference.
    (ii) In a planned economy, production is organised by firms owned by the government. The government sets each factory a production target.

(c) In a market where demand exceeds supply the price of the good will rise. In the next time period firms will decide that the higher price of the good makes it profitable to put extra resources into its manufacture.

(d) In a planned economy the state has to anticipate the likely demand for a good and set the necessary production targets. If in the meantime consumer preferences change or if factories do not meet their output targets, then shortages of some goods will occur.

(e) The UK is a mixed economy where the private sector allocates resources to the production of non-essential items such as cars. The private sector uses prices and profits as a signal to switch resources between the manufacture of different commodities.

The state directly allocates resources in the production of essential commodities such as defence and law and order. The level of resources used by the state is a political decision of the government of the day.

There are a number of state-owned firms (nationalised industries) which allocate resources in basic industries such as coal. The government has the final say on the amount of resources used by public corporations.

1.5 Questions

1 Which of the following would you consider to be consumer goods?:
   A coal stocks at a power station   B coal stocks at your home
   C your personal calculator   D your school's computer
   E your family's TV set   F a security TV camera in a shop
   G a postman's bicycle   H your bicycle
                                         (WJEC specimen GCSE)

2 Which of the following would you consider to be providing a service:

   A coal miner   B teacher   C farmer   D fisherman

3 What do economists mean by the word ' production'?

4 Resources are sometimes called:
   A profits   B transfer earnings
   C factors of production   D wages and salaries

5 The payment made to entrepreneurs for taking on the risk of production is called
   ....

6 State the four rewards to the factors of production.

7 Which one of the following is an economic good?
   A sun in the desert   B air
   C coal that has been mined   D sea water in the ocean

8 Which one of the following is a free good?
   A air   B street lighting
   C television programmes   D your birthday present

9 Which one of the following is normally called a consumer good?
   A an office word processor   B a salesman's car
   C an office   D a private telephone

10 Which one of the following is the best example of a capital good?
   A a motor cycle   B a radio
   C a gun   D a delivery van

11 When a business man buys a new machine it is known as ....

12 The economic problem facing all economies is:
   A inequality   B value
   C scarcity of resources   D low economic growth

13 All wants cannot be met because of the problem of:
   A unemployment   B inflation
   C greed   D scarcity

14 Opportunity cost is the:
   A unit cost of the good   B total cost of the good
   C cost of producing one more of   D loss of the next best alternative
      the good

15 Your school decides to invest in building a new library. Suggest what the opportunity cost might be.

16 If a man buys a new computer he may not be able to afford to go on holiday. This is an example of:
    A social cost   B opportunity cost
    C total cost   D variable cost

17 In a capitalist economy the price mechanism:
    A allocates resources   B raises taxes
    C reduces competition   D measures national income

18 Market economies do *not* have:
    A stock exchange   B prices
    C public corporations   D exchange rates

19 A mixed economy has:
    A private and public enterprise   B imports and exports
    C large and small firms   D industrial and agricultural sectors

20 The problem of what to produce in a command economy is mainly solved by:
    A supply and demand   B the profit motive
    C government instructions   D consumer wants

21 Which one of the following countries has a centrally planned economy?
    A Portugal   B Nigeria   C China   D Chile

1.6 Answers

1 **B, C, E, H**   2 **B**
3 The manufacture of a good or a service.
4 **C**   5 Profit
6 Wages, rent, interest and profits.   7 **C**   8 **A**
9 **D**   10 **D**   11 Investment   12 **C**
13 **D**   14 **D**
15 Any alternative that could have been made with the same resources, e.g. a swimming pool.   16 **B**   17 **A**   18 **C**
19 **A**   20 **C**   21 **C**

2 Population

2.1 Population Size

(a) Method of Calculation

The study of population statistics is called *demography*. Since 1801 a population *census* (survey) of the UK has been held every ten years to count the number of people in the country. The growth of the UK population over the last 180 years is discussed in Example 2.1.

A census is carried out because the government needs to plan ahead. The figures can be used to estimate the number of roads, schools, hospitals, etc. likely to be needed in the future.

(b) Birth Rate

The *birth rate* is the number of births per thousand of the population in a year. The birth rate has fallen from 28.6 in 1900 to 12.8 in 1986. This dramatic fall has been caused by:

(i) Improved birth control. Contraceptives are now more available and socially accepted.
(ii) Women choosing to continue working, or waiting before raising smaller families.

(c) Death Rate

The *death rate* is the number of deaths per thousand of the population in a year. The death rate has fallen from 18.4 in 1900 to 11.7 in 1986. This fall has been caused by:

(i) Improved housing, diet and sanitation.
(ii) Improved health care through medical discoveries and introduction of the National Health Service.

(d) Migration

Migration happens when people either permanently leave a country (*emigration*) or enter it (*immigration*). *Net migration* is the difference between the number of people emigrating and immigrating.

People usually want to leave countries (*voluntary emigration*) for two reasons:

(i) *Push factors* which include high unemployment, low living standards or poor climate in their own country.

(ii) *Pull factors* which include good job prospects, and high living standards in a new country.

Figure 2.1 sums up the factors influencing population size.

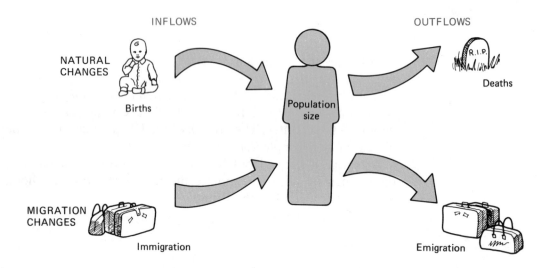

Figure 2.1   Population changes

2.2   Population Structure

(a) Population Structure by Sex and Age

Population pyramids can be used to show the sex and age structure of a particular country. Figure 2.2 gives two examples. Developed countries tend to

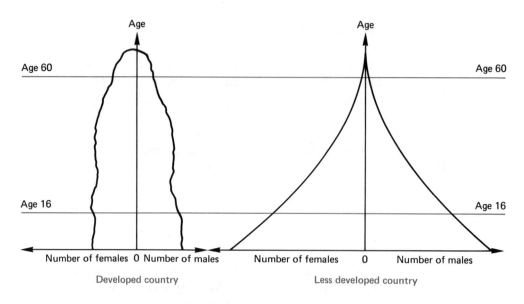

Figure 2.2   Population pyramids

have an even sex and age structure while less developed ones have over half their population aged under 16.

An *ageing population* occurs when the average age per person is rising.

(b) Population Structure by Area

There is an uneven spread of population about the country because:

 (i) Some areas are remote, hilly or uninhabitable.
 (ii) Farming areas employ few people.
(iii) Industry is concentrated in towns.

80 per cent of the UK population live in England, largely in the south-east and midlands. 80 per cent of people live in *urban* (built-up) areas. 20 cities have a population of more than 250 000. The seven UK *conurbations* (several towns joined together) house a third of the population but they occupy only 3 per cent of the land area.

2.3 Optimum Population

(a) T. R. Malthus

Writing at the end of the eighteenth century, Malthus argued that:

 (i) Population rises in a *geometric way*, i.e. 1, 2, 4, 8, 16.
 (ii) The food supply rises *arithmetically*, i.e. 1, 2, 3, 4, 5.

Only war, famine and plague would prevent absolute poverty.

Malthus did not take into account the spread of birth-control techniques which reduced the rate of population growth. Malthus also overlooked the effects of future farming inventions, and the development of foreign trade which dramatically increased the food supply.

(b) Optimum Population

 (i) *Optimum* (best) *population* occurs when *productivity* output per person) is highest.
 (ii) An *under-populated* country can increase productivity by increasing its population.
(iii) An *over-populated* country can increase productivity by reducing its population.

2.4 Worked Examples

Example 2.1

The table shows the number of people living in each country in the United Kingdom in various years. Study the information and answer all the questions which follow.

	Population (in thousands) of				
Year	United Kingdom	England	Wales	Scotland	N. Ireland
1801	unknown	8 306	587	1 608	unknown
1851	22 259	16 765	1163	2 889	1 442
1901	38 237	30 515	2 013	4 472	1 237
1951	50 225	41 159	2 599	5 096	1 371
1981	55 848	46 363	2 792	5 131	1 562

Source: Adapted from *Annual Abstract of Statistics*, No. 122, HMSO, 1986

(a) Name the country in the UK with:

    (i) the largest population in 1981; **(1 mark)**
    (ii) a declining population between 1851 and 1901. **(1 mark)**

(b) From the table:
    (i) Find the number of people living in Scotland in 1981. **(1 mark)**
    (ii) Calculate the percentage increase in population of England between 1801 and 1981. **(2 marks)**
    (iii) Find the country with the most stable population since 1951. **(2 marks)**
(c) What is a census? **(1 mark)**
(d) Why do you think the size of population sometimes falls? **(4 marks)**
(e) Give three reasons why the government carries out a census. **(3 marks)**

Solution 2.1

(a)   (i) The country with the largest population in 1981 was England.
    (ii) Northern Ireland had a declining population between 1851 and 1901.

(b)   (i) The number of people living in Scotland in 1981 was 5 131 000.
    (ii) The percentage increase in the population of England between 1801 and 1981 can be found using the equation:

$$\text{Population increase} = \frac{1981 \text{ population} - 1801 \text{ population}}{1801 \text{ population}} \times 100$$

$$= \frac{46\ 363 - 8306}{8306} \times 100 = 458\%$$

    (iii) The country with the smallest percentage change in population since 1951 will have the most stable population. This was Scotland, where the increase between 1951 and 81 was

$$[(5131 - 5096) / 5096] \times 100 = 0.69\%.$$

(c) A census is a survey carried out by the government every ten years which counts the number of people living in the UK.
(d) Population size depends on the number of inflows and outflows from a country over a given period of time. If the number of births and immigrants is smaller than the number of deaths and emigrants then the population size will fall.

(e) A census is carried out so that the government knows the total number and age of people living in the country and in each region. Census information allows the government to plan ahead and anticipate the amount of social services to be provided. The government may decide on the basis of population trends revealed in the census that a series of new towns is needed to cope with an increasing number of young families or that some secondary schools need to be closed because of fewer pupils in the 11 to 16 age category.

Example 2.2

The table shows the number of people living in the UK, the number of births, and the number of deaths for three different years. Study the information carefully and answer all the questions which follow.

Year	Population (thousands)	Total births (thousands)	Total deaths (thousands)
1901	38 237	1095	341
1951	50 225	803	307
1981	55 848	731	332

Source: *Annual Abstract of Statistics*, No. 122, HMSO, 1986

(a) Name the year with:

    (i) the lowest number of deaths; **(1 mark)**
    (ii) the largest natural increase in population; **(2 marks)**
    (iii) the lowest birth rate. **(2 marks)**

(b) What has happened to the number of births between 1901 and 1981? Give three reasons to explain your answer. **(6 marks)**

(c) How can the size of population increase between 1951 and 1981 while at the same time the number of deaths is rising and the number of births is falling? **(4 marks)**

Solution 2.2

(a)   (i) 1951 saw the lowest number of deaths.

    (ii) The natural increase in population in any one year can be found by subtracting the number of births from the number of deaths. In 1901 the natural increase in the population was the largest for any year in the table at:

$$1\ 095\ 000 - 341\ 000 = 754\ 000.$$

    (iii) The birth rate is the number of births per thousand of the population in a year and is found using the equation:

$$\text{Birth rate} = \frac{\text{Number of births}}{\text{Size of population}} \times 1000.$$

In 1981 the birth rate was lowest at $\dfrac{731\ 000 \times 1000}{55\ 848\ 000} = 13.1.$

(b) The number of births fell between 1901 and 1981 mainly because of the greater availability and greater social acceptance of contraceptive techniques

The twentieth century has also seen a radical change in society's attitude to the economic role of women, who are now far less prepared to act as unpaid housekeepers. As a consequence of women continuing in their careers the birth rate has fallen.

Social attitudes to large families have also changed over the last eighty years. Households are electing to reduce the number of children in the family and enjoy a higher standard of living.

(c) While an increase in the number of deaths and a fall in the number of births will tend to reduce the size of the population, the total number of births and deaths must be compared. If the number of births is still larger than the number of deaths then there has been a natural increase in the size of population.

The overall change in population will take account of natural changes and net migration.

Example 2.3

Study diagrams A and B which show natural changes and net migration trends for the population of the United Kingdom. Answer all the questions which follow.

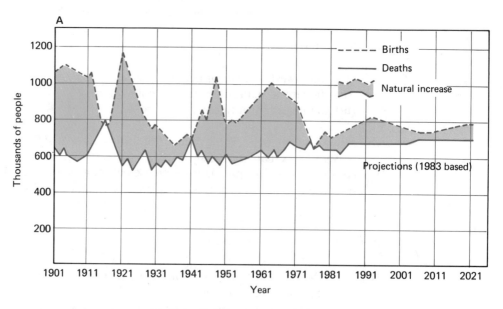

A   United Kingdom natural increase

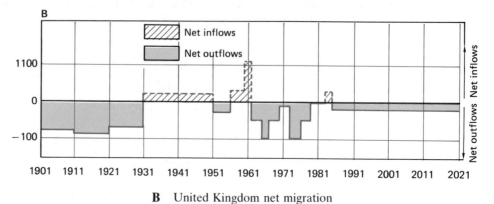

B   United Kingdom net migration

Source: Adapted from *Social Trends 16*, HMSO, 1986

(a) What was the number of deaths in 1981? **(1 mark)**
(b) In what year was the number of births highest? **(1 mark)**
(c) Calculate the natural increase in population in 1951. **(1 mark)**
(d) In what years was net migration positive? **(1 mark)**
(e) During what period after 1945 did the population size fall? **(2 marks)**
(f) Use the data provided to comment briefly on the economic effects of net migration from 1961 to 1987. **(6 marks)**
(g) The graphs show possible future changes in population. Comment briefly on the possible economic effects after 1985 of the trends in:

     (i) births, (ii) deaths. **(8 marks)**

Solution 2.3

(a) There were 640 000 deaths in 1981.
(b) The number of births was highest in 1921.
(c) The natural increase in population is found by measuring the vertical distance between the births and deaths lines in graph A. In 1951 the natural increase in population was approximately 190 000.
(d) Positive net migration means more people have come to live in a country than have left to live abroad. This is shown by the net inflow areas on graph B, i.e. 1931–51; 1956–62; and 1983–5.
(e) There was a net decrease in population in the mid-1970s when net migration was negative and larger than the natural increase in the population.
(f) With the exception of 1983–5 there have been a larger number of people permanently leaving the country than entering. The economic effects of net emigration depends on the type of person leaving.

    If an emigrant is highly skilled then the country loses the benefit of his training and output. Moreover, those people who used to supply goods and services to the emigrant will suffer a fall in their sales and income. The government will receive less tax revenue.

    If an emigrant is a dependant (i.e. not engaged in the production of commodities) then there will be reduced state expenditure on welfare services such as education and pensions.

(g) (i) There may be a continual increase in the number of births up to the year 1993. Initially, this may require greater provision of maternity services. After a few years there may be a surge in the demand for primary school places which may require greater resources being devoted to education.

      After 1993 there may be a decline in the number of births until 2005, after which the trend may once again be upwards. This suggests that from 1993 until the turn of the century child-related industries may suffer a period of decline.

   (ii) In spite of the overall increase in the size of population over the next forty years the number of deaths may be stable. This suggests that the average age of the population may increase. This involves increasing the provision of elderly-related products such as health and social care. There may also be a larger amount of pension payments to be found from the income of the employed.

Example 2.4

Population pyramids show the sex and age structure of a country. Diagram A shows the sex and age structure of the UK in 1984. Diagram B shows the likely structure in 2001. Study the diagrams and answer all the questions which follow.

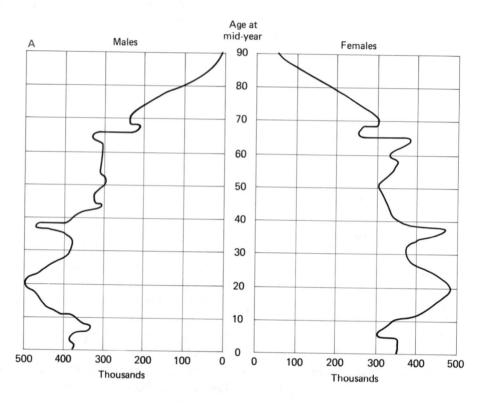

A   United Kingdom population by sex and age, 1984

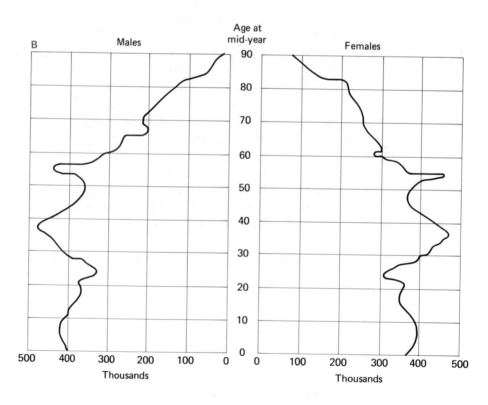

B   United Kingdom population by sex and age, 2001

(a) Which age has the largest number of females in 1984? **(1 mark)**

(b) How many males are aged 20 in (i) 1984 and (ii) 2001? **(2 marks)**

(c) Using the information given in the diagram suggest the likely changes between 1984 and 2001 in:

    (i) the number of school children; **(2 marks)**

    (ii) the number of people older than 75. **(1 mark)**

(d) Using the information given in the diagram advise the government on its future policy for each of the following:

    (i) education provision for the 16–21 age group; **(5 marks)**

    (ii) welfare services for the over 65s. **(4 marks)**

Solution 2.4

(a) The age 20 has the largest number of females in 1984.

(b) There are 500 000 males aged 20 in 1984 and 360 000 males aged 20 in 2001.

(c)   (i) Given that the compulsory school qualifying and leaving age stays at 5 and 16, the number of school children under the age of 11 will increase while the number aged between 12 and 16 will fall.

    (ii) The diagram suggests an increase in the number of people living past the age of 75.

(d)   (i) Between now and the end of the century there will be a very large fall in the number of young people of both sexes aged 16 to 21. Falling rolls can be used to save money through the amalgamation or closure of colleges. This money can then be used to increase the provision of other welfare services or to reduce taxation. Alternatively, the fall in the number of students can be used to reduce class sizes thereby increasing the standard of tuition.

    (ii) The number of people aged between 65 and 75 will fall over the next 17 years. This suggests scope for reducing the provision of resources for the active retired. However, the number of elderly aged over 75 will increase. This will require a significant increase in the provision of medical and welfare care. There will be an increased demand for hospital beds and health visitors. The old particularly feel the effect of cold weather and there will be an increased demand for heating.

Example 2.5

A

B

Study the photographs here. Picture A shows a bazaar area in New Delhi, India, picture B a shopping precinct in Tokyo, Japan.

(a) Which photograph suggests that the people have a low standard of living?

(1 mark)

(b) State two pieces of evidence in the photograph to support your answer to question (a). **(2 marks)**
(c) Account for the absence of motor cars in each photograph. **(2 marks)**
(d) Both countries have a high population. One has an *optimum population* while the other is *over-populated*.

    (i) Which photograph shows optimum population? **(1 mark)**
    (ii) Which photograph shows over-population? **(1 mark)**
    (iii) What do the words *in italics* mean? **(4 marks)**

(e) Suggest why one country has become over-populated. **(4 marks)**

Solution 2.5

(a) Picture A suggests a low standard of living.
(b) The woman carrying the basket has no shoes and the buildings look run down.
(c) There are no cars in picture A because few citizens in Delhi can afford to maintain one. The shopping area in picture B has no cars but this is probably because they have been banned to make way for a pedestrian precinct.

(d) (i) Picture B shows optimum population.
    (ii) Picture A shows over-population.
    (iii) Optimum means the best. Optimum population occurs when a country's population combines with resources to give the highest possible output per person.
    Over-population occurs when a decrease in population would result in an increase in productivity.

(e) Over-population is caused by too large an increase in the number of people in a country. This could be the result of a high birth rate caused by early marriage and the absence of birth control techniques. Medical advances have reduced the death rate, further adding to the natural increase in the population.

A second reason why a country becomes over-populated is through a large number of immigrants. If one country suffers a disaster such as a famine, many people will be forced to seek refuge in a neighbouring country. If their stay becomes permanent, over-population may result.

2.5 Questions

1 State two reasons why a census is carried out.
2 What is meant by the phrase 'birth rate'?
3 State two reasons why the birth rate might fall.
4 What is meant by the term 'death rate'?
5 State two reasons why the death rate might rise.
6 Emigration refers to:
    A the number of people permanently living in a country
    B the number of people permanently leaving a country
    C the number of people permanently entering a country
    D the natural increase in the population
7 State three factors which determine the size of a country's population.

8 Total population: 60 000 000.
   Live births: 800 000.
   Registered deaths: 600 000.

   Calculate:

   (a) the death rate;
   (b) the birth rate;
   (c) the natural increase in population.

9 A population pyramid usually shows:
   A the birth rate   B the death rate
   C the geographical distribution of population
   D the age and sex distribution of population
10 State two reasons for the uneven spread of population about the UK.
11 A population which gives maximum output per person is known as ....
   population.
12 What is meant by the phrase 'ageing population'?
13 Optimum population is reached when:
   A emigration and immigration are in balance
   B real income per head is at the highest level
   C birth rates and death rates are equal
   D there is the same number of women as men

14 Size of population (millions)	10	20	20	40	50
Total output (£ billions)	40	110	180	200	200

   What is the optimum size of the population?

2.6 Answers

1 Any two of the following:
   (a) To find the number of people living in the country.
   (b) To calculate changes in population since the last census.
   (c) To find the geographical distribution of people
   (d) To plan the type of social services needed in the future.
2 The number of births per thousand of the population in a year.
3 See section 2.1(b).
4 The number of deaths per thousand of the population in a year.
5 Any two of the following: (a) an outbreak of war, famine, disease or some other
   natural disaster; (b) a fall in living standards.
6 **B**
7 Any three factors which affect the number of births, deaths or migration.

8 (a) $\dfrac{\text{Registered deaths}}{\text{Population}} \times 1000 = \dfrac{600\ 000}{60\ 000\ 000} \times 1000 = 10.$

   (b) $\dfrac{\text{Live births}}{\text{Population}} \times 1000 = \dfrac{800\ 000}{60\ 000\ 000} \times 1000 = 13.33.$

   (c) Live births – Registered deaths = 800 000 – 600 000 = 200 000.
9 **D**   10 See section 2.2(b).   11 optimum
12 The average age of the population is rising.   13 **B**
14 By dividing each population level into each output level you will find that output
   per person is highest at £6000 when the population size is *30 million*.

3 Production

3.1 Specialisation

Specialisation happens when one individual, region or country concentrates in making one good.

(a) Division of Labour

The *division of labour* is a particular type of specialisation where the production of a good is broken up into many separate tasks each performed by one person. An early economist, Adam Smith, suggested that without any help one worker could produce only ten pins in one day. However, in a pin factory where each worker performs only one task, ten workers using the division of labour principle, could produce a daily total of 48 000 pins. Output per person (*productivity*) rose from 10 to 4800 when the division of labour principle was used.

(b) Advantages of the Division of Labour

The division of labour raises output, thereby reducing costs per unit, for the following reasons:

   (i) Continually repeating a task improves the skill of the worker.
   (ii) Time is not wasted setting up tools for different tasks and in moving between jobs.
   (iii) Workers can specialise in tasks best suited to their abilities.
   (iv) Expensive machinery can be used all the time.
   (v) Each task requires little skill, so workers are more easily trained.

(c) Disadvantages of the Division of Labour

Eventually the division of labour will actually reduce productivity and increase unit costs for the following reasons:

   (i) Continually repeating a task may become boring.
   (ii) Workers begin to take less pride in their work.
   (iii) If one machine breaks down then the entire factory stops.
   (iv) Some workers receive a very narrow training and may not be able to find alternative jobs.
   (v) Mass-produced goods lack variety.

(d) Limits to the Division of Labour

   (i) Mass production requires mass demand.
  (ii) The transport system must be good enough to reach a large number of consumers (*mass market*).
 (iii) *Barter* is the direct exchange of goods for other goods. Each worker creates only part of the finished goods, therefore the division of labour cannot be used in a barter society.

(e) Automation

The introduction of conveyor belts at the turn of the century allowed *mass production* (very large output). *Automation* refers to intensive use of machinery in production.

3.2 Costs of Production and Revenue

(a) Total Costs

A *firm* organises the manufacture of a good or service. An *industry* is made up of all those firms producing the same commodity. The amount spent on producing a given amount of a good is called *total cost*, *TC*, and is found by adding together variable and fixed costs.

(b) Variable Costs

Variable costs, *VC*, depend on how many goods are being made (*output*). If just one more unit is made then total variable costs rise. Variable costs include the following:

  (i) weekly wages paid to the shop floor workers;
 (ii) the cost of buying raw materials and components;
(iii) the cost of electricity and gas.

(c) Fixed Costs

Fixed costs, *FC*, are totally independent of output. Fixed costs have to be paid out even if the factory stops production. Fixed costs include the following:

  (i) monthly salaries paid to managers;
 (ii) rent paid for the use of premises;
(iii) rates paid to the council;
(iv) any interest paid on loans;
 (v) insurance payments in case of accidents (see section 20.3);
(vi) money put aside to replace worn-out machines and vehicles sometime in the future (*depreciation*).

(d) Average Cost

Average cost, *AC*, or *unit cost* is the cost of producing one item and is calculated by dividing total costs by total output.

(e) Marginal Cost

Marginal cost, *MC*, is the cost of producing one **extra** unit and is calculated by dividing the change, Δ, in total costs by the change in output.

(f) Revenue

   (i) *Total revenue*, *TR*, is the money the firm gets back from selling goods and is found by multiplying the number sold, *Q*, by the selling price, *P*.
   (ii) *Average revenue*, *AR*, is the amount received from selling one item and equals the selling price of the good.

(g) Equations

$$TC = VC + FC \qquad VC = TC - FC \qquad FC = TC - VC$$

$$AC = TC\,/\,Q. \qquad TR = P \times Q. \qquad AR = TR\,/\,Q.$$

$$MC = \Delta TC\,/\,\Delta Q.$$

3.3 Social Cost

The *private cost* to a motorist of driving from Cornwall to Scotland is the cost of petrol and oil and the wear and tear on his car. However, other people have to put up with the *externalities* of the journey, for instance the noise, smell, pollution and traffic congestion the motorist helps to cause along the way.

   If we add on to private cost an amount of money to compensate for the inconvenience caused, the overall figure will be the *social cost* of the journey:

Private costs	+	Externalities	=	Social cost
(Cost to individual)		(Cost to other people)		(Cost to everyone)

3.4 Worked Examples

Example 3.1

Study the photograph on the next page which was taken inside a blanket factory. Some firms use the division of labour principle and split up the manufacture of a good into separate tasks, each performed by one worker.

(a) Briefly describe the job of the worker in the picture.   (1 mark)
(b) Explain how the division of labour can be applied to the manufacture of blankets.
                                                                                (4 marks)
(c) Are the blankets in the picture more likely to have been
        (i) made by a small number of workers, or   (ii) mass produced?
        Explain your answer.   (5 marks)
(d) What type of good is a blanket?   (1 mark)
(e) What do economists call the place where a blanket is made?   (1 mark)
(f) What are the problems of specialisation for:
        (i) consumers, and   (ii) workers?   (4 marks)

Solution 3.1

(a) The machinist in the picture has the job of sewing on the ribbon edges.

(b) Applying the division of labour principle to the manufacture of blankets involves splitting up the work into separate tasks with only one worker performing each operation. One worker concentrates on weaving the wool into lengths of cloth, another spends all day cutting the wool into blanket size, the machinist in the photograph sews on the ribbon edges, and so on.

(c) The number of workers used to manufacture blankets depends mainly on the demand for the final product. The higher the demand for blankets the higher the demand for workers. Many consumers have switched to using duvets instead of blankets. This reduces the scope for mass production using large numbers of workers.

  The picture suggests that this is a small factory using only a few workers to produce a limited number of blankets. There is no evidence of the conveyor belts and expensive machinery associated with mass production.

(d) A blanket is an example of a consumer good.

(e) Blankets are made in a factory.

(f) (i) Specialisation results in the mass production of goods. Consumers who have special requirements may be dissatisfied with the standardised output of factories.

   (ii) Specialisation allows workers to concentrate on one task. This may result in the workers becoming bored with their occupation.

     Specialists also run the risk of remaining unemployed should they lose their job. The skills learned in one occupation are not necessarily required in another job. An unemployed machinist must be retrained before filling a vacancy as a computer programmer.

Example 3.2

(a) State briefly what you understand by the division of labour. **(2 marks)**
(b) Giving examples, explain two advantages in using the division of labour in the production of televisions. **(4 marks)**
(c) How will the division of labour be affected by:

    (i) the size of the market; **(3 marks)**
    (ii) a country's transport system; **(2 marks)**
    (iii) the use of barter as the only method of exchange. **(4 marks)**

Solution 3.2

(a) The division of labour occurs when the production of a good is broken down into separate operations with one worker performing each task.
(b) The production of televisions requires the use of expensive machinery. Without the division of labour a testing machine in the quality control section would stand idle for part of the day when workers changed tasks. By using the division of labour one worker operates the tester for the entire shift so that a more intensive use is made of the machine.

    Each worker performs the same task each day. A worker who concentrates on connecting the tube to the control panel soon becomes an expert and performs the task in a fraction of the time taken by a non-specialist.

(c) (i) The division of labour results in a large increase in output. There is little point in mass-producing a good if there is only a limited market. The larger the market, the greater the demand for the good and the greater the scope for the division of labour.

    (ii) Before the industrial revolution there was a limited transport network in the UK. This meant that goods could not reach a large enough market to justify the use of the division of labour in production. Today an efficient transport system allows isolated factories to reach world-wide markets.

    (iii) Barter is the exchange of goods directly for other goods. Barter works in a simple economy where workers specialise in the entire production of one good.

    The division of labour is a special type of specialisation where workers contribute to only one small part of a mass produced good. A worker does not have a complete and finished good to offer in exchange. Hence the division of labour is impossible in a barter economy.

Example 3.3

Read the following passage carefully and then answer all the questions that follow.

Until recently the production of newspapers required the use of hot-metal type set by highly paid and *highly skilled printers*. The prospect of a large wage bill and the very high cost of setting up *plant and equipment* deterred many would-be publishers in the 1970s from launching their own paper.

The advent of information technology has opened the possibility of *automated production* bypassing the traditional skills of printers. Journalists now have the opportunity of typing their articles directly into a computer which then automatically sets out each page before printing the complete newspaper.

Automated production benefits the consumer in the form of better quality and lower priced papers. However, society has to meet the cost of increased unemployment payments to those printers no longer required.

(a) Give briefly the meaning of the following terms:

     (i) highly skilled printers   (ii) plant and equipment
    (iii) automated production   **(3 marks)**

(b) State one example given in the passage of: (i) a fixed cost,   (ii) a variable cost and (iii) a social cost.   **(3 marks)**

(c) Using the information given in the passage:
    (i) Give two reasons why so few newspapers were launcheed in the 1970s.
                                                        (1 mark)
    (ii) Give two reasons why the cost of producing a newspaper is likely to fall.
                                                        (1 mark)
    (iii) State two advantages of automation for the consumer.   **(1 mark)**

(d) What are the likely effects of the new method of publishing papers on:

    (i) competition in the newspaper industry;   **(2 marks)**
    (ii) the profits of newspapers not using the new technology.   **(3 marks)**

Solution 3.3

(a) (i) 'Highly skilled printers' are workers who use specialist techniques to print newspapers.
    (ii) 'Plant and equipment' are the factory premises and machines used to print newspapers.
  (iii) Automated production is the use of machines to produce newspapers without the direct use of labour.

(b) (i) A fixed cost given in the passage is the cost of installing a computer.
    (ii) A variable cost given in the passage is the cost of wages.
  (iii) A social cost given in the passage is the cost of unemployment benefit.

(c) (i) Few newspapers were launched in the 1970s because the high cost of wages and premises made it most unlikely that the owner would make a profit.
    (ii) Automation requires fewer workers so that the wage bill will be reduced. Journalists will be able to save time by writing directly into a computer.
  (iii) Automation will result in lower priced and better quality products.

(d) (i) As the cost of setting up and running a newspaper has fallen, so there is likely to be an increase in the number of newspapers on sale.
    (ii) Newspapers which stick to the traditional method of printing will have higher production costs than their competitors. For a given level of sales the traditionally produced newspaper will make a smaller profit than a competitor produced by electronic presses.

Example 3.4

Sydney runs a fish and chip shop. His profit is the difference between his costs and revenue. At the end of one week Sydney writes down the following figures:

Costs (per week)		Item	Weekly sales	Price
Advertising	£200	Cod	600	£1.00
Fish and pies	£200	Pies	200	£0.50
Potatoes	£100	Portion of		
Electricity	£ 50	chips	800	£0.40
Rent	£150			
Wages	£300			

(a) Calculate:
    (i) fixed costs,   (ii) total costs, and   (iii) total revenue.   **(4 marks)**

(b) Is the fish and chip shop making a profit? Explain your answer.   **(2 marks)**

(c) What would be the likely effects on the shop's profit of each of the following:

    (i) a 10 per cent fall in the price of potatoes;   **(2 marks)**
    (ii) the opening of a new café nearby.   **(2 marks)**
    (iii) The introduction of VAT on the sale of takeaway food.   **(1 mark)**

(d) Sydney reduces the price of pies by 20 per cent. Sales increase by 10 per cent.

    (i) Calculate the effect on total revenue   **(2 marks)**
    (ii) Would you advise Sydney to continue to offer pies at a reduced price? Explain your answer.   **(2 marks)**

Solution 3.4

(a)   (i) Sydney's fixed costs are advertising (£200) and rent (£150) making a total of £350.

    (ii) Adding together fixed (£350) and variable (£650) costs means that total costs equal £1000.

    (iii) The income from the sale of each item is found by multiplying sales by price. Adding together the income received from the sale of cod (£600), pies (£100) and chips (£320) means that total revenue is £1020.

(b) Profit can be calculated by subtracting total costs (£1000) from total revenue (£1020), which means the shop has made a small profit of £20.

(c)   (i) A 10 per cent fall in the price of potatoes will reduce costs and so increase profits by £10 per week.

    (ii) The opening of a new café will offer customers an alternative source of food. If some customers prefer to sit down for their meal then sales and hence profits from the shop will fall.

    (iii) The introduction of VAT will increase the price of fish and chips and so sales and profits will fall.

(d)   (i) The initial income from the sale of 200 pies at 50p each is £100. The new income from the sale of 220 pies at 40p each is £88.

    (ii) While the sale of pies has increased following the reduction in price the *extra* sales have not been enough to make up the lost revenue involved in selling *every* pie at a lower price. I would advise Sydney to stop selling pies at a reduced price.

Example 3.5

Study the information given below concerning the cost and output schedule for a particular firm. The market price of the good is always £10.

Output (units)	0	1	2	3	4	5
Total costs (£)	10	12	15	19	32	40

(a) What is the total cost of producing 3 items? **(1 mark)**
(b) Why do total costs increase as the level of output increases? **(2 marks)**
(c) Calculate:

    (i) fixed costs; **(1 mark)**
    (ii) average cost of producing 2 units; **(1 mark)**
    (iii) total variable cost of producing 4 units; **(1 mark)**
    (iv) the most profitable level of output. **(3 marks)**

(d) If the marginal cost of producing the sixth unit is £20, calculate the total cost of producing 6 units. **(1 mark)**
(e) Using examples, describe the major fixed and variable costs involved in owning a house. **(5 marks)**

Solution 3.5

(a) The total cost of producing 3 units is £19.
(b) Total costs increase with the level of output because the firm has to pay more to use the additional resources needed to produce more goods.

(c) (i) When output is zero there are no variable costs but the firm still has to pay out fixed costs. Hence the total costs of £10 incurred when output is zero can only be the firm's fixed costs.
    (ii) The average cost of producing 2 units is found by dividing total cost (£15) by the level of output (2) and is £7.50.
    (iii) Fixed costs (FC) remain £10 no matter what the level of output. If the total cost (TC) of producing 4 units is £32, and fixed costs are £10, then total variable costs (VC) are:

$$VC = TC - FC = £32 - £10 = £22.$$

    (iv) The mosts profitable level of output is where the difference between total revenue and total cost is largest.
        The total revenue received from the sale of 3 units is found by multiplying price (£10) by quantity (3), which equals £30. Total cost is £19. The largest profit (£11) is made by producing 3 units.

(d) Marginal cost is the cost of producing the extra unit. If the total cost of producing 5 units is £40 and it costs another £20 to produce one more unit, then the total cost of producing 6 units is £60.
(e) The fixed costs involved in owning a house have to be met even if the owner is not living there because, say, he is away on holiday. Fixed costs include mortgage repayments to the building society; insurance payments on the building and its contents; and rates to the local authority.

The variable costs in owning a house have to be met only when the owner is in residence. Variable costs mainly consist of the gas and electricity bills from heating.

Example 3.6

A haulage company specialises in transporting coal by road from the local pit to a power station 50 miles away.

(a) Give two examples of the fixed costs involved in running a lorry.   **(2 marks)**
(b) Give two examples of:

    (i) the private costs of transporting coal by road;   **(2 marks)**
    (ii) the social costs of transporting coal by road.   **(2 marks)**

(c) Explain clearly the difference between opportunity cost and social cost   **(4 marks)**
(d) Advise the government on the likely costs and benefits following the construction of a third London airport.   **(5 marks)**

Solution 3.6

(a) A road haulage company has to meet the cost of taxing and insuring a lorry even if it is off the road.

(b) (i) The private cost involved in transporting coal by road is met by the haulage company and includes the cost of fuel and the driver's wages.
   (ii) Social costs consist of the private cost of transporting coal plus an allowance for externalities, i.e. the damage done to the environment by large lorries. Transporting coal by road results in traffic congestion, and increased health risks for society at large.

(c) Opportunity cost is the cost of consuming or producing a good in terms of the next best foregone alternative. For example, the opportunity cost of building a new swimming pool is the sports hall that could have been built instead.

    Social cost is the cost to society of an individual's economic activity. For example, the social cost of smoking cigarettes is the cost of the tobacco plus an allowance for the discomfort caused to non-smokers.

(d) If a third London airport results in an increase in the number of flights then there will be an increase in the amount of noise and environmental pollution caused by aeroplanes. This represents an increased social cost.

    If, however, the extra airport results in the same number of flights spread over a larger number of sites then residents around Heathrow and Gatwick will enjoy increased social benefits in the form of reduced noise and pollution.

    The third airport will also have the benefit of increasing employment opportunities for the unemployed in the area.

Example 3.7

Look at the photograph on the next page of Ravenscraig works in Motherwell, Scotland, which is one of the most modern steel plants in the world. The costs of building and running the plant are high.

(a) From the photograph, give an example of:

    (i) a variable cost;   **(2 marks)**
    (ii) a fixed cost;   **(2 marks)**
    (iii) a social cost.   **(2 marks)**

(b) Before the plant was built at Ravenscraig the land was used for farming. How does this example illustrate the principle of opportunity cost? **(4 marks)**

(c) What would be the effects of closing down Ravenscraig on:

    (i) the environment;   **(2 marks)**
    (ii) the local coal industry?   **(3 marks)**

Solution 3.7

(a) (i) The amount of coal used depends on the amount of steel being made and is therefore a variable cost.

    (ii) The actual buildings in which the manufacture of steel takes place is an example of a fixed cost.

    (iii) The smoke entering the atmosphere and causing pollution is an example of a social cost.

(b) The opportunity cost of employing resources for one use is the alternative foregone. The land taken up in building Ravenscraig had an alternative use as farm land. Therefore, the opportunity cost of using the land for building is the foregone agricultural use.

(c) (i) Ravenscraig helps to create pollution by spilling waste products from the manufacture of steel into the atmosphere. A closure of Ravenscraig will reduce the damage done to the environment.

If the plant is then pulled down and the area is landscaped then there will be an additional improvement in the environment.

(ii) From the picture, the steel works at Ravenscraig uses a large amount of coal. If this is bought from local coal mines then the closure of the works will mean a drastic loss of sales. Local pits will have to close if no replacement customers are found. This will result in heavy local unemployment.

3.5 Questions

1 Define production.
2 Jill can produce two spears and one axe in a day's work. David can produce one spear and two axes in a day's work. How could the production of spears and axes be increased?
3 State one advantage of specialisation.
4 The system of work where each worker concentrates on a single task is known as
……………………………………………………………

5

Output (£)	10	18	28	24	18
Employment	5	6	7	8	9

At what level of output is the productivity of labour highest?
6 An advantage of the division of labour is:
  A a fall in the level of production   B a fall in unit costs
  C the need for more training   D a loss of craftsmanship
7 Which one of the following does *not* occur when division of labour is introduced?
  A output rises   B some tasks become more repetitive
  C workers need a wider range of skills D production time is saved
8 Automation is ……………………………………………………………………………
9 In one month a firm produces 400 units of output and its costs of production are:

mortgage repayments on factory	£2000
wages to workers	£9000
rates on factory building	£1000
electricity bill	£2500
raw materials	£2500
wages of cleaning staff	£1000

What are the firm's (a) fixed costs, (b) variable costs, (c) total costs of production?
10 The total cost divided by the total level of output equals the:
  A marginal cost   B fixed cost
  C variable cost   D average total cost
11 The following figures are the weekly costs of a firm:

wages	£2500
power	£200
rent and rates	£230
raw materials	£1700

Calculate the firm's (a) variable costs, (b) total costs.
12 Which one of the following costs will not change as output and sales increase?
  A the rates on the factory   B the wages of the workers
  C the cost of power   D the cost of raw materials

13 Which one of the following is a fixed cost of production?
  A money spent on repairs
  B the electricity bill
  C the wages paid to the workers in the packing department
  D the interest paid on a bank loan
14 The cost of producing the extra unit is known as ....
15 A firm sells 100 teddy bears each week for £15 each.
  (a) What is the firm's average revenue?
  (b) What is the firm's total revenue?
16 Give one example for each of the following:
  (a) a variable cost, (b) a fixed cost, (c) a social cost.
17 Ignoring transport costs, the private cost of dumping toxic waste on a public rubbish tip is:
  A zero
  B the cost of disposing of the waste safely
  C the cost of landscaping the rubbish tip
  D B and C
18 Social cost equals:
  A total cost
  B private cost
  C private cost plus external cost
  D private cost minus external cost
19 Give two examples of external costs following the construction of a new airport.
20 What is the social benefit of living next door to a keen gardener?
21 Lowering underground fares will:
  A increase the number of cars on the road
  B redistribute income towards the less well off
  C reduce the external cost of traffic congestion
  D increase the use of inner-city car parks.

3.6 Answers

1 The manufacture of a good or a service.
2 Each should specialise in the production of the good they are best at making. Production will rise if Jill makes only spears and David makes only axes.
3 See section 3.1(b).   4 The division of labour.
5 For each level of you should divide total output by the level of employment. Productivity is highest when output is £28.
6 B   7 C
8 The intensive use of machinery in production.
9 (a) Add together mortgage repayments, rates and cleaning wages to give total fixed costs of £4000.
  (b) Add together wages of workers, electricity and raw materials. Variable costs are £14 000. Note that cleaning staff have to be paid even if the factory stops production and are therefore a fixed cost.
  (c) Add together fixed and variable costs: £18 000.
10 D   11 (a) £4400 (b)£4630   12 A   13 D
14 Marginal cost.
15 (a) £15. Average revenue and price are the same thing. (b) £1500.
16 (a) See section 3.2(b). (b) See section 3.2(c). (c) See Section 3.3.
17 A.   18 C.
19 Noise and pollution.   20 Your free view of the garden.
21 C.

4 Economies of Scale

4.1 Economies of Scale

These occur when mass producing a good results in lower average cost. Economies of scale occur within a firm (*internal*) or within an industry (*external*).

(a) Internal Economies of Scale

These are economies made within a firm as a result of mass production. As the firm produces more and more goods, so average costs begin to fall because of:

(i) *Technical economies* made in the actual production of the good. For example, large firms can use expensive machinery, intensively.
(ii) *Managerial economies* made in the administration of a large firm by splitting up management jobs and employing specialist accountants, salesmen, etc.
(iii) *Financial economies* made by borrowing money at lower rates of interest than smaller firms.
(iv) *Marketing economies* made by spreading the high cost of advertising on television and in national newspapers, across a large level of output.
(v) *Commercial economies* made when buying supplies in bulk and therefore gaining a larger discount.
(vi) *Research and development economies* made when developing new and better products.

(b) External Economies of Scale

These are economies made outside the firm as a result of its location and occur when:

(i) A local skilled labour force is available.
(ii) Specialist local back-up firms can supply parts or services.
(iii) An area has a good transport network.
(iv) An area has an excellent reputation for producing a particular good. For example, Sheffield is associated with steel.

(c) Internal Diseconomies of Scale

These occur when the firm has become too large and inefficient. As the firm increases production, average costs begin to rise because:

(i) The disadvantages of the division of labour take effect (see section 3.1(c)).
(ii) Management becomes out of touch with the shop floor and some machinery becomes over-manned.

(iii) Decisions are not taken quickly and there is too much form filling.
(iv) Lack of communication in a large firm means that management tasks sometimes get done twice.

(d) External Diseconomies of Scale

These occur when too many firms have located in one area. Unit costs begin to rise because:

  (i) Local labour becomes scarce and firms now have to offer higher wages to attract new workers.
 (ii) Land and factories become scarce and rents begin to rise.
(iii) Local roads become congested and so transport costs begin to rise.

4.2   Integration

(a) Integration

This occurs when two firms join together to form one new company. Integration can be voluntary (a *merger*) or forced (a *takeover*). Figure 4.1 shows the three main types of integration.

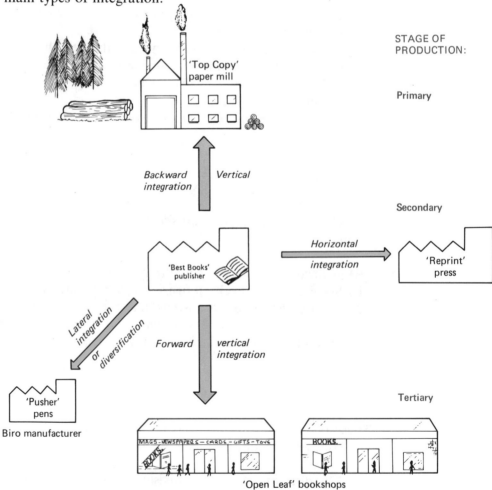

Figure 4.1   Types of integration

(b) Motives for Integration

(i) Integration increases the size of the firm. Larger firms can achieve more internal economies of scale.

(ii) One firm may need fewer workers, managers and premises (*rationalisation*).

(iii) Large domestic firms are then more able to compete against large foreign multinationals.

(iv) Integration allows firms to increase the range of products they manufacture (*diversification*). Diversified firms no longer have 'all their eggs in one basket'.

(c) Survival of the Small Firm

Small firms are able to compete with large firms because:

(i) Some products cannot be mass produced, e.g. contact lenses.

(ii) Some products have only a limited demand, e.g. horse shoes.

(iii) Some products require little capital, e.g. window cleaning.

(iv) Small firms receive grants and subsidies from the government.

4.3 Market Structure

Market structure refers to the number of firms in an industry. In *perfect competition* there are a large number of small firms in the industry, each producing identical products. Very few markets are perfectly competitive but one example is wheat.

In a *monopoly* one firm supplies 25 per cent or more of a market. The Ford Motor Company is an example of a monopoly firm. A *pure monopoly* is a special type of monopoly where one firm supplies the entire market. British Rail is an example of a UK pure monopolist.

4.4 Worked Examples

Example 4.1

Study the photographs on the next page. Picture A shows the servicing of an Alfa Romeo car, picture B the production of Maestro cars.

(a) Which of the photographs shows conveyor belt production? Explain your choice of photograph. **(2 marks)**

(b) Economies of scale are the savings made by a firm when it manufacturers a good in large quantities. Would you expect to find economies of scale in a motor car factory? Use one of the photographs to help explain your answer. **(4 marks)**

(c) Would you expect to find economies of scale in a motor car repair garage? Use one of the photographs to help explain your answer. **(4 marks)**

(d) Does the introduction of robot arms in the production of Maestro cars remove the need for human workers? **(2 marks)**

(e) What are the disadvantages of producing wheat on a small farm? **(5 marks)**

A

AUSTIN ROVER THE MAESTRO BODY PRODUCTION LINE IS EQUIPPED WITH 14 ROBOTS CAPABLE OF WELDING FIVE DIFFERENT BODY TYPES. OVER 60% OF SPOTWELDS ON THE MAESTRO BODY ARE APPLIED BY AUTOMATIC MULTIWELDERS AND ROBOTS.

B

Solution 4.1

(a) Picture B shows the production of motor cars on a conveyor belt. A conveyor belt is a system of manufacture where products move along a mechanical track. While there is a track in picture B, there is none shown in picture A.

(b) A motor car factory offers considerable possibilities for economies of scale. Picture B shows that technical economies can be made by making intensive use of automated conveyor belts and expensive machines such as robot arms.

Managers can concentrate on one task, e.g. buying components. Commercial economies from buying large quantities of steel at low prices are available. The company can afford to spread the high cost of television advertising across a large volume of sales.

(c) Most motor car repair garages have little opportunity for achieving economies of scale. Picture A shows that car repair requires individual attention and personal service. One job may require the fitting of a set of brake pads while another requires an adjustment of the steering.

If the garage in picture A is specialising in only one type of repair (e.g. replacing exhaust systems) then you can expect to find more economies of scale. The job becomes more or less standardised and components can be bought in bulk and at a discount.

(d) Automation does not entirely remove the need for human workers, who will be needed to control the machines and to check the quantity of work. Also, some jobs are too intricate for robot arms and can be done only by skilled workers.

(e) Small-scale production often results in higher unit cost. A farmer producing wheat on a small holding is unable to make use of efficient machinery such as combine harvesters. He is unable to use large lorries and so the unit cost of getting his wheat to market is high. There is only a limited scope for the use of the division-of-labour principle on a small farm and some workers do jobs they are not particularly skilled in performing.

In short, the major disadvantage of small-scale production is that unit costs of production tend to be higher than for firms manufacturing the same good in bulk.

Example 4.2

Economies of scale occur when a firm reduces the cost of producing each item by manufacturing a large quantity of a good.

(a) Give an example of a good which is usually produced in large quantities.
                                                                        (1 mark)
(b) Give one reason why you think the good chosen in (a) is usually produced in bulk.
                                                                        (2 marks)
(c) How could producing shirts in bulk affect:

    (i) the manufacture of shirts;   **(4 marks)**
    (ii) the management of a shirt factory;   **(3 marks)**
    (iii) the purchase of raw materials?   **(2 marks)**

(d) Can the shirt factory benefit by being in the same area as other firms?   **(4 Marks)**
(e) Why do you think some goods are usually produced by small firms?   **(4 marks)**

Solution 4.2

(a) Manufactured goods such as motor cars are usually produced in bulk.
(b) Goods in mass demand such as motor cars almost always have to be manufactured in bulk.

(c) (i) Technical economies can be made in the actual manufacture of a good. The shirt factory can apply the division-of-labour principle far more extensively than a small manufacturer. One worker can stitch the sleeves while another packs the finished shirts into a box.

    Mass production allows the company to link manufacturing processes. Costs could be reduced by organising the spinning and weaving of cotton into shirts in one factory.

 (ii) Doubling output does not necessarily result in twice as much paper work. The shirt firm may be large enough to employ specialist managers in charge of individual departments. The transport manager may have enough work in a large company to keep him busy all day.

(iii) The shirt factory may be able to buy raw materials in bulk and at a discount.

(d) External economies of scale are the savings made outside the firm as a result of its location. A firm, irrespective of its size, may find that a particular area has an efficient transport network, or that the local workforce already possesses the necessary skill and training.

An area may have a specialist bulk producer of parts (e.g. Lucas which can supply each individual car manufacturer in the area with low-cost components (e.g. headlights)).

(e) Goods are usually supplied by small firms in industries where there are no real opportunities for economies of scale. This can be because the demand for a product is so limited that there is little point in mass-producing a good, e.g. luxury yachts.

Some products can be supplied only by small firms because each item has to be made to individual requirements. Many service industries such as hairdressing are dominated by a large number of small firms.

Example 4.3

Assess the advantages for a washing machine manufacturer of each of the following:
(a) producing goods in bulk;   **(4 marks)**
(b) introducing robot machines on the production line;   **(4 marks)**
(c) vertical integration;   **(4 marks)**
(d) taking over a company manufacturing pens.   **(3 marks)**

Solution 4.3

(a) The main advantage of producing a good in bulk is the opportunity for economies of scale. A washing machine manufacturer can organise production using an extensive division of labour. Output will be large enough to justify the use of highly expensive machines. Managers can be employed to do one specific task such as supervising quality control.

Large output requires a large amount of raw materials which can be bought at a discount. The manufacturer can afford to advertise his products in national newspapers, and on television. He can employ his own fleet of lorries to transport the goods to the retailers cheaply.

(b) Robot arms are machines operated by computers which perform simple and repetitive tasks quickly and efficiently. The manufacturer can use the workers once employed to perform the tasks now done by the robot arm somewhere else in the factory. Alternatively he can reduce his wage bill by making surplus workers redundant.

(c) Vertical integration occurs when one firm merges with a second firm at a different stage of production. If the washing machine manufacturer joins together with a components company, then he has a guaranteed source of supplies. If the washing machine manufacturer merges with an electrical retailer, then he has a guaranteed market for his goods.

(d) Diversification occurs when one firm takes over a second company producing an unrelated product. The washing machine manufacturer benefits by spreading business risks over a larger range of products. If the market for washing machines suddenly collapses he can still produce pens and is not necessarily faced with financial ruin. There may also be limited scope for commercial and financial economies.

Example 4.4

Read the following passage carefully and then answer the questions that follow.

Hanson Trust is a highly *diversified* company manufacturing a range of products from bricks to batteries. Hanson has grown as a result of a series of takeovers. In the 1970s Hanson bought two companies—London Brick and Ever Ready Batteries–and managed to increase overall profits by reducing the labour force and cutting overheads. In April 1986 Hanson made a £2.3 billion *bid* for the Imperial Group, manufacturers of tobacco.

The electrical retailer, Dixons, have also followed a path of expansion through *takeover*. Having recently acquired their chief competitor, Currys, Dixons next engaged in a multi-billion pound *bid* for the Woolworth chain of high street shops.

(a) Which company now owns Ever Ready Batteries?   **(1 mark)**

(b) Give briefly the meaning of the following terms:

    (i) diversified, (ii) takeover, (iii) bid.   **(4 marks)**

(c) Give two examples of horizontal integration discussed in the passage.
                                                                  (2 marks)

(d) Using the information given in the passage explain how Hanson increased overall profits after buying London Brick and Ever Ready.   **(2 marks)**

(e) How will the merger between Currys and Dixons affect:

    (i) Currys shareholders;   **(2 marks)**
    (ii) consumers of electrical goods;   **(2 marks)**
    (iii) the profits made by manufacturers of electrical goods?   **(3 marks)**

Solution 4.4

(a) Ever Ready Batteries is now owned by Hanson Trust.

(b) (i) Diversified means a company does not concentrate in the production of one particular type of commodity but manufacturers several different, unrelated, products.
  (ii) A takeover occurs when one firm buys another.
  (iii) A bid is when one company offers to buy another company.

(c) Horizontal integration occurs when two firms at the same stage of production join together to form one new company. Two examples discussed in the passage are the merger of Currys and Dixons, and the proposed merger of Dixons and Woolworth.

(d) Hanson increased the profit made by London Brick and Ever Ready Batteries by cutting each group's workforce and by using the existing Hanson Trust's administration to cut managerial overheads.

(e) (i) Some Currys shareholders may have sold their shares to Dixons and made a profit. The remaining Currys shareholders will benefit only if Dixons are able to increase company profits and dividends.
  (ii) Consumers will find that some branches of Currys and Dixons will close. This means a loss of competition which may result in higher prices and reduced choice.
  (iii) The manufacturers of electrical goods will find that there are now fewer retailers buying their products. Currys may use their increased buying power to negotiate even bigger discounts on their purchase. This will reduce the profit of the manufacturers.

Example 4.5

(a) Using examples, explain the difference between a perfectly competitive firm and a monopoly.   **(4 marks)**

(b) Give two reasons why a monopolist cannot charge very high prices.   **(2 marks)**

(c) Using examples, explain why a monopolist may be able to stop competitors from entering the industry for a particular good.   **(5 marks)**

(d) Can a firm become too large to be efficient?   **(5 marks)**

Solution 4.5

(a) A perfectly competitive firm tends to be small in size and produces a good for which there are many readily available substitutes. Because of his size, a barley farmer is unable to have any impact on the world price of his grain. Moreover, he is unable to stop other farmers producing barley should he begin to earn abnormally high profits.

A monopolist is a large firm supplying 25 per cent or more of a market. Unilever are one of only two manufacturers of soap powder. Unilever can influence the price at which it sells its product and has been successful in excluding competitors from entering the industry. A special type of monopoly is a pure monopoly such as British Rail, which is the sole supplier of a good.

(b) Consumers do not have to buy a product if the price is set too high. Government legislation allows the Office of Fair Trading or the Monopolies Commission to investigate any firm abusing its monopoly power.

(c) A monopolist may be able to exclude competitors from manufacturing its product because the monopolist owns the copyright, patent or trademark. For example, it is illegal to produce pirated videos of popular films or imitations of branded products such as Levi's jeans.

If an industry offers significant economies of scale then new firms have difficulty competing with an established monopolist. The monopolist has a low unit cost of production which a new firm cannot match until it is successful.

New firms are unable to enter an industry if the monopolist owns all the sites of a raw material needed to manufacture a particular product.

(d) A firm can become too large to be efficient. Managers may find that they are unaware of over-manning on the shop floor. A lack of communication between workers and managers can result in jobs being done either twice or incorrectly. A large firm may become over-concerned with form filling and red tape. The resulting internal diseconomies of scale result in an increase in average cost and inefficiency.

4.5 Questions

1 Define economies of scale.
2 As output rises, a firm benefiting from economies of scale finds that its ....
    .... costs are falling.
3 Where costs per unit of production decrease as the scale of production increases the firm enjoys the advantages of ....
4 Which of the following actions could result in a publishing firm benefiting from an internal economy of scale?:
    A it buys its paper in bulk
    B specialist transport firms are established in its locality
    C a new motorway is built near to its factory
    D a competitor locates in the same area
5 Name two internal economies of scale.
6 Give one example of a technical economy of scale.
7 Explain the difference between commercial and marketing economies of scale.
8 Which one of the following is an example of an external economy of scale?
    A development of a pool of skilled labour in the locality
    B borrowing money on favourable terms
    C employment of specialist managers
    D bulk purchase of materials at a discount

9   Explain the difference between internal and external economies of scale.
10   State two external economies of scale.
11   Where unit costs rise as the scale of production increases the firm is experiencing
     ....
12   Give two examples of internal diseconomies of scale.
13   How can external diseconomies of scale arise?
14   Two firms at the same stage of production merge. What form of integration is this?
15   A brewery taking over a chain of public houses is an example of:
     A horizontal integration   **B** backward vertical integration
     C forward vertical integration   **D** lateral integration
16   Distinguish between vertical and horizontal integration.
17   State two advantages for a company of vertical integration.
18   State two reasons why small firms can compete with larger firms.
19   Define market structure.
20   If all of the firms supplying one good merge they have a .... in that market.
21   A monopolist supplies .... per cent or more of a market.
22   Which of the following is a monopoly industry?
     A insurance   **B** carrots   **C** motor cars   **D** hairdressing

4.6   Answers

1   The reduced unit cost from manufacturing a good in bulk.
2   Unit or average.
3   Economies of scale or internal economies of scale.
4   **A**   5   See section 4.1(a).   6   See section 4.1(a)(i)
7   Commercial economies of scale are savings made in the buying of raw materials whereas marketing economies of scale are savings made in the cost of advertising.
8   **A**
9   Internal economies of scale occur *within* the firm as a result of mass production. External economies of scale occur *outside* the firm as a result of its location.
10   See section 4.1(b).
11   Diseconomies of scale or internal diseconomies of scale.
12   See section 4.1(c).
13   See section 4.1(d).
14   Horizontal integration.   15   **C**
16   Vertical integration is a merger between two firms at *different* stages of production while horizontal integration is a merger between two firms at the *same* stage of production.
17   See section 4.2(b).   18   See section 4.2(c).
19   The number of firms in one industry.   20   Monopoly.
21   25 per cent   22   **C**

5 Business Organisation

5.1 Private- and Public-sector Firms

(a) The Private Sector

The economy can be divided into the private and public sectors. The *private sector* is made up of members of the general public and firms owned by the general public (Fig. 5.1).

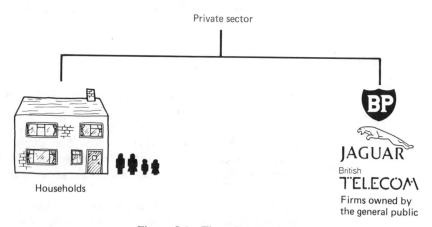

Figure 5.1   The private sector

(b) The Public Sector

The *Public Sector* is made up of the central government in London, various local councils, and firms owned by the government (*nationalised industries*) such as British Rail and the Post Office (Fig. 5.2).

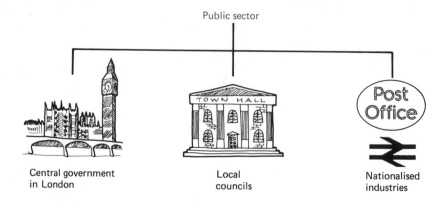

Figure 5.2   The public sector

5.2 Private-sector Firms

(a) Types of Private-sector Firm

Table 5.1 summarises the main types of firm owned by members of the general public.

Table 5.1 Private-sector firms

Type	Example	Owners	Control	Advantages	Disadvantages
Sole trader	Corner shop	1	With sole trader	Requires little capital. Incentive to work hard. Regular customers known. Owner can make quick business decisions.	Unlimited liability. Difficult to find capital. Long hours worked. Holidays or illness cause problems.
Partnership	Firm of doctors	2 to 20	Shared equally between partners	Each partner contributes capital. Each partner specialises. Regular customers known.	Unlimited liability. One partner's mistake affects all partners. Partners may disagree.
Private limited company (Ltd)	Small family business	2 or more	Directors elected by shareholders	Limited liability. Shareholders contribute capital. Protected from takeovers.	Still limited capital for expansion. Limited economies of scale.
Public limited company (plc)	Boots	2 or more	Directors elected by shareholders	Limited liability. Large amount of capital can be raised. Economies of scale.	Unwanted takeover possible. Can be remote from customers. Potential diseconomies of scale.
Co-operative	Oxford and Swindon	2 or more	Committee	Profits returned to customers. Democratic.	Committee may lack business experience.

(b) Liability

The owners are *liable* or responsible for the debts of a company.

  (i) *Unlimited liability* means the owner may have to sell some or all of his personal possessions to help pay off the company's debts.
 (ii) *Limited liability* means that the owner loses only the money he has put into the company and no more. He does not have to sell personal belongings.

(c) Establishing a Limited Company

Limited companies have their own legal identity. They can sue people and other companies and be sued themselves. Anyone wanting to establish a limited company must issue:

  (i) A *memorandum of association* stating the name, aims, and address of the company and the amount of capital to be raised.

(ii) *Articles of association* stating the internal organisation of the company.

The Registrar of Companies then issues a *certificate of incorporation* which permits the company to trade.

The limited company then prepares a *prospectus* describing the history and prospects of the firm and inviting individuals to buy their shares. Only a public limited company can advertise its prospectus.

Each share allows one vote and pays one *dividend* (profit payment). Each year the shareholders elect a chairman and a board of directors who control the everyday running of the firm.

5.3 Public-sector Firms

(a) Types of Public-sector Firm

Each nationalised industry (or *public corporation*) has its own Act of Parliament and its own government minister. Firms owned by the government aim to operate in the public interest and do not necessarily try to make maximum profits.

(b) Public Limited Companies and Public Corporations

These are compared in Table 5.2.

Table 5.2   Differences between public limited companies and public corporations

Feature	Public limited company	Public corporation
Ownership	General Public	Government
Control	Chairman elected by shareholders	Chairman selected by the government
Size	Large	Very large
Capital	Raised by issuing shares	Raised by issuing stocks
Profits	Go to the shareholders	Go to the government
Aim	Make a large profit	Serve the public interest

5.4 Privatisation

The Thatcher administration (1979 to date) has followed a course of selling state-owned firms such as British Telecom back to the private sector. This is called *privatisation*.

(a) Arguments for Privatisation

(i) Firms operate more efficiently in the private sector because they are trying to maximise profits.
(ii) Money can be raised to increase government services or to pay for tax cuts.
(iii) Ordinary people become shareholders and take a greater interest in economic matters (*'people's capitalism'*).

(b) **Arguments Against Privatisation**

(i) Public monopolies simply become private monopolies.
(ii) Socially necessary but unprofitable services may not now be provided.
(iii) Nationalised industries are already owned indirectly by the general public.

5.5 Multinationals

A *multinational corporation* is a very large firm with a head office in one country and several branches operating overseas.

(a) Advantages of Multinationals

(i) Investment by multinationals creates jobs for the host country.
(ii) The multinational will introduce new production techniques and managerial skills.
(iii) New or better goods may now become available in the host country.

(b) Disadvantages of Multinationals

(i) Profits are returned to the overseas head office.
(ii) The multinational may operate against the interest of the host country.
(iii) The multinational may force its overseas branches to buy supplies from the head office.

5.6 Worked Examples

Example 5.1

(a) What is meant by the term 'limited liability'? **(2 marks)**
(b) State two types of business organisation where the owner(s) have unlimited liability. **(2 marks)**
(c) Give two differences between private and public limited companies. **(4 marks)**
(d) What is a public-sector firm? **(1 mark)**
(e) Give two examples of goods sold by public-sector firms. **(2 marks)**
(f) How do public-sector firms raise capital for investment? **(4 marks)**

Solution 5.1

(a) Limited liability means that the owner loses only the money he has used to buy shares in a company should that company go bankrupt.
(b) Sole traders and partnerships have unlimited liability.
(c) A private limited company cannot advertise its shares for sale to the general public, while a public limited company can issue a prospectus inviting anyone to buy shares. Shares in a private company cannot be sold without the permission of the rest of the shareholders, while shares in a public company can be freely bought and sold on the stock exchange.
(d) A public-sector firm is owned by the government.
(e) Nationalised industries sell essential goods such as electricity and rail transport.

(f) Public-sector firms raise capital for investment by re-investing profits or by borrowing money. One method of borrowing money is to approach the government for a loan. A second method is to sell stocks to the general public. These are certificates which pay a fixed rate of interest every year to the holder who can sell the stock at any time on the Stock Exchange.

Example 5.2

(a) Using examples state three advantages of the sole proprietor (or sole trader) as a type of business organisation. **(3 marks)**
(b) Why might a sole proprietor consider entering into a partnership? **(4 marks)**
(c) What legal formalities are required in setting up a partnership? **(2 marks)**
(d) Name two types of business where you would expect to find partnerships trading. **(2 marks)**
(e) What happens if a partnership incurs losses and becomes bankrupt? **(4 marks)**

Solution 5.2

(a) A sole proprietor needs little capital to establish a business. For example, a window cleaner needs only a few inexpensive items to carry out his trade. The same window cleaner will soon be on first-name terms with most of his customers and will be able to make quick business decisions because he has no one else to consult.
(b) A sole trader may take on a partner whose expertise will improve the running and efficiency of the company. Each partner can specialise in one part of the business.
   A partner will introduce more capital into the firm which can be used to expand the business. A partner will also help the sole trader by sharing the burden of organisation and by allowing the sole trader to take holidays.
(c) There are no legal formalities required by law. However, most people entering a partnership prepare a deed of partnership setting out the duties and responsibilities of each partner.
(d) Partnerships are most common in professional occupations where each partner can specialise in one area of practice. Many groups of doctors and solicitors are organised as partnerships.
(e) Each partner has unlimited liability and could have to sell some or all of his personal possessions to help pay off the debts incurred by the company. This could involve the forced sale of all the assets owned by the partnership and also the forced sale of each partner's house.

Example 5.3

Read the following passage carefully and then answer the questions below.

When a company sets up in business people get together to contribute the money which it needs to buy buildings, equipment and raw materials. They share together in providing the money—'capital'—from their savings. They become shareholders.
   A share represents a part of the company. A shareholder is part owner of that company. If a company's capital is divided up into 100 shares and a person holds one of them then he owns one hundredth of the assets of that company. When a company makes a profit it pays a dividend to its shareholders as a reward for putting their savings to work in the company. A dividend is like the interest a bank or a building society pays on your deposit. But there is a difference. The dividend is much less certain than interest on a bank deposit because profits

are uncertain. In good years the dividend can be high, in poor years it may be reduced; indeed a dividend may not be paid at all.

There is a risk, just as there is a risk in building a factory. The dividend is part of the reward for the risk.

(a) What is meant by 'capital' from the point of view of an investor? **(2 marks)**
(b) What is the minimum number of shareholders permissible in a public limited company? **(2 marks)**
(c) What risks are involved in share ownership? **(2 marks)**
(d) What are the differences between 'interest' and a 'dividend'? **(3 marks)**
(e) Is there any limit to the risk involved in being a shareholder? **(3 marks)**
(f) Give two reasons why investors might prefer to hold preference shares rather than ordinary shares. **(4 marks)**
(g) Describe four advantages of public limited companies as a form of business ownership. **(4 marks)**

(NI GCE 1985)

Solution 5.3

(a) The capital of an investor is his savings which he can either leave in a bank or building society earning interest or invest in buying shares in a new company.
(b) By law a public limited company must have at least two shareholders.
(c) Shareholders run two risks. First, the company may do badly and not pay out any dividend. Second, the company may do very badly and go into liquidation. The shareholder will then probably lose all the money he has paid out buying the company's shares.
(d) A dividend is a variable payment linked to the profit made by the company. If the company makes a large profit then there will be a high dividend for each share held. No company profit means no shareholder's dividend.

Interest is the payment given by debtors to their creditors and is a percentage of the amount that has been borrowed.
(e) Shareholders enjoy the privilege of limited liability. They risk the money they have spent on buying the shares of a company and no more. Shareholders do not risk losing their personal possessions.
(f) A preference share pays a fixed dividend each year, providing the company makes a profit. Preference shareholders are paid before ordinary shareholders receive their dividend. Investors who prefer to have a fixed and more or less certain income will buy preference rather than ordinary shares.
(g) A public limited company is able to sell shares to the general public and can raise millions of pounds' worth of capital. A public limited company is controlled by a professional board of directors elected each year at a meeting of all shareholders. Each shareholder has only limited liability and can sell his shares at any time on the Stock Exchange.

Because of its large size a public limited company is better able to compete with large foreign multinationals because it is able to benefit from economies of scale.

Example 5.4

Read the following newspaper report and answer all the questions that follow:

The Dwindling Power of the Co-operative Retail Movement
by David Churchill

The co-operative movement grew up during the harsh conditions of Victorian Britain. Groceries were especially expensive and of poor quality. In 1840 28 Lancashire people banded together to start a co-operative society. They bought and sold food to ensure that members could buy cheap produce. The society provided much-needed social and educational facilities, and any *financial surplus* was given back to members in proportion to their purchases—the famous co-op 'divi'.

By 1900 there were 1400 retail societies with *boards of directors* elected by more than 12 million customer members.

The societies are still Britain's biggest *retailer* with more than 6000 shops. However, Tesco and Sainsbury now have a bigger market share with only a tenth of the number of supermarkets operated by co-ops.

Every other type of retail operator has outperformed the co-ops in the 1980s. Since 1980 grocers have increased sales by 46 per cent while the co-ops sales have increased by only 15 per cent. The number of customer shareholders has fallen from 10 to 8 million. Co-operative retailing to many appears a spent force.

Source: Adapted from *Financial Times*, 24 May 1986

(a) What is meant by:

    (i) financial surplus;   (ii) board of directors;
    (iii) retailer?   **(3 marks)**

(b) State two economic reasons given in the passage for joining a co-operative society.   **(2 marks)**

(c) Has the increase in the UK standard of living affected the co-operative movement?   **(3 marks)**

(d) Which organisation has the largest number of supermarkets in the UK?
    (1 mark)

(e) How many customer members has the Co-op lost since 1980?   **(1 mark)**

(f) The Co-op has increased its sales by 15 per cent and yet David Churchill says they are being outperformed. Why is this?   **(2 marks)**

(g) Why do you think the Co-op is unable to sell as much as Tesco and Sainsbury even though the Co-op has more stores?   **(3 marks)**

Solution 5.4

(a)   (i) A financial surplus is the profit made by a co-op.
    (ii) A board of directors is a committee of members elected to run the everyday affairs of the society.
    (iii) A retailer is an organisation which sells goods to customers from shops.

(b) A co-operative society offers educational facilities, and allows its members to have a say in the running of the business.

(c) As people become better off they do not need to form self-help groups such as the Co-operative Society. Therefore fewer people join or use the Co-op.

(d) The Co-op still has the largest *number* of supermarkets in the UK.

(e) The Co-op has lost 2 million members since 1980.

(f) Although the sales of the Co-op have gone up by 15 per cent this is well below the growth of the rest of the retail industry which increased its sales by almost half.

(g) The Co-op has a large number of small stores where people do not spend very much money. Tesco and Sainsbury have concentrated on establishing a small number of very large stores where people go to buy their weekly shopping. One of these large stores takes more than ten times the amount of money spent in the average Co-op supermarket.

Example 5.5

(a) Explain the main differences between a public limited company and a public corporation over:

(i) ownership;	**(2 marks)**
(ii) everyday control of the company;	**(3 marks)**
(iii) raising capital for expansion;	**(3 marks)**
(iv) the amount of profit made.	**(4 marks)**

(b) Public corporations sometimes run up a loss in the public interest.

(i) What do you understand by the economic term 'loss'?   **(2 marks)**

(ii) Are the losses of public corporations in the public interest? Explain your answer.   **(4 marks)**

Solution 5.5

(a) (i) A public limited company is a private-sector firm owned by shareholders. A public corporation is a public-sector firm owned by the state.

(ii) A public limited company is controlled by a chairman and board of directors elected every year by the shareholders at an annual general meeting. A public corporation is controlled by a chairman appointed by the government of the day. The chairman of a public corporation works closely with a government minister who decides the general policy of a nationalised industry.

(iii) Public limited companies raise their capital by selling shares and debentures to the public while public corporations raise money by issuing stocks. The profits of a public limited company are paid out to shareholders while the profits of nationalised industries are used by the government to help finance its expenditure.

(iv) Public limited companies usually aim to make as large a profit as they can. Failure to do so may result in the board of directors being replaced at the next shareholders' meeting or an unwanted takeover bid from a rival. Public corporations do not necessarily attempt to earn as large a profit as is possible. Instead they operate in the public interest, often supplying subsidised but socially necessary services.

(b) A loss occurs when the income from the sale of goods and services is less than the cost of supplying those commodities.

(c) Losses can be in the public interest. The electricity boards make a loss supplying power to remote regions of the country. However, it would be socially unacceptable if people living in the Highlands of Scotland were to be without electricity, or if they were to be asked to pay far more than those living in Edinburgh.

If, on the other hand, the losses are the result of over-manning and managerial inefficiencies then the losses of a public corporation are not in the public interest.

Example 5.6

Some important sectors of industry are nationalised but the Conservative government elected in 1979 decided to 'privatise' certain of these public corporations.

(a) Explain the meaning of the term privatisation.
(b) Name three undertakings within the public sector which have been wholly or partly privatised during the last four years.
(c) Explain three economic reasons why the government thinks it is advantageous to privatise certain nationalised industries.

(EAEB CSE 1984)

Solution 5.6

(a) Privatisation occurs when state-owned companies are sold to the private sector.
(b) Jaguar Cars (1984), British Telecom (1984) and Britoil (1985).
(c) The government believes that firms operate more efficiently in the private sector. A privatised firm will now try to maximise profits by reducing labour costs and overheads.

   Privatisation raises large sums of money for the government which can be used either to increase its provision of welfare services or as a method of reducing personal taxation.

   The government is committed to the idea of 'people's capitalism' where a large number of the public own a direct stake in British industry. This will increase general awareness of economic matters and encourage firms to be more accountable to the public.

Example 5.7

The Conservative government is seeking to privatise some of the nationalised industries in the United Kingdom. In 1984 British Telecom was privatised.

(a) Explain what is meant by the privatisation of British Telecom.   **(2 marks)**
(b) Analyse the likely consequences of the privatisation of British Telecom on:

    (i) the telecommunications market;   **(3 marks)**
    (ii) ownership of the company;   **(3 marks)**
    (iii) future investment in capital equipment by British Telecom.   **(3 marks)**

(c) What economic and social effects might a policy of selling *all* nationalised/public sector assets have on:

    (i) employment,
    (ii) the price of goods or services supplied?   **(9 marks)**

(NISEC specimen GCSE)

Solution 5.7

(a) Privatisation refers to sale of shares in state-owned firms such as British Telecom (BT) to private owners.

(b) (i) The telecommunications market is made up of the buyers and sellers of telephone-related services. The privatisation of BT will replace what was once a state-run monopoly with a private one. If, however, BT operates more efficiently in the private sector then consumers will benefit from a better and cheaper product.

(ii) Privatisation will mean a large number of ordinary people will either own shares directly in the company or indirectly through pension funds and trade union ownership of BT shares.

(iii) BT will not now be able to borrow funds directly from the government but may have higher profits with which to buy new capital equipment.

(c) (i) Nationalised industries employ millions of people. If the privatised industry decides to increase profits by cutting back on socially necessary but unprofitable activities then there will be an increase in unemployment.

For example, a large number of coal mines are 'uneconomic' and would be closed by a private company determined to make maximum profits. The social cost of massive unemployment to the nation and individual mining communities would run into millions of pounds.

(ii) The privatisation of all public-sector firms might lead to an increase in the prices of a whole range of necessary goods and services such as water and electricity. This is because private firms might want to raise their prices to make maximum profits.

Moreover, the price of some goods in some areas might go up drastically. Before privatisation, public corporations will have used the profits made from successful operations to subsidise the running of loss-making services. Privatised industries might well decide to increase the prices of loss-making services or even cut them out all together.

Consumers living in prosperous areas would continue to enjoy cheap gas, rail travel, etc., while people living in remote areas would be faced with higher prices and reduced services. This would make the regional problem worse.

5.7 Questions

1 What is meant by the phrase 'unlimited liability'?
2 The word limited after the name of a company suggests that:
   A shareholders have a limited number of shares in the company
   B the shareholder's loss is limited to what he has paid for the shares
   C its shares are quoted on the stock exchange
   D there is a limit to the number of shareholders
3 What is the difference between limited and unlimited liability?
4 Industries owned by members of the general public form part of the .... sector.
5 State three main advantages of the sole trader as a form of business organisation.
6 A disadvantage of the sole trader is that:
   A extra workers cannot be employed
   B the owner is personally liable for any debts
   C banks will not lend to this type of business
   D output cannot be sold nationally
7 Which type of firm is likely to choose a partnership as a form of business organisation?
8 If a partnership became a limited company what advantages would it gain?
9 In which of the following types of business is/are the owner/owners liable for all company losses:
   A   public limited company   B private limited company
   C   co-operatives   D partnerships
10 Co-operative societies are controlled by an elected.....................................

11 What happens to any profits made by a co-operative retail society?
12 What happens to any profit made by a public limited company?
13 Name two of the documents which must be completed by the promoters of a limited company.
14 Which of the following types of business organisation has shares quoted on the stock exchange?
    A a co-operative society   B a public joint-stock company
    C a private joint-stock company   D a public corporation
15 The main difference between a private limited company and a public limited company is that:
    A only one is financed by government loans
    B only the shareholders in one have limited liability
    C only one is owned by the government
    D only one can offer its shares for sale on the stock exchange
16 The legal owners of a public limited company are:
    A the government   B the shareholders
    C the debenture holders   D the directors
17 Industries owned by the government are called...
18 Nationalised industries form part of the .... sector.
19 British coal can be regarded as a firm in the public ....
20 What are the differences between a public corporation and a public limited company over:
    (a) finance   (b) ownership   (c) management (d) aims
21 What is meant by 'privatisation'?
22 Give one reason for the privatisation of British Telecom
23 Give one reason for the nationalisation of British Rail.
24 What is a multinational?
25 State two disadvantages of multinationals.

5.6 Answers

1 The owner is fully responsible for the debts of the company. He may be required to sell his own personal property to help pay creditors.
2 **B**   3 See section 5.2(b).   4 Private
5 See Table 5.1.
6 **B. A** is incorrect because a sole trader can employ any number of people. **C** is incorrect because banks will lend some money to sole traders if security is offered. **D** is incorrect because there is nothing to stop sole traders selling anywhere within the United Kingdom.
7 Any professional group of people who work together, e.g. a firm of lawyers.
8 Partners would gain limited liability. The new company could raise more capital and would have its own legal identity.
9 **D**   10 Committee
11 Some profit may be kept back for reinvestment. Part of the profit goes to shareholders in the form of an interest payment. The rest is returned to customers as dividend stamps.
12 Some profit may be kept back for reinvestment. Part of the profit is interest payments to debenture holders. The rest is paid out as dividends to shareholders.
13 Articles and Memorandum of Association   14 **B**
15 **D**   16 **B**   17 Nationalised industries or public corporations.
18 Public   19 Corporation or sector company.

20 See Table 5.2.
21 Selling state-owned firms to the general public.
22 See section 5.4(a).   23 See Section 5.4(b).
24 A firm with branches in many countries.
25 See section 5.5(b).

6 Industrial Location

6.1 Factors Influencing Location

Sometimes firms have to decide where to build a new factory. It is important to consider the different costs of different locations. Businessmen take into account the natural and acquired advantages of a particular area.

(a) Natural Advantages

(i) An area may have a water source for waste disposal or cooling.
(ii) An area may be flat or isolated and attract dangerous or unpleasant industries.
(iii) An area may have the right climate for the production of a good.
(iv) *Weight-losing* industries use bulky raw materials to produce a compact finished product and tend to locate near the source of raw materials.

(b) Acquired Advantages

An area may have developed a number of advantages as the result of firms locating in the region. These are called *external economies of scale* and are explained in section 4.1(b).

Weight-gaining industries use compact raw materials to produce a bulky finished product and tend to locate near the major market for the good.

(c) Footloose Industries

A *footloose industry* gains no particular advantage from any one location usually because transport costs are the same for each site.

Industrial inertia occurs when a firm continues to expand on its existing site even though there are cheaper alternatives.

6.2 Structure of UK Industry

(a) Regional Structure of UK Industry

The *localisation of industry* occurs when there is a concentration of producers of a particular product in one area. See Table 6.1.

Table 6.1 Structure of UK industry by region

Region	Type of industry
North	Traditional heavy industry concentrated around Tyneside and Teeside
Yorks and Humber	Iron and steel; textiles and clothing; coal; fishing
East Midlands	Diverse industry but specialises in hosiery, footwear and clothing
East Anglia	Agriculture and food processing; footwear and tourism
South East	Financial and commercial centre; technological and light engineering
South West	Agriculture and food processing; tourism; aerospace; tobacco
West Midlands	Mechanical and electrical engineering; vehicles; iron and steel; potteries
North West	Heavy engineering; cotton; clothing; glass; chemicals; vehicles
Wales	Coal, iron and steel in S. Wales. Agriculture; light engineering
Scotland	North Sea oil; agriculture; shipbuilding; tourism
Northern Ireland	Shipbuilding; textiles

(b) Recent Changes in the Structure of UK Industry

(i) Declining industries. Since 1973 manufacturing output has been falling by 2 per cent each year. The shipbuilding, textile and motor vehicle industries have suffered particularly.

(ii) Expanding industries. The energy crisis and discovery of North Sea oil has increased the output of the mining industry, dramatically. However, the collapse of oil prices in 1986 may see a reversal of this trend. Service industries including banking, communications and insurance have expanded rapidly.

6.3 Regional Policy

(a) Regional Problem

The regional problem refers to the uneven spread of living standards between different regions of the UK. Areas with below-average income per person are *depressed regions*. They usually have a large concentration of declining industries and are remote from the major markets. New firms prefer to locate in the expanding South East.

The gap between the prosperous South East and the rest of the country is growing. New firms are attracted to the South East by the extensive motorway and air links and the availability of workers familiar with the new technologies. For example, computer-based, high-technology firms have located along the M4 motorway corridor west of London.

(b) Government Regional Policy

Footloose firms can be attracted to depressed regions by government grants. The government offers:

(i) *Regional development grant (RDG)*. Firms locating in special development areas receive grants to pay for factories and machinery up to a limit of £10 000 per new job created.

(ii) *Regional selective assistance*. Firms locating in intermediate development areas may receive a grant towards machinery and training costs.

(iii) *Enterprise zones*. These are small areas situated mainly in inner-city areas where rate and rent allowances are provided by the government.

6.4 Worked Examples

Example 6.1

Look at the two photographs; picture A shows the location of a cement factory, picture B that of a power station.

A

B

(a) From picture A, give two reasons why the cement factory is built in a remote area?   **(4 marks)**
(b) From picture B, give two reasons why the power station is sited near water.
                                                                       (4 marks)
(c) Using examples, explain why it is necessary to consider the type of product when choosing the location for a new factory.   **(4 marks)**
(d) What do you understand by the term 'footloose industries'? Give an example of a footloose industry.   **(3 marks)**

Solution 6.1

(a) The cement works is located in a remote area because a large amount of dust is pumped into the atmosphere during manufacture. If the cement works were to be situated in a built-up area the local residents would suffer from pollution.

   The cement works takes up a lot of space, and money can be saved by building the factory in a remote area where rents are low.

(b) The power station is located near water so that coal can be easily unloaded by ship. Picture B shows a jetty containing five cranes which unloads the coal straight onto a coal conveyor system.

   The power station is built near the river so that water can be used to cool down the turbines housed in the main buildings.

(c) Some products use vast amounts of raw material to produce a much smaller finished product. Weight-losing industries such as steel will reduce their costs of production by locating a new factory close to the major source of raw materials, i.e. coal.

Some products turn compact raw materials into a bulky finished product. Industries involved in light engineering (e.g. a dishwasher manufacturer) can produce goods far more cheaply if they build a new factory close to the major market for their product.

(d) A footloose industry is neither bulk-gaining nor bulk-losing and has no reason to choose one site rather than another. Several locations offer the same costs of production. The manufacture of shirts is an example of a footloose industry.

Example 6.2

Read the following passage and answer all the questions which follow.

Aberdeen has become an expert in supplying the services needed by North Sea oil companies. As production reaches its peak in 1986 the collapse of oil prices to $15 a barrel has cast a shadow over the future prosperity of the region. However, nearly all the drilling rigs are producing oil at less than $5 a barrel. While there have been some 500 redundancies following the closure of 4 uneconomic platforms, there are over 22 000 employed offshore. 60 per cent of North Sea workers usually live outside the Aberdeen area.

There has been a collapse in the number of drilling explorations for new fields and no new orders have been received by Scottish rig-building yards. The trend is towards smaller floating platforms which could be built by the work-starved shipbuilding yards of Clydeside.

Aberdeen remains an important fishing town and has one of the busiest airports in Europe. Local unemployment at 8 per cent is well below the national average.

(a) What do you understand by the term 'localisation of industry'?   **(2 marks)**
(b) Name two industries given in the passage which are highly localised in Aberdeen.
                                                                                        (2 marks)
(c) What evidence is there in the passage of a high standard of living in Aberdeen?
                                                                                        (2 marks)
(d) What is meant by 'uneconomic platforms'?   **(3 marks)**
(e) The passage suggests that 500 offshore workers lost their jobs in 1986. How many of these are likely to have been local people?   **(2 marks)**
(f) At what price would oil production stop in the North Sea?   **(1 mark)**
(g) Using the information in the passage, assess the likely economic effects of a permanent fall in the price of oil for Clydeside shipbuilders.   **(3 marks)**

Solution 6.2

(a) The localisation of industry is where a large number of firms, supplying the same type of good, build factories in the same area.

(b) Industries supplying services to the oil fields and fishing are highly localised in Aberdeen.

(c) Aberdeen has a below-average rate of unemployment for the UK. This suggests that average incomes in the area are higher than in those areas where there is high unemployment.

(d) An uneconomic platform is a loss-making rig which costs more to maintain than the revenue received from the sale of its oil.

(e) Only 40 per cent of the total North Sea oil workforce is made up of local people. Therefore 40 per cent of the 500 redundancies are likely to be local residents, i.e. 200.

(f) If the world price of oil fell below $5 a barrel then no North Sea platform could produce oil at a profit and production would stop.

(g) As the price falls oil companies are less prepared to build and maintain large and expensive platforms. An alternative given in the passage is for shipbuilding companies to build smaller floating platforms which are cheaper to maintain. Clydeside shipbuilders may win the contract to build these new stations and this would increase employment and profitability in the yards.

Example 6.3

Study the information in the map and the table opposite and answer all the questions which follow.

- (a) From the map, name a city in a development area. **(1 mark)**
- (b) How much money would a firm locating in Norwich receive from the government? **(1 mark)**
- (c) From the table, what is the major difference between a special development area and an intermediate area? **(3 marks)**
- (d) Using examples, give three reasons why some regions are more depressed than other regions. **(6 marks)**
- (e) Which of the measures given in the table is most likely to attract a large manufacturer of cars to a development area? Explain your answer. **(4 marks)**

Solution 6.3

- (a) Glasgow is a city in a development area.
- (b) Since Norwich is not in a development area there would be no government grants available.
- (c) In a special development area the government guarantees payment for buildings and capital while in an intermediate area grants are not guaranteed and are related to the number of jobs created.
- (d) Some regions such as Northern Ireland are depressed because of their remoteness from the major markets of Europe.

  Some regions such as the North East have a heavy concentration of traditional heavy engineering industries such as shipbuilding which are no longer in demand. As a result the region suffers from above-average levels of unemployment.

  An area in decline suffers from a downward business spiral. As factories and shops close so the income and expenditure of local people decline. Shopkeepers find their business is falling off and reduce their demand for locally made goods. This in turn reduces total spending within the region and accelerates the process of decline.
- (e) A car manufacturer is more likely to be attracted to a special development area where he will receive a 15 per cent allowance on money spent on buying buildings and machines. The production of cars uses a large number of expensive machines. A 15 per cent subsidy will reduce the cost of building a new factory in a special development area by many millions of pounds.

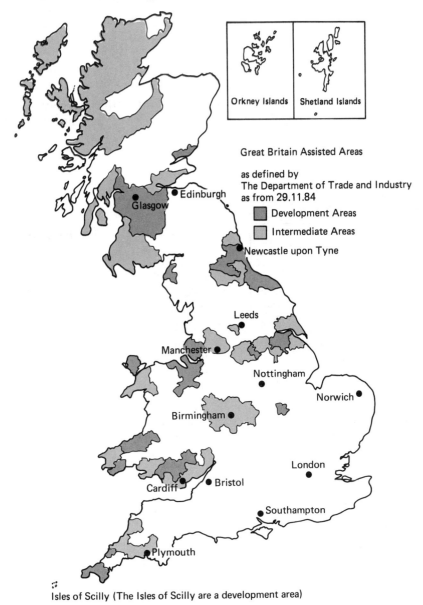

Great Britain assisted areas

Type of incentive	Development areas	Intermediate areas	Non-development areas
Guaranteed grants for buildings, machinery and equipment	15%	Nil	Nil
Selective grants for buildings, machinery and equipment	Additional assistance may be given towards the fixed costs of a project. The level is related to the amount of employment created.		Nil
Training grants	40% of basic wages and training costs.		Nil
Help for transferred key-worker	Grants, free fares and lodging allowances. Help with finding houses.		Nil
Factory rents	Rents may be free at first.		Nil
Loans	Government loans may be given.		Nil

Source: Adapted from Barry Harrison, 'Recent developments in regional policy', in *Economics—the Journal of the Economics Association*, vol. 23, No. 93, 1986

Example 6.4

Study the diagram and the table. Use the information in them about fourteen of the most popular relocation centres in Britain to answer all the questions which follow.

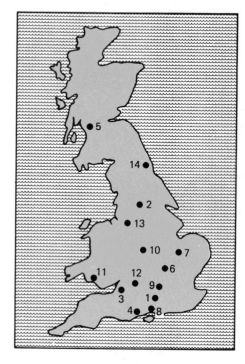

Area	Office rent (£ per sq. ft)	Commercial rates (£ per sq. ft)	House prices (£)
1 Basingstoke	10.50	2.80	43 549
2 Bradford	2.50	2.00	19 760
3 Bristol	7.00	2.70	32 390
4 Bournemouth	6.50	2.50	38 207
5 East Kilbride	4.50	3.85	29 918
6 Milton Keynes	9.00	2.60	46 250
7 Peterborough	6.50	2.40	32 024
8 Portsmouth	6.00	2.25	32 609
9 Reading	13.00	3.20	51 476
10 Redditch	4.50	1.90	30 221
11 Swansea	4.00	1.20	34 068
12 Swindon	8.00	2.50	40 799
13 Warrington	6.50	2.30	31 673
14 Washington	4.50	1.90	26 619

Source: 'A relocation reckoner', by Erik Brown, *The Observer*, 18 May 1986

A relocation reckoner

(a) How much does it cost to rent one square foot of office space in Milton Keynes?

(1 mark)

(b) Which area has the least expensive house prices? **(1 mark)**

(c) What is meant by the term 'commercial rates'? **(2 marks)**

(d) Briefly describe the likely saving to a firm of moving from Basingstoke to East Kilbride

(2 marks)

(e) Calculate from the table the *total* cost of hiring a 500 square foot office in Portsmouth

(4 marks)

(f) How will a house-owning employee be affected by a move from site 14 to site 12?

(5 marks)

(g) Why do firms still locate in expensive areas such as Reading? **(5 marks)**

Solution 6.4

(a) It costs £9.00 to rent one square foot of office space in Milton Keynes.

(b) The cheapest house in the table is found in Bradford.

(c) Commercial rates are the tax on offices collected by the local council to pay for local services.

(d) A firm moving to East Kilbride from Basingstoke will find that the cost of renting falls from £10.50 to £4.50 a square foot.

(e) The cost of hiring the office will be the rent (£6.00) multiplied by the square footage used (500), making a total of £3000.

   The rate bill will be £2.25 × 500, i.e. £1125. The total cost of renting and rates is £4125.

(f) The average cost of a house in Washington is £26 619. The same-sized house in Swindon costs over £40 000. The house-owning employee would have to find almost £14 000 or move to a smaller house.

The house owner will also be affected by the high costs of actually moving. Legal fees, stamp duty and estate agent commissions can add up to £3000. Then there is the expense of paying a removal firm to move the house owner's possessions.

The total cost of the move may be in excess of £18 000 and this may discourage workers from moving from one area of the country to another. This is known as the *geographical immobility of labour.*

(g) A firm may still locate near Reading if the higher sales and profits from being in a prosperous area outweight the high cost of offices.

A firm may need a particular type of skilled labour which is only available in the area. Many high-tech firms in the computer industry locate near Reading for this reason.

Reading will have a number of specialist firms offering back-up services not found in other parts of the country. Reading also has excellent motorway links and is close to Heathrow Airport.

Example 6.5

Look at the advertisement here.

(a) List three advantages given in the advertisement for locating in Medway.

(3 marks)

(b) What type of development area is found in Medway? (1 mark)

(c) Why does the government offer money to firms setting up new factories in development areas? (4 marks)

(d) Why would an electrical goods manufacturer be particularly interested in moving to Medway? (4 marks)

(e) What do you understand by the term industrial inertia? (3 marks)

Solution 6.5

(a) Medway is close to motorways, airports and seaports. It can offer low rates and attractive rentals. It has a lot of young and skilled workers looking for employment.

(b) The advertisement states that Medway includes five prime-site enterprise zones.

(c) The government is concerned about the uneven spread of employment and income about the country. One way of making income more even is to encourage firms to move to high-unemployment areas such as Medway by offering grants.

(d) An electrical goods manufacturer produces bulk increasing products and so can reduce his costs of production by locating near to the market. The advertisement suggests that Medway is close to many important British and European markets.

(e) Industrial inertia occurs when firms expand on their existing site even though there are cheaper alternative locations in other parts of the country. Industrial inertia is usually the result of managers preferring the environment they know to the risk of major change and upheaval.

Example 6.6

Look at the aerial picture of East Kilbride, Scotland, opposite.
Features shown in the photograph include:

– the Inland Revenue computer centre;
– an Olympic-length swimming pool and youth centre;
– existing shops and offices;
– a proposed site for a £6m air-conditioned shopping mall and offices with parking spaces for 1300 cars.

(a) Imagine you are the development officer of the local council. Write a publicity handout to go with the photograph explaining the economic advantages of setting up a shop or office in the area. Make use of the following headings:

    (i) advantages of a new site; (2 marks)
    (ii) existing local business; (2 marks)
    (iii) local workforce (2 marks)
    (iv) transport links; (2 marks)
    (v) recreational facilities; (2 marks)
    (vi) countryside. (2 marks)

(b) What is 'the regional problem'? (3 marks)

Solution 6.6

(a) If you're planning to develop your business you need look no further than East Kilbride. Consider the following features:

New site We can offer you all the advantages of selecting brand new premises to fit your own needs. The new centre contains all types and sizes of office and shop to suit your requirements.

Existing business The picture shows that important employers and customers have already moved to the area and are just waiting to buy your produce.

Local work force Kilbride has a wealth of workers trained in the latest office and shop techniques, anxious to join your company.

Transport links The picture shows that the new centre is slap bang next to an extensive network of roads. This allows direct and speedy access to your premises for both customer and supplier.

Recreational facilities Note the Olympic-sized swimming pool and local youth centre for you and your employees to use on your days off.

Countryside And if it is the countryside you want to live and work in, Kilbride has the answer. Large areas of great natural beauty are but a couple of minutes drive from the heart of the city.

(b) The regional problem refers to different standards of living in different parts of the country. Depressed regions have lower average incomes and higher unemployment than the more prosperous regions of the country.

6.5 Questions

1 List four natural advantages of an area affecting the location of industry.
2 Weight-gaining industries locate near ....
3 Give two reasons why a shoe manufacturer might site a factory in your area.
4 A manufacturing industry which locates near to its market is a/an
   A footloose industry   B bulk-increasing industry
   C inert industry   D bulk-decreasing industry
5 Weight-losing industries locate near..
6 .... occurs when a firm expands on its existing site even though there are cheaper alternatives.
7 Give two reasons why some industries are scattered throughout the country.
8 What do you understand by a localised industry?
9 Distinguish between the 'location of industry' and the 'localisation of industry'.
10 Why is pottery a highly localised industry in the UK?
11 Which one of the following industries is most localised in the UK?
   A wholesaling   B farming
   C car manufacturing   D construction
12 State two UK industries which in recent years have experienced growth.
13 State two UK industries which in recent years have experienced decline.
14 Industry has tended to locate in the South East of England because of:
   A low rents   B large markets
   C low wages   D government financial assistance
15 Explain why most high-technology industry is located in the South East.
16 Why does the government adopt a location of industry policy?
17 State two incentives available to firms locating in enterprise zones.

6.6 Answers

1 See section 6.1(a).   2 The market.
3 Any two of the following: (a) Near a large market.   (b) Good local communication links with the rest of the country.
   (c) Near a source of raw materials.   (d) A skilled labour force is available.   (e) Rents and rates are low in the area.
   (f) Government grants may be available.
4 B   5 The source of raw materials.
6 Industrial inertia.
7 Any two of the following: (a) The industry is footloose.
   (b) The source of raw materials is scattered.
   (c) The market is scattered.   8 See section 6.2(a).
9 The location of industry means where firms are situated. Localisation means a large number of firms producing the same good in one area.
10 Only a few areas have the natural and acquired advantages needed to produce pottery.
11 C
12 North Sea oil; electronics and computers; most services.
13 Most traditional manufacturing and heavy engineering industries.
14 B   15 See section 6.3(a)
16 To reduce differences in the standard of living between different parts of the country.
17 See section 6.3(b)(iii).

7 Supply and Demand

7.1 Demand

(a) Definition

Desire refers to people's willingness to own a good. *Demand* is the amount of a good that consumers are willing and able to buy at a given price.

(b) Utility

Utility is the satisfaction people get from *consuming* (using) a good or a service. Utility varies from person to person. Some people get more satisfaction from eating chips than others. Even the same person can gain greater satisfaction by eating chips when hungry than when he has lost his appetite.

(c) Factors Influencing Demand

The amount of a good demanded depends on:

  (i) the price of the good;
 (ii) the income of consumers;
(iii) the demand for alternative goods which could be used (*substitutes*);
 (iv) the demand for goods used at the same time (*complements*);
  (v) whether people like the good (*consumer taste*).

The *demand curve* labelled *DD* in Fig.7.1 on the next page shows the amount of a good one or more consumers are willing and able to buy at different prices.

(d) Movements Along and Shifts in Demand Curves

A change in price *never* shifts the demand curve for that good. In Fig. 7.1 an increase in price results in a *movement* up the demand curve. The fall in the quantity demanded from Q_1 to Q_2 is sometimes called a *contraction* in demand.
   A demand curve *shifts* only if there is a change in income, in taste or in the demand for substitutes or complements. In Fig. 7.2 a decrease in demand has shifted the demand curve to the left.

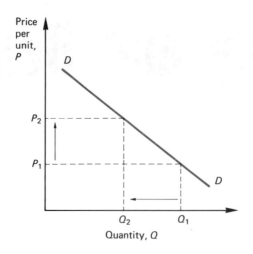 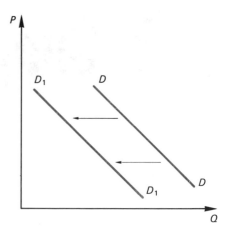

Figure 7.1 A decrease in quantity demanded

Cause: a rise in price.

Figure 7.2 A decrease in demand

Cause: a decrease in income;
or more substitutes bought;
or fewer complements bought;
or the good is now less popular.

7.2 Supply

(a) Factors Influencing Supply

Supply is the amount of a good producers are willing and able to sell at a given price. Supply depends on:

(i) the price of the good;
(ii) the cost of making the good;
(iii) the supply of alternative goods the producer could make with the same resources (*competitive supply*);
(iv) the supply of goods actually produced at the same time (*joint supply*);
(v) unexpected events that affect supply.

The *supply curve* labelled *SS* in Fig. 7.3 opposite shows the amount of a good one or more producers are prepared to sell at different prices.

(b) Movements Along and Shifts in Supply Curves

A change in price *never* shifts the supply curve for that good. In Fig. 7.3 an increase in price results in a *movement* up the supply curve. The increase in quantity supplied from Q_1 to Q_2 is sometimes called an *expansion in supply*.

A supply curve *shifts* only if there is:

(i) a change in costs;
(ii) a change in the number of goods in competitive or joint supply; or
(iii) some unforeseen event which affects production.

In Fig. 7.4 an increase in supply shifts the supply curve to the right.

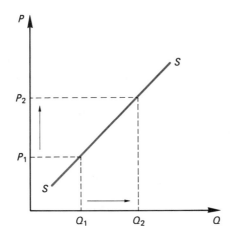

Figure 7.3 An increase in quantity supplied

Cause: a rise in price

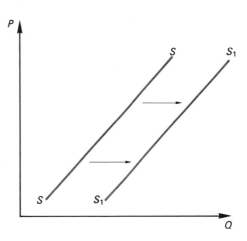

Figure 7.4 An increase in supply

Cause a fall in costs of production;
or firms switch from alternatives
into making this good;
or more goods in joint supply;
or an unexpected event (e.g. good
weather) increases production.

7.3 Market Price

At prices above £3 there is *excess supply* while at prices below £3 there is *excess demand*. The price where the amount consumers want to buy equals the amount producers are prepared to sell is the *equilibrium market price*.

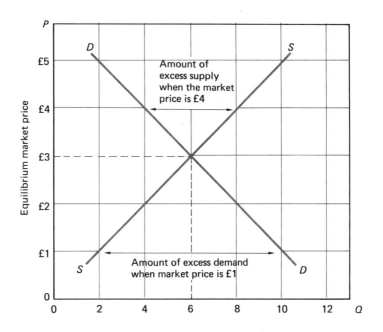

Figure 7.5 Excess supply and demand

7.4 Indirect Taxes and Subsidies

In Fig. 7.6 an indirect tax of £1 has been added to *SS*. Note that price increases by only 50p. This suggests that part of the tax is paid by the firm.

In Fig. 7.7 a subsidy of £1 has been taken from *SS*. Note that price falls by only 50p. This suggests that the firm keeps part of the subsidy.

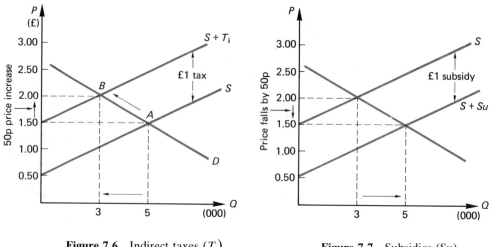

Figure 7.6 Indirect taxes (T_i) **Figure 7.7** Subsidies (Su)

7.5 Elasticity

(a) Price Elasticity of Demand

Price elasticity of demand (PED) measures the responsiveness of demand to a given change in price and is found using the equation:

$$\text{PED} = \frac{\text{Percentage change in quantity demanded}}{\text{Percentage change in price}},$$

or

$$\text{PED} = \frac{P}{Q} \times \frac{\Delta Q}{\Delta P}$$

where P = the original price,
  Q = the original quantity
and Δ = 'the change in'.

See Table 7.1.

Table 7.1 Features of price elasticity of demand

Feature	Elastic goods	Inelastic goods
PED value	Greater than 1	Less than 1
A rise in price means	A larger fall in demand	A smaller fall in demand
Slope of demand curve	Flat	Steep
Number of substitutes	Many	Few
Type of good	Luxury	Necessity
Price of good	Expensive	Cheap
Example	Maestro cars	Petrol

(b) Price Elasticity of Supply

Price elasticity of supply (PES) measures the responsiveness of supply to a given change in price.

$$\text{PES} = \frac{\text{Percentage change in quantity supplied}}{\text{Percentage change in price}},$$

or

$$\text{PES} = \frac{P}{Q} \times \frac{\Delta Q}{\Delta P}$$

See Table 7.2.

Table 7.2 Features of elasticity of supply

Feature	Elastic goods	Inelastic goods
PES value	Greater than 1	Less than 1
A rise in price means	A larger rise in supply	A smaller rise in supply
Slope of supply curve	Flat	Steep
The good is produced	Rapidly	Slowly
The time period is	Months	Days
The firm has	Large stocks	Limited stocks
Example	Screws	Beef

(c) Income Elasticity of Demand

Income elasticity of demand (YED) measures the responsiveness of demand to a given change in income:

$$\text{YED} = \frac{\text{Percentage change in quantity demanded}}{\text{Percentage change in income}}.$$

If YED is negative then the good is *inferior*. People use an increase in income to buy less of this good and more of a superior substitute.

If YED is positive then the good is *normal*. Consumers use an increase in income to buy more of the good.

(d) Cross Elasticity of Demand

Cross elasticity of demand (XED) measures the responsiveness of demand for one good (*z*) to a given change in the price of a second good (*w*):

$$\text{XED} = \frac{\text{Percentage change in quantity demanded of good } \mathbf{z}}{\text{Percentage change in the price of good } \mathbf{w}}$$

If XED is positive then the two goods are substitutes. If XED is negative then the two goods are complements.

7.6 Worked Examples

Example 7.1

(a) Explain clearly the difference between wants and demand. **(4 marks)**

(b) With aid of diagrams, distinguish between:

    (i) an increase in the quantity of tape cassettes demanded, and

    (ii) an increase in the demand for tape cassettes. **(6 marks)**

(c) Assess the influence on the price of tape cassettes of each of the following circumstances:

    (i) an increase in unemployment among young workers.

    (ii) a major cut in the cost of electronic components used to manufacture tape recorders.

    (iii) a successful advertising campaign for compact discs. **(6 marks)**

(WJEC specimen GCSE)

Solution 7.1

(a) Wants refer to people's desire for a good while demand refers to desire backed up by the ability to pay for a good.

(b) (i) An increase in the quantity of tape cassettes demanded is sometimes called an expansion in demand and is the result of a fall in price. In diagram A, the fall in price from P_1 to P_2 increases the quantity of tape cassettes demanded from Q_1 to Q_2.

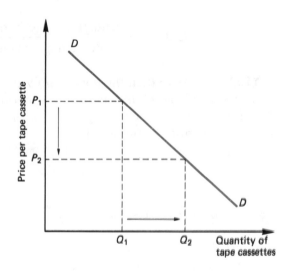

A

    (ii) An increase in demand means an increase in demand at all prices. In diagram B, an increase in demand will shift the demand curve for tape cassettes labelled DD to D_1D_1.

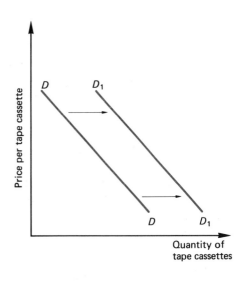

Price per tape cassette

Quantity of
tape cassettes

B

(c) (i) A large number of cassettes are bought by young workers and if some
         were to lose their jobs then they would have less money to spend on
         tapes. Demand would fall, causing the price of tapes to fall.
    (ii) A major cut in the cost of electronic components used to manufacture
         tape recorders would encourage the producer to increase supply. The
         price of recorders would fall, leading to an increase in the quantity of
         machines demanded.
            Since tape recorders and cassettes are complements, the demand for
         tapes would increase, resulting in an increase in the price of tapes.
   (iii) A successful advertising campaign for a substitute for tape recorders
         would reduce the demand for both tape recorders and the cassettes to
         go with the recorders. The demand for tapes would decrease, resulting
         in a fall in price.

Example 7.2

The following questions are based on the information given in the table below.

The market for apples

Price per lb (pence)	Quantity demanded (000)	Quantity supplied (000)
50	100	700
40	200	600
30	300	500
20	400	400
10	500	300

(a) What is the equilibrium price?   (1 mark)
(b) Give two reasons why the demand for apples might increase.   (2 marks)
(c) Give two reasons why the supply of apples might fall.   (2 marks)
(d) If the market price was 50p, how many apples would be demanded?   (1 mark)
(e) If the market price was 30p, how many apples would be supplied?   (1 mark)
(f) If the price of apples fell from 20p to 10p, calculate the price elasticity of demand.
    Show all your working.   (3 marks)
(SREB 1985)

Solution 7.2

(a) The equilibrium price is where the amount supplied and demanded is the same. From the table this price is 20p.
(b) The demand for apples may increase if there is an increase in consumers' income or if the demand for a substitute good such as pears goes down. (Alternatively, if the demand for a complement such as cheese increases or if apples become more popular.)
(c) The supply of apples may fall if there is a frost which damages the crop or if producers use the apples to produce an alternative good such as cider. (Alternatively, following an increase in the costs of production.)
(d) 100 000 apples are demanded at price 50p.
(e) 500 000 apples are supplied at price 30p.

(f) $\text{PED} = \dfrac{P}{Q} \times \dfrac{\Delta Q}{\Delta P} = \dfrac{20}{400} \times \dfrac{100}{10} = 0.5$. Demand is inelastic.

Example 7.3

You are given the information in the table about the market for potatoes.

Price per kilo (pence)	Amount demanded per (kg)	Amount supplied per week (kg)
7	30	62
6	35	60
5	41	57
4	45	53
3	49	49
2	53	45
1	57	41

(a) Using this information draw the supply and demand curves. **(2 marks)**
(b) What would be the equilibrium price and why? **(1 mark)**
(c) Suppose the government were to say to the seller: 'the minimum price you can charge is 4 pence per kg'. What would be the short-term effect? **(2 marks)**
(d) If the amount demanded increased by 8 kg, at all prices, what would be the effect on equilibrium price (assuming supply remains the same)? **(3 marks)**
(e) Imagine that the government gave potato farmers a subsidy of 2 pence per kg. What would be the new equilibrium price using the above information? **(2 marks)**

(NISEC specimen GCSE)

Solution 7.3

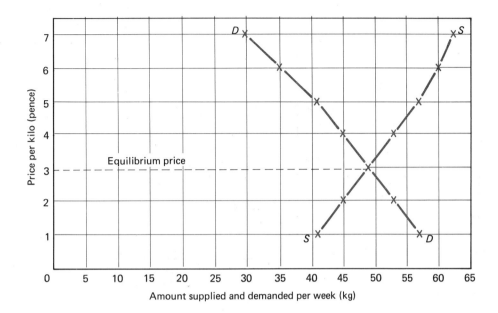

(b) The equilibrium price is given by the intersection of *S* and *D* in the diagram. 3 pence is the only price at which the amount consumers are willing and able to buy coincides with the amount producers are willing and able to sell.

(c) From the supply schedule, producers are willing to sell 53 kg at the minimum price of 4 pence. From the demand schedule, consumers are willing to buy only 45 kg at this price. There will be an excess supply of 8 kg.

(d) If demand increases by 8 kg at all prices then the demand curve shifts to the right and price increases. To calculate the new price you could redraw the demand curve in the diagram, adding on 8 kg at all prices. It is quicker simply to add 8 kg to the amount stated in the demand schedule.

   At 4 pence consumers now demand 45 + 8 = 53 kg—which is also the amount producers want to sell at this price.

   Equilibrium price increases from 3 to 4 pence.

(e) A subsidy has the effect of increasing supply. At 4p producers are initially prepared to sell 53 kg. A 2p subsidy means they are now willing to sell 53 kg for only 2p. At 2p consumers are prepared to buy 53 kg and this is the new equilibrium price.

Example 7.4

Study the information in the passage and graph on the next page and then answer the questions below.

> While on holiday in Grimsby a young boy notices that at the beginning of the day fish sellers manage to sell some fish at a high price. As the day goes on, fish sellers lower their price to increase sales and avoid being left with old and worthless fish. Just before the end of the day the same clever pensioner appears and almost always buys the last few scraps of fish for his cat at a very low price.
>
>   The boy draws a graph, shown here, which gives the demand for fish, *D*, and supply of fish, *S*, at different prices.

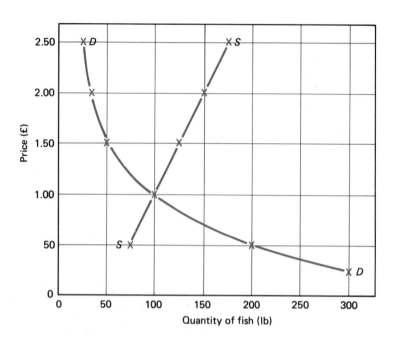

(a) What is the price at which the amount of fish supplied equals the amount of fish demanded? **(1 mark)**

(b) What is the name given to this price by economists? **(1 mark)**

(c) Why does the pensioner wait until the market is almost closed before he buys his fish? **(1 mark)**

(d) Can the pensioner be sure he will always be able to buy fish at this time of the day? Explain your answer. **(2 marks)**

(e) Why can fish sellers sell at a higher price in the morning than in the afternoon? **(3 marks)**

(f) What happens to the amount spent on fish if the price falls from £1.50 to £1.00. **(2 marks)**

(g) Calculate the elasticity of demand when price changes from £1.50 to £1.00. **(2 marks)**

(h) Why does the price of fresh fish vary more than the price of frozen fish? **(4 marks)**

Solution 7.4

(a) The price at which the amount of fish supplied equals the amount of fish demanded is £1.00.

(b) This is called the equilibrium market price.

(c) The pensioner hopes to pay a very low price for his fish.

(d) The pensioner has no guarantee of being able to buy fish at this time because the stalls may have been able to sell all their fish for a higher price earlier in the day.

(e) Earlier in the day consumers determined to buy fish, even at a high price, will have made their purchases in case the fish becomes sold out.

(f) The amount spent on a good is found by multiplying price by the quantity sold. When the price is £1.50 consumers buy 50 lb of fish. Their total expenditure on fish is £75. When the price is £1.00 consumers buy 100 lb of fish, i.e. they spend £100.

(g) $\text{PED} = \dfrac{P}{Q} \times \dfrac{\Delta Q}{\Delta P} = \dfrac{1.5}{50} \times \dfrac{50}{0.5} = 3$. Demand is elastic.

(h)

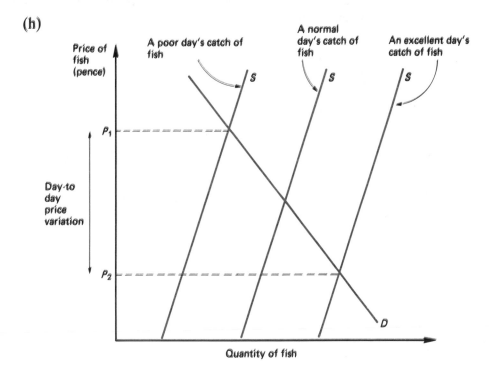

The supply of fresh fish can vary from day to day, depending on the weather and the fishermen's luck. In the diagram, changes in the size of each day's catch have the effect of shifting the supply curve to the right when an unexpectedly large numbers of fish are caught, and to the left when the catch is poor. Hence the price of fresh fish is highly unstable.

The supply of frozen fish is more certain than that of fresh fish. In times of great demand fish can be taken out of a freezer and sold. If there is a fall in demand then the fish can be put into cold storage for many months. Hence the price of frozen fish is relatively stable.

Example 7.5

In the United Kingdom, when value added tax (VAT) at 15 per cent was first put on takeaway food, it was estimated that demand fell by 25 per cent.

(a) Explain why the introduction of VAT should cause the demand for takeaway meals to fall. **(6 marks)**
(b) Explain, or show by diagrams, the effect on the price and output of takeaway meals of:

   (i) a fall in the price of potatoes and rice;
   (ii) advertising which leads customers to believe that takeaway food is unhealthy. **(4 marks)**
(c) Explain briefly how the owner of a takeaway food restaurant could calculate the price elasticity of demand for his/her takeaway meals. **(2 marks)**
(d) Using the idea of price elasticity of demand, explain why the government, in seeking to raise large amounts of revenue from taxation, might prefer to raise taxes on cigarettes or petrol rather than on takeaway food. **(4 marks)**

(SEG specimen GCSE)

Solution 7.5

(a) Diagram A shows the effect of introducing VAT on the demand for takeaway food.

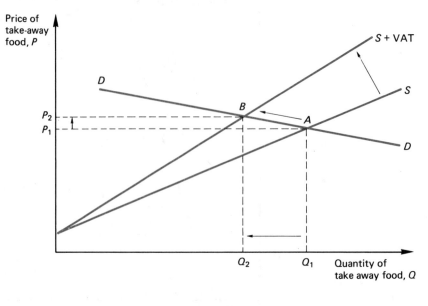

A

The amount of VAT has been added to the supply curve to give a new curve, S + VAT. There is a decrease in demand through a movement along the curve from A to B. The actual decrease in the quantity demanded is $(Q_1 - Q_2)$.

(b) (i) The price of potatoes and rice represents a cost of production for takeaway food. A fall in costs will encourage the producer to increase supply. The supply curve S in diagram B shifts to the right to S_1. Price falls from P_1 to P_2 while output increases from Q_1 to Q_2.

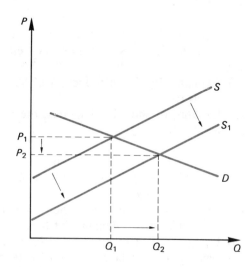

B

(ii) A successful advertising campaign which leads customers to believe that takeaway food is unhealthy will reduce demand; the demand curve D in diagram C shifts downwards to D_1. Price falls from P_1 to P_2 and output also decreases from Q_1 to Q_2.

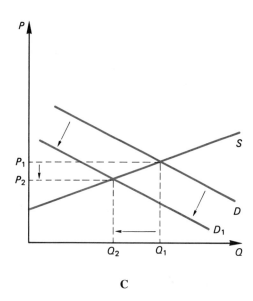

C

(c) Price elasticity of demand (PED) measures the responsiveness of demand to a given change in price and can be calculated using the equation

$$\text{PED} = \frac{\text{Percentage change in quantity demanded}}{\text{Percentage change in price}}.$$

(d) A 15 per cent tax on takeaway food results in a proportionately larger fall in quantity demanded of 25 per cent. People can stop buying takeaway food because there are many close substitute goods such as meals in restaurants. A big fall in consumption means that the government does not raise large amounts of revenue by taxing takeaway food.

The government would raise more money tax by increasing VAT on the purchase of inelastic goods. Cigarettes and petrol have no close substitutes so that consumers continue to buy roughly the same quantity as before the price increase.

Example 7.6

(a) Briefly *explain* the difference between a contraction in supply and a decrease in supply. **(4 marks)**

(b) With the aid of diagrams explain the following statements:

(i) The supply of tickets to a pop concert is totally inelastic. **(3 marks)**
(ii) The demand for a supermarket brand of soap powder is quite elastic. **(3 marks)**

(c) An inferior good is a product bought by consumers only because they cannot afford a better alternative.

(i) Give an example of an inferior good. **(1 mark)**

(ii) What will be the effect of an increase in income on the demand for an inferior good? **(2 marks)**

Solution 7.6

(a) A contraction in supply occurs when a fall in price results in a movement down a supply curve. A contraction in supply does not result in a shift in a supply curve.

A decrease in supply means a decrease in supply at all market prices, which causes the supply curve for a good to shift to the left. A decrease in supply is the result of a change in a factor influencing supply apart from price, e.g. an increase in unit costs.

(b) (i) Diagram A shows a totally inelastic supply curve. The vertical shape of the supply curve S means that if the price is £1 or £50 then supply remains fixed. The concert hall can hold only 10 000 fans irrespective of the entry price.

(ii) The demand curve for supermarket soap powder in diagram B is elastic because there are many substitutes for the good. A small increase in price (P_1 to P_2) results in a large number of consumers buying alternative products. There is a proportionately larger fall in quantity demanded (Q_1 to Q_2).

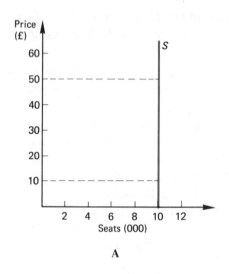
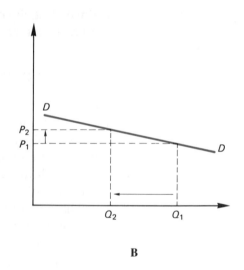

A   B

(c) (i) A good which most consumers stop buying in bulk once their income increases is margarine.

(ii) An increase in income reduces the demand for inferior goods. For example, as their income increases wealthy households reduce their consumption of margarine because they can now afford to consume quality alternatives such as butter.

7.7 Questions

1 What is the main difference between demand and desire?
2 A consumer always attempts to maximise his:
    A income   **B** utility   **C** demand   **D** savings

3 State two goods which are complementary to each other.
4 What is the economic term used to describe the quantity people are prepared to buy in a market at any price?
5 A demand curve for a commodity is drawn on the assumption that all influences on demand are held constant except ....
6 An increase in demand for a good may follow:
   A a rise in the price of a complement
   B an increase in income
   C an unsuccessful advertising campaign
   D an increase in the demand for a substitute
7 A demand for a good shifts to the right following:
   A a fall in income
   B an increase in the price of a complementary good
   C an increase in the price of a substitute good
   D a fall in the price of the good
8 What is the main difference between supply and a supply curve?
   Use the following pairs of commodities to complete each of the sentences given in questions 9 to 12:
      pipes and tobacco
      yoghurt and butter
      butter and margarine
      beef and hides
9 .... are substitute goods.
10 .... are complementary goods.
11 .... are goods in joint supply.
12 .... are goods in competitive supply
13 The supply of a good will fall at all prices following:
   A the introduction of automation   B a fall in the price of the product
   C a decrease in VAT on the good   D a fall in productivity

Price (pence per lb)	Demand (tonnes)	Supply (tonnes)
120	3	40
100	9	32
80	15	25
60	20	20
40	25	13
20	35	7

The figures in the table refer to the demand and supply for carrots. Use them to answer questions 14 to 16.
14 What is the equilibrium price?
15 Calculate the elasticity of supply if the price of carrots falls from 80p to 60p.
16 What situation exists in this market if the price is fixed at 40p?
17 Draw a graph to illustrate the effect of an indirect tax on the price and output of a good.
18 What is the main difference in effect between an indirect tax and a subsidy?
19 Price elasticity of demand is the responsiveness of demand to a change in:
   A income   B the price of substitutes
   C the price of complements   D the price of the product
20 The demand curve for a certain good will be very price elastic if:
   A it has a very close substitute   B it is a very popular item
   C it is in very short supply   D it is a necessity
21 The price of shirts in a market rises from £4.00 to £5.00 and the demand falls from 800 to 600 shirts. The elasticity of demand for shirts is:
   A one-quarter   B one-half   C one   D two

22 The responsiveness of supply to a change in price is known as ....
    ....
23 Income rises by 20 per cent. As a result video recorder sales double. This means:
    A   price elasticity of demand is inelastic
    B   price elasticity of demand is elastic
    C   income elasticity of demand is inelastic
    D   income elasticity of demand is elastic
24 Which of the following items would you expect to have a negative income
    elasticity of demand value?
    A   potatoes   B   beer   C   meat   D   yachts
25 If the cross elasticity of demand value is negative then the two goods are:
    A   unrelated   B   normal   C   complements   D   substitutes

7.8 Answers

1   Desire is *willingness* to acquire a good. Demand is *willingness and ability* to
    acquire a good.   2 **B**
3   Any two goods you have stated which are consumed at the same time, e.g. bread
    and butter.
4   Demand curve or demand schedule.
5   Price   6 **B**   7 **C**
8   Supply is the amount of a good producers are willing and able to sell at a *given*
    price. A supply curve is the amount of a good producers are willing and able to
    sell at *different* market prices.
9   Butter and margarine   10 Pipes and tobacco
11 Beef and hides   12 Yoghurt and butter
13 **D**. Note answer **B** is wrong because a fall in price results in a movement down a
    supply curve and does not cause the 'fall at all prices' stated in the question.
14 The price where supply equals demand is the market price, i.e. 60p.

15 PES $= \dfrac{P}{Q} \times \dfrac{\Delta Q}{\Delta P} = \dfrac{80}{25} \times \dfrac{5}{20} = \dfrac{4}{5}$ or 0.8. Supply is inelastic.

16 At 40p, 25 tonnes would be demanded while only 13 tonnes would be supplied
    and there would be a state of excess demand.
17 See Fig. 7.6.
18 Generally, indirect taxes increase prices while subsidies lower prices.
19 **D**   20 **A**

21 PED $= \dfrac{P}{Q} \times \dfrac{\Delta Q}{\Delta P} = \dfrac{4}{800} \times \dfrac{200}{1} = \dfrac{4}{4} = 1$. Therefore answer **C**.

22 Elasticity of supply or price elasticity of supply.
23 A 20 per cent increase in income results in a proportionately larger increase of
    100 per cent in the quantity of videos demanded. Therefore answer **D**.
24 Potatoes are an inferior good which consumers will switch out of once their
    incomes begin to increase. Therefore answer **A**.
25 **C**

8 Income and Wealth

8.1 Income

(a) Types of Income

Income is the amount of money received by a household over a period of time. Figure 8.1 shows the various types of income and their source.

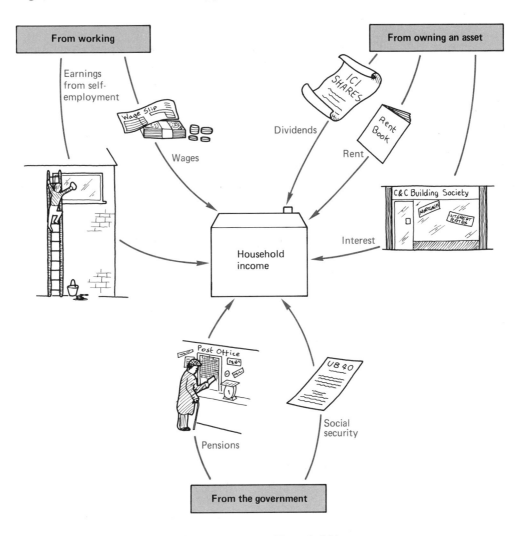

Figure 8.1 Sources of household income

(b) Distribution of Income

Income distribution is the way in which total income is shared out between households. Not everyone receives the same amount of money each year because of wage differences and the uneven ownership of wealth.

8.2 Wages

(a) Methods of Payment

Workers sell their labour to employers in return for:

  (i) *Salaries*. Usually salaries are paid monthly to non-manual workers such as managers irrespective of the number of hours worked.
 (ii) *Wages*. Wages are weekly payments for work done and are paid by:

   (1) *Piece rate* or *piece work*: an amount for every item made.
   (2) *Time rate*: an amount for every hour worked.

(b) Deductions

The *gross wage* is made up of basic wages plus overtime and bonus payments. Deducting income tax and national insurance contributions leaves *net wages* or *take-home pay*.

(c) Money and Real Wages

Money wages refers to pay without any adjustment for inflation.
  Real Wages are the amount of goods and services money wages can buy; this is given by the equation:

$$\text{Real wages} = \frac{\text{Money wages}}{\text{Retail price index}} \times 100.$$

8.3 Wage Differences

The wage for a job is determined by the supply and demand for labour in that particular occupation. A job where labour is in high demand but in short supply will pay higher wages.

(a) Demand for Workers

The demand for labour is found (*derived*) from the demand for the finished good. There will be an increased demand for workers if:

  (i) There is an increased demand for the finished good.
 (ii) Workers increase their productivity.

(b) Supply of Workers

There will be a limited supply of workers if the job:

  (i) requires special qualifications, skills, training or ability;
 (ii) is unpleasant, dirty or boring;

(iii) is stressful or carries great responsibility.
(iv) involves antisocial hours.

(c) Wage Drift

Wage drift occurs when the earnings of some workers rise above the average for the industry. Workers doing the same job within the same industry may be paid differently because:

  (i) Workers in cities are sometimes paid more to meet the higher cost of living.
 (ii) In spite of equal-opportunities legislation women tend to earn less because their careers are interrupted by family commitments, or they suffer from sex discrimination.
(iii) Older workers tend to earn more because they are paid a bonus to reward their experience.
(iv) Some workers are paid more for working harder.
 (v) Some workers receive overtime, bonuses, etc.

8.4 Wealth

(a) Types of Wealth

Wealth is the value of all the *assets* (items) owned by a household at a particular moment in time. Figure 8.2 illustrates the main types of wealth.

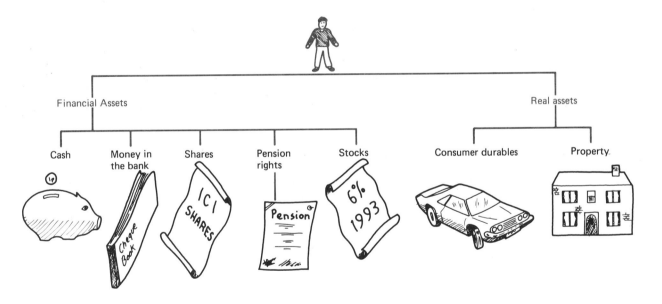

Figure 8.2 Types of wealth

(b) Wealth Distribution

Wealth Distribution means the way the ownership of assets is shared out between households.

Table 8.1 suggests that while the top 1 per cent and 10 per cent now own a smaller share of total wealth than in 1971, half the population still own only 4 per cent of all assets.

Table 8.1 Wealth trends

	Share of total wealth	
	1971	*1983*
Most wealthy 1%	31%	20%
Most wealthy 10%	65%	54%
Most wealthy 50%	95%	96%

8.5 Worked Examples

Example 8.1

Income distribution means the way in which total earnings are divided between different groups. The following table shows six sources of income and the percentage of total income each source provides. Study the table and answer all the questions that follow.

Type of income	Share of total income	
	1974	*1984*
Wages and salaries	67%	61%
Self-employment	9%	9%
Rent, dividends and interest	7%	7%
Private pensions	5%	7%
Social security benefit	9%	13%
Other	3%	3%

Source: Adapted from *Social Trends*, 16, HMSO, 1986

(a) From the table give one example of income earned from:
   (i) employment, and   (ii) owning property.   **(2 marks)**
(b) What has happened to the percentage share of total income received by the self-employed between 1974 and 1984?   **(1 mark)**
(c) What do you understand by the terms:
   (i) self-employment and   (ii) private pensions?   **(3 marks)**
(d) What evidence is there in the table for believing that there has been an increase in the number of unemployed?   **(2 marks)**
(e) What would be the likely effect on the share of total income earned from rent, dividends and interest following:

   (i) an increase in savings;
   (ii) an increase in the number of homeowners?   **(4 marks)**

(f) The table suggests that the share of total income received as wages and salaries has gone down between 1974 and 1984. Does this mean the standard of living has also fallen during the same period? Explain your answer.   **(4 marks)**

Solution 8.1

(a) Wages are an example of income earned from working, and rent is earned from owning property.

(b) The percentage share of total income received by the self-employed did not change between 1974 and 1984.

(c) (i) Self-employment refers to those people who do not work for others but work for themselves.

   (ii) Private pensions are received by retired people who contributed to their own savings scheme. Private pensions do not include state pension payments.

(d) The unemployed receive benefits. The percentage share of benefits in total income has risen sharply in the period from 9 per cent to 13 per cent. This suggests a probable increase in the number of employed.

(e) (i) Interest is earned from lending money. An increase in savings will mean an increase in interest payments which, in turn, will increase the share of interest in total income.

   (ii) Rent is earned from letting out property. An increase in the number of house owners suggests that fewer people will be renting property. The income of landlords falls, reducing the share of rent in total income.

(f) Only a fall in the *value* of total income will reduce the standard of living. Given the same value for total income, a fall in the share of wage earners between two years will be cancelled out by an increase in the share of other groups. A fall in the share of wages and salaries in total income does not necessarily result in a fall in the standard of living

Example 8.2

The diagram on the next page shows the average weekly pay of different occupations. Manual occupations involve mainly physical work. Study the information and answer all the questions.

(a) From the diagram, how much do teachers receive each week? **(1 mark)**

(b) On average, how much more each week does the non-manual worker earn than the manual worker? **(1 mark)**

(c) Give an example of manual work shown in the diagram. **(1 mark)**

(d) Both doctors and teachers provide a social service. For what economic reasons do you think that they do not earn the same wage? **(4 marks)**

(e) What do you understand by the term gross pay? **(2 marks)**

(f) How can the government use each of the following to make wages more equal:

   (i) income tax; **(3 marks)**
   (ii) social security benefits; **(3 marks)**
   (iii) social services? **(3 marks)**

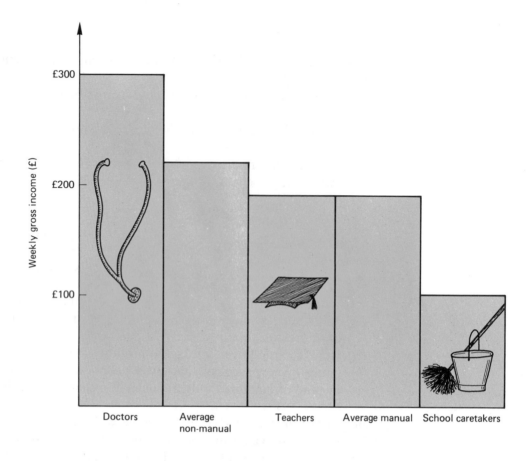

Solution 8.2

(a) On average, teachers receive a gross weekly wage of £190.

(b) The difference in average weekly gross income between non-manual and manual workers is £30 a week.

(c) A caretaker is an example of a manual worker.

(d) Both jobs require qualifications and a period of training. However, the entrance requirements and training period for doctors is more demanding than for teachers. Hence there are fewer people with the skill and training necessary for a medical career. Since the supply of doctors is more limited than that of teachers, doctors tend to earn more.

(e) Gross pay is the income of a worker before any deductions have been made for income tax and national insurance.

(f)   (i) For a doctor earning £300 a week and paying 50 per cent income tax, take-home pay will be only £150. For someone earning £150 and paying 10 per cent income tax, take-home pay will be just £15 a week less than a doctor's. Progressive income tax makes income more even.

 (ii) If benefits are given only to the lowest-paid then the gap between high- and low-income groups will be reduced. Rent subsidies and rate rebates are examples of benefits which make income more equal.

(iii) Social services are provided to everyone by the government irrespective of income. If the lowest-paid make more use of these facilities than the highest-paid, then by providing a benefit in kind the government has made income more equal.

Example 8.3

(a) A manager is paid a gross monthly salary of £1000 but takes home a net monthly salary of £700. Why is there a difference between gross salary and net salary?

(2 marks)

(b) Give one example of a non-monetary reward sometimes given by a firm to:

    (i) a manager; **(1 mark)**

    (ii) a shop-floor worker. **(1 mark)**

(c) Some workers are paid according to the number of items they make (piece rate) and others are paid according to the number of hours they work (time rate). If you were a manager of a shirt factory, by which method would you pay the following? Give a reason in each case.

    (i) a machinist; **(2 marks)**
    (ii) a supervisor of the machinists; **(2 marks)**
    (iii) a secretary in the accounts office. **(2 marks)**

(d) Explain why workers doing the same job are paid different wages. **(5 marks)**

Solution 8.3

(a) The manager has to pay income tax and national insurance contributions out of his income. Once these deductions have been made from the manager's gross salary, the remainder is called net salary.

(b) (i) Non-monetary rewards are items provided by firms to employees at little or no cost. For example, companies sometimes provide a manager with a company car for business and private use.
    (ii) Companies sometimes provide workers with subsidised meals at lunch time.

(c) (i) If a machinist is paid for every item made then there is an incentive to produce as many items as possible during one shift.
    (ii) A supervisor does not actually produce a finished good. Therefore it is better to pay an hourly wage rate.
    (iii) A secretary in the accounts department could be paid for every letter sent out but this might result in rushed, incorrect correspondence. It is better to pay the secretary according to the hours worked.

(d) Wage drift occurs when workers doing the same job receive different wages. This may come about because one worker is given a bonus payment for working harder or longer hours. Many firms reward workers who have been with the company for many years with a higher wage. Some workers are paid an allowance if they work in cities where the cost of goods and services is higher than average.

In spite of legislation some disadvantaged groups such as women and racial minorities still tend to earn less than other workers doing the same job. This may be because these groups are reluctant to seek promotion, or because of discrimination.

Example 8.4

(a) Explain the differences between income and wealth. **(4 marks)**
(b) What part is played in the creation of *both* income and wealth in:

    (i) a brickworks; **(4 marks)**
    (ii) a bank? **(4 marks)**

(c) (i) Explain *two* factors which affect the distribution of income in the United Kingdom. **(4 marks)**
    (ii) Explain *two* factors which affect the distribution of wealth in the United Kingdom. **(4 marks)**

(SEG specimen GCSE)

Solution 8.4

(a) Income is a flow value and is the amount of money a person receives *each time period*. For example, a plumber may have an income of £200 each week.

    Wealth is a stock value and is the value of all the assets owned by a person at a *particular moment in time*. If the plumber adds up the money held in his bank account and the second-hand value of all the goods he owns then this gives the total amount of wealth owned.

(b) (i) A brickworks uses raw materials to turn into bricks. The difference between the cost of producing and the revenue from selling the bricks is called value added. The value added is the firm's contribution to wealth creation.

       The land, labour and capital used in production will receive income in return for their factor services in making bricks.

    (ii) Wealth is created by specialists who use money to purchase goods they have not had time to make themselves. Banks offer payment services such as cheques, and this improves the use of money as a medium of exchange and so contributes towards wealth creation.

       The land, labour and capital used in providing banking facilities receive income in return for their factor services.

(c) (i) The distribution of income refers to the way earnings are shared out between people. Income distribution is affected by the type of job people do and the amount of assets they own. Some people have highly paid jobs and receive an income from owning assets. Other people own no assets and have low paid jobs.

    (ii) People can use their income to buy assets such as a house or non-durable consumer goods such as a holiday. Therefore, the ownership of wealth varies between households. Assets can be passed on to children, which tends to maintain the uneven spread of wealth.

Example 8.5

Study the two photographs which show two different families outside their own homes.

Family A

Family B

(a) Name one luxury good shown in the photographs. **(1 mark)**
(b) From the photographs, write a brief account of the type of leisure activity available to each family. **(4 marks)**
(c) What economic reasons could you give to explain the different standard of living enjoyed by each family? **(4 marks)**
(d) Advise the government on the action it could take to:

    (i) make income more even; **(3 marks)**
    (ii) make wealth more even. **(3 marks)**

Solution 8.5

(a) There are no luxury goods shown with family A. The swimming pool of family B is an example of a luxury good.
(b) Leisure time is time used for relaxation. Family A have few belongings to help them enjoy their free time. The poor state of their clothes suggests that they do not have sufficient income to buy the necessities of life, let alone spend money on leisure pursuits.

    Family B are surrounded by many luxuries and seem well fed. They have enough money to maintain an expensive swimming pool and so can probably afford to follow many leisure activities.
(c) The amount of wealth owned by a family depends on their past income and whether they received an inheritance. Family A probably earned little income in the past and received no money on the death of relatives. Family B probably earned a large income in the past or inherited money.
(d) (i) Income can be made more even by making income tax more progressive. This means taking a larger percentage of income in tax as income rises. Taxes taken from the most wealthy can then be transferred to the least wealthy, either directly as benefit payments or indirectly in the form of free social services.

    (ii) Wealth can be made more even by taxing the transfer of capital between people. If the government takes 90 per cent of any inheritance or gift then wealth differences will eventually be reduced—although this will take a long time. Progressive income tax reduces the opportunity for people to build up wealth.

8.6 Questions

Use each of the following phrases to complete questions 1 to 5.

    A earned income   **B** net income
    C transfer income   **D** real income
    E gross income

1 Social security benefits are examples of ....
2 Take-home pay is called ....
3 Money received for producing a good is known as ....
4 .... refers to the amount of goods wages can buy.
5 Basic wages plus overtime gives ....
6 Incomes will be more equal if the government:
    A makes income tax more progressive **B** lowers income tax allowances
    C increases indirect taxation   **D** lowers transfer payments
7 State two differences between salaries and wages.
8 What is the name given to wages which are calculated according to the amount of goods made?
9 State two deductions from a pay packet likely to be made by an employer.
10 Explain what is meant by the phrase 'real income'.
11 If prices increase but money income remains constant then there has been:
    A a fall in production   **B** a decrease in real income
    C an increase in living standards   **D** a decrease in the cost of living
12 The demand for workers depends on:
    A effective demand   **B** competitive demand
    C derived demand   **D** joint demand
13 Production line workers are poorly paid because:
    A the work is unskilled   **B** the work is tiring
    C they work long hours   **D** the work is boring
14 What do you understand by wage drift?
15 Which of the following is an example of wealth?
    A the rent paid to a landlord   **B** the profit earned by ICI
    C the wages of a factory worker **D** some ICI shares held by an individual
16 Explain the main differences between income and wealth.
17 State two methods the government could use to make wealth more equal.

8.7 Answers

1 **C**   2 **B**   3 **A**   4 **D**   5 **E**   6 **A**
7 Salaries are paid monthly: do not depend on the hours worked; and are a fixed cost.
    Wages are paid weekly; do depend on the hours worked; and are a variable cost.
8 Piece rate or piece work.
9 Employers may deduct income tax, national insurance, pension, trade union and insurance subscriptions.
10 See section 8.2(c).
11 **B**   12 **C**   13 **A**
14 See section 8.3(c).   15 **D**
16 Income is a flow value and refers to money received each time period. Wealth is a stock value and refers to the value of all assets owned by an individual at a particular moment in time.
17 The government can tax the ownership and transfer of valuable assets such as houses.

9 Trade Unions

9.1 Features of Trade Unions

(a) Types of Trade Union

A *trade union* is an organisation which represents workers. There are four main types:

(i) *Craft unions* representing skilled workers from one occupation. For example, SOGAT 82 (printers) and the AEU (engineering).
(ii) *General unions* representing mainly unskilled workers from many occupations. For example, the TGWU (Transport and General Workers' Union).
(iii) *Industrial unions* representing mainly workers in one industry. For example, the NUM (miners' union).
(iv) *Professional* or *white-collar unions* representing skilled workers in mainly service industries. For example, the NUT (teachers' union).

(b) Functions of Trade Unions

Trade unions aim to:

(i) Improve the pay of workers.
(ii) Improve working conditions and secure longer holidays.
(iii) protect members' jobs.
(iv) Provide local, social and welfare facilities.
(v) Influence government policy by sponsoring Members of Parliament and contributing money to political parties.

(c) Organisation of Trade Unions

Each trade union has its own internal organisation. Generally:

(i) Small groups of workers elect a local spokesman (*shop steward*).
(ii) Every area has a *branch* which sends *delegates* (representatives) to a yearly *national conference*.
(iii) Conference passes *resolutions* (policies) and elects a *national executive*. Only the national executive can call an official strike.
(iv) The entire membership elects a *general secretary*. The general secretary acts as the union's spokesman and manages everyday affairs, usually until he reaches retirement age.

(d) The Trades Union Congress

The *Trades Union Congress* (TUC) is made up of over 90 unions representing more than 11 million members. An annual conference decides overall union policy and elects the General Council. The General Secretary of the TUC is the trades union spokesman in any negotiations with the government or employers' organisations. The TUC has no power to initiate or halt an individual union's industrial action.

9.2 Employers' Associations

Employers' associations represent the employers in a particular industry and negotiate with unions.

The Confederation of British Industry (CBI) is made up of over 300 employers' associations and nearly 14 000 individual firms. The CBI represents employers in negotiations with the government and the TUC. The Director General acts as spokesperson for the CBI.

9.3 Wage Negotiations

(a) Collective Bargaining

In the nineteenth century workers used to negotiate their own pay and conditions with their employer. *Collective bargaining* occurs when workers allow the union to negotiate on their behalf. Negotiation can be with an individual employer or an employers' association.

(b) Types of Dispute

Disputes can arise over pay, working conditions, redundancies or *restrictive practices* which include:

(i) A *closed shop* when a union insists that all workers in a place of work are members.
(ii) *Demarcation* when a union insists that only their members do certain jobs.
(iii) *Blacking* goods when the union refuses to handle goods produced by a firm in dispute with a union.
(iv) *Over-manning* when the union insists on a large number of workers for one job.

(c) Industrial Action

If negotiations break down employers may lose output while workers may lose some pay. More often than not a compromise is found. However, sometimes one party resorts to industrial action. Unions can:

(i) *Work to rule* and do the bare minimum of work.
(ii) Impose an *overtime ban* and refuse extra work.
(iii) *Strike* and refuse to work altogether.

(iv) Mount a *picket line* outside their place of work and ask other trade unionists not to enter.

Employers can operate a *lockout* and refuse workers entry or they can dismiss striking workers for breach of contract.

(d) Recent Legislation

Recent legislation has severely weakened trade union power as follows:

(i) An employer can now sue a union for lost profits if industrial action is taken without an initial secret ballot of workers.
(ii) Industrial action can be taken only against the original employer and not against his suppliers or buyers.
(iii) Mass picketing is unlawful. Only a handful of strikers are allowed to man a picket line, peacefully.

(e) Arbitration

Arbitration is when employers and the unions agree to an independent referee to try to find common ground.

(i) Since 1974 an independent Advisory Conciliation and Arbitration Service (ACAS) has been available to help solve disputes.
(ii) In the 1980s there have been an increasing number of *single-union agreements* where employers negotiate with only one union. *Pendulum arbitration* is used to settle a dispute where an independent referee chooses one side or the other.

9.4 Worked Examples

Example 9.1

To answer questions (a) to (c), study the two photographs on the next page which show different types of trade union activity. For each photograph:
(a) Name the union shown.   **(2 marks)**
(b) State the type of union.   **(2 marks)**
(c) Explain the type of trade union activity.   **(4 marks)**

(d) Assess the likely effect of each of the following on the number of people belonging to trade unions. Explain your answers.

   (i) An increase in unemployment.   **(2 marks)**
   (ii) An increase in the number of closed shops.   **(2 marks)**

A company which has just increased its profits is faced with a wage demand from the union.
(e) How might an employer describe the likely economic effects of a strike over pay?
                                                                             (4 marks)
(f) What might a trade union official say in reply?   **(4 marks)**

A A massed crowd of printing workers confront police outside the news International plant at Wapping in pursuit of their claim.

B The Durham annual gala with miners on their way to be addressed by union and Labour Party leaders.

Solution 9.1

(a) Photograph A shows SOGAT 82 and photograph B shows the NUM.
(b) SOGAT 82 is a craft union representing skilled printers and the NUM is an industrial union representing most of the workers in mining.
(c) Photograph A shows a union in dispute mounting a picket line in pursuit of their claim.

   Photograph B shows local union members rallying to demonstrate mutual strength and support, and to listen to their leaders.

(d) (i) Unemployed people may be unable to afford to continue paying union subscriptions and may therefore decide to leave the union. However, an increase in the number of people unemployed may make those still in work afraid for their jobs. Workers who do not at present belong to a union may now decide to join in case they too are made redundant.
   (ii) A closed shop is when a union insists that all employees in a place of work belong to a union. This will have the effect of increasing the number of people belonging to trade unions.

(e) The increased profits are needed to pay for new investment and expansion. A successful firm means job security for the workers.

   If the strike halts production, the firm will have no revenue coming in to pay for fixed costs such as rent and rates which still have to be paid. If the strike continues for any length of time, then losses will build up and the company may be forced into liquidation. Striking workers will then have lost their jobs as a result of their own action.

(f) The increased profits of the company are the result of the extra efforts of the work force. It is only fair that workers should share in the success of the company through higher wages.

   The company does not have to suffer a strike. The extra cost of the pay increase can be met by the company's increased profits and will be a far smaller sum than the losses from an all-out strike.

Example 9.2

   (a) Give three reasons why a trade union might ask for a wage increase. **(3 marks)**
   (b) In the event of a dispute over a trade union demand for higher wages what action could:

   (i) the trade union take to support its wage claim; **(4 marks)**
   (ii) the employer take to oppose the wage claim? **(3 marks)**

   (c) Why do many trade unions belong to the Trades Union Congress? **(2 marks)**
   (d) A productivity deal is when an increase in wages is linked to an increase in workers' output. Assess the likely effect of a productivity deal on:

   (i) the price of the firm's product; **(5 marks)**
   (ii) the number of workers employed by the firm. **(3 marks)**

Solution 9.2

   (a) A trade union might ask for a pay increase in times of inflation to restore the purchasing power of their members. The union might ask for an increase if the company has made bigger profits. A union might also ask for an increase in wages if workers in other occupations have received an increase. (Alternatively if productivity increases.)

(b) (i) A union can work to rule and do only those tasks set down in their contract. This involves refusing to do voluntary tasks. An overtime ban is effective if the company is anxious to increase production. A strike has the effect of bringing the entire factory to a halt. These measures reduce the firm's profits.

(ii) An employer can reduce the pay of workers not working normally or even sack employees in dispute. The employer would then take on new staff.

(c) The Trade Union Congress represents the union movement in negotiations with the government and the CBI. Unions who belong to the TUC have a say in deciding its overall policy.

(d) (i) The price of a product is partly affected by the firm's costs of production. An increase in wages raises costs and hence prices. If, however, a 10 per cent increase in wages is matched by a 10 per cent increase in productivity then unit cost is unaffected and there is no reason why price should rise.

If the increase in wages is accompanied by a proportionately greater increase in output then average cost is reduced and price may well fall.

(ii) A productivity deal increases output. If the firm is able to sell all the extra units which have been produced then there will be no change in the number of employees.

If the firm is unable to increase its sales, then the old level of output can now be met using fewer workers and a number of people may lose their jobs.

Example 9.3

Read the following publicity handout prepared by a local union which describes some recent changes in trade union activity.

One way a trade union in dispute with a particular firm can take industrial action is by placing pickets outside the factory gates. Pickets ask workers not to 'cross the line' and go to work.

Until recently, a mass picket could prevent any supplies getting into or out of the factory and it was one of the most powerful weapons at the disposal of a large union. However, in the early 1980s the government passed a law banning picket lines made up of more than six strikers.

Recent legislation also means that a strike must be supported by a majority of members in a secret ballot. Any union taking 'secondary' action against companies not directly involved in the strike (e.g. the firm's main customer) could be fined millions of pounds.

Mass unemployment has strengthened the hand of the employers. Some unions are reacting by signing no-strike agreements which involve all disputes being decided by an outside body. Employers and the union have to follow the decision of the independent arbitrators.

(a) From the passage what does the trade union mean by:

    (i) industrial action; **(1 mark)**
    (ii) mass picket; **(1 mark)**
    (iii) no-strike agreements. **(1 mark)**

(b) According to the passage, what type of union was once able to use mass picketing in a dispute? **(1 mark)**

(c) Using the information in the passage, explain how government legislation has reduced union power. **(2 marks)**

(d) Give one other reason suggested in the passage for reduced union power.
(1 mark)

(e) You are an officer of the union. The union is in dispute with a local firm. Write a report describing the type of action you think your union could legally take.
(4 marks)

(f) The union ignores your advice and decides to mount a mass picket. What are the likely economic results for:

    (i) your union; **(3 marks)**
    (ii) your local community. **(3 marks)**

Solution 9.3

(a) (i) Industrial action is when the union asks its members to do something against the company, e.g. banning overtime.
    (ii) A mass picket is when a large number of workers on strike prevent goods leaving or entering the factory.
    (iii) A no-strike agreement is when all disputes are referred to an outside body whose decision is binding.

(b) Mass picketing was once used by large unions with many members.

(c) The government has passed two laws which have reduced union power. Mass picketing is now illegal. Unions can now be sued if they disrupt the normal working of another firm not directly involved in the strike.

(d) Mass unemployment has made workers reluctant to take strike action in case they lose their jobs.

(e) The union should consider imposing a 'work to rule' with each employee only doing those jobs laid down in his contract. An overtime ban will hit the company's profits and make it difficult to meet delivery deadlines.

The union could ballot all members over possible strike action.

(f) (i) The union would find itself in court for breaking the law. The courts have the power to fine the union, and to seize all the assets of the union until it agrees to cease mass picketing. The union would then be unable to pay its members' strike pay. This may reduce the number of people on strike.
    (ii) Mass picketing involves thousands of strikers and a large number of policemen. The local community may witness violent scenes resulting in damage to property.

Mass pickets on strike will not be receiving very much income and will have to cut back on their expenditure in shops.

9.5 Questions

Pair each of the following:

1	professional association	A	GMWU (municipal workers)
2	general union	B	SOGAT 82 (printers)
3	industrial union	C	APEX (clerks)
4	white-collar union	D	BMA (doctors)
5	craft union	E	NUM (miners)
	(e.g. 1—E)		

(WJEC specimen GCSE)

1........ 2........ 3........ 4........ 5........

6   What is the main difference between an industrial and a craft trade union?
7   State two functions of a trade union.
8   Why might craft unions resist the introduction of technology?
9   Describe two possible benefits of belonging to a trade union.
10 Describe two possible disadvantages of belonging to a trade union.
11 The .... is often a trade union's chief spokesman.
12 Most UK trade unions are members of the:
    A CBI   **B** TUC   **C** GATT   **D** ACAS
13 The Confederation of British Industry is an example of:
    A a multinational corporation   **B** a trade union
    C an employers' association   **D** a public corporation
14 What is meant by collective bargaining?
15 Which of the following would most help a trade union in negotiating a wage rise:
    A the industry is increasing the use of labour-saving machinery
    B the industry is making large losses
    C the industry is located in a special development area
    D the union has a large number of members in that industry
16 In a .... all who work in a particular industry must belong to a trade union.
17 What is a demarcation dispute?
18 State two courses of action available to a trade union in an effort to force management into accepting their wage claim.
19 The Advisory, Conciliation and Arbitration Service aims to:
    A take sides in a dispute   **B** negotiate terms for redundant workers
    C suggest compensation for unfair dismissal   **D** find common ground in a dispute

9.6 Answers

1   **D** 2 **A** 3 **E** 4 **C** 5 **B**
6   Industrial unions represent all workers in a particular industry. Craft unions represent workers in a particular occupation.
7   See section 9.1(b).
8   This may result in the loss of jobs in that occupation.
9   The union represents you in pay negotiations or if you have an argument with your employer. The union has social and educational facilities.
10 It costs money to belong to a union and you may have to go along with majority decisions, even if you disagree.
11 General secretary.
12 **B**   13 **C**
14 All workers are represented by unions in wage negotiations.
15 **D**. Unions with many members in an industry can organise effective industrial action if employers fail to offer an adequate wage rise.
16 Closed shop.
17 A disagreement over who does a particular job.
18 See section 9.3(c).
19 **D**

10 National Income

10.1 Circular Flow of Income

(a) Real and Money Flows

Figure 10.1 divides the economy into two sections or *sectors* made up of households and firms.

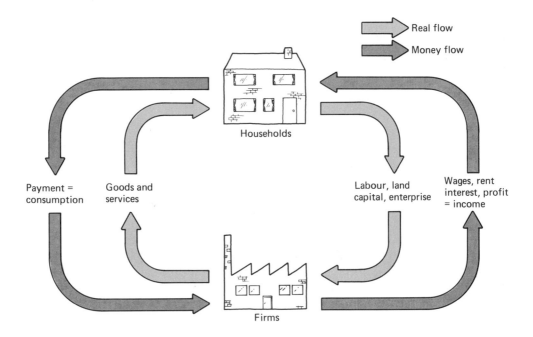

Figure 10.1 The circular flow of income

There are two types of *flow* (an amount per time period) between these groups:

(i) A *real flow*. Households own factor services which they hire out to firms. Factor services are then used to manufacture goods and services.
(ii) A *money flow*. Households receive payments for their services (*income*) and use this money to buy the output of firms (*consumption*).

(b) Leakages or Withdrawals From the Circular Flow

Figure 10.2 on the next page shows that some part of household income will be:

(i) Put aside for future spending, i.e. *saved*.
(ii) Paid to the government in *taxes*.
(iii) Spent on foreign made goods *imported* into the country.

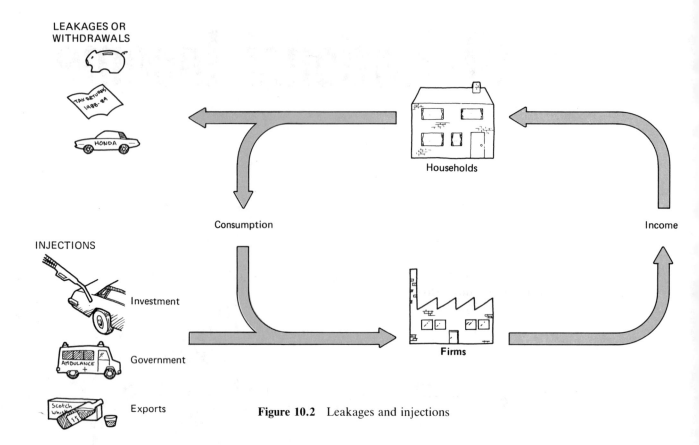

INJECTIONS

Investment

Government

Exports

Consumption

Households

Income

Firms

Figure 10.2 Leakages and injections

(c) Injections Into the Circular Flow

Figure 10.2 shows that some goods will be sold to:

   (i) other firms, i.e. *investment* expenditure;
  (ii) the government, i.e. *government* expenditure;
 (iii) foreigners, i.e. *export* expenditure.

(d) The Multiplier Effect

In Figure 10.3 an increase in government spending is received by a household as extra income. Part of this extra income is then spent and part is saved.

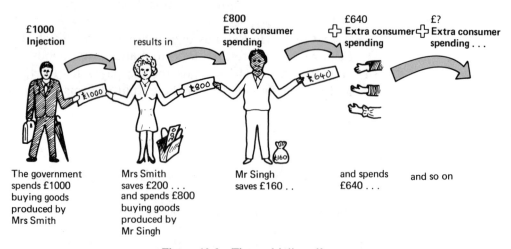

£1000
Injection

results in

£800
Extra consumer
spending

£640
✚ Extra consumer
spending

£?
✚ Extra consumer
spending . . .

The government
spends £1000
buying goods
produced by
Mrs Smith

Mrs Smith
saves £200 . . .
and spends £800
buying goods
produced by
Mr Singh

Mr Singh
saves £160 . .

and spends
£640 . . .

and so on

Figure 10.3 The multiplier effect

Extra consumer spending then gives rise to a series of further incomes and expenditures. The overall increase in spending is much higher than the initial injection.

10.2 National Income Accounts

The relationships explained in section 10.1 form the basis of national income accounting. The aim of *national income accounting* is to place a money value on this year's output. There are three methods of calculation.

(a) Income Method

Figure 10.4 shows the procedure followed in using the income method.

Note that only incomes earned from supplying a factor service are counted. Unearned incomes such as pensions and *transfer payments* are ignored.

Figure 10.4 The income method

(b) Expenditure Method

The government adds up all the money spent in buying this year's output and ignores:

 (i) indirect taxes and subsidies included in the selling price;
 (ii) spending on second-hand goods.

(c) Output Method

The economy is broken up into twelve different sectors (e.g. manufacturing). The money spent on making the goods (*inputs*) is taken away from the money received from the sale of the goods (*outputs*) to give each sector's *value added*. Taking final output or adding up each sector's value added gives national income.

Unpaid output such as the work of housewives is not recorded.

10.3 Standard of Living

(a) Measurement of the Standard of Living

The value of this year's national income is a useful measure of how well-off a country is in material terms. However, inflation increases the *money* value of national income but does not provide us with any more goods to consume. *Real national income* is found by applying the equation:

$$\text{Real national income} = \frac{\text{Money national income}}{\text{Retail price index}} \times 100.$$

The *standard of living* refers to the amount of goods and services consumed by households in one year and is found by applying the equation:

$$\text{Standard of living} = \frac{\text{Real national income}}{\text{Population}}.$$

A high standard of living means households consume a large number of goods and services.

A second method of calculating living standards is to count the percentage of people owning consumer durables such as cars, televisions, etc. An increase in ownership indicates an improved standard of living.

A third method of calculating living standards is by noting how long an average person has to work to earn enough money to buy certain goods. If people have to work less time to buy goods, then there has been an increase in the standard of living.

(b) Interpretation of the Standard of Living

An increase in the standard of living may not mean a better life-style for the majority if:

(i) Only a small minority of wealthy people consume the extra goods.
(ii) Increased output of certain goods results in more noise, congestion and pollution.
(iii) Leisure time is reduced to achieve the production increase.
(iv) There is an increase in the amount of stress and anxiety in society.

10.4 Worked Examples

Example 10.1

The diagram shows a simple circular flow of income for an economy made up of households and firms only. Households earn their income by supplying factor services such as labour to firms. Firms use the efforts of households to make goods and services which are then sold back to consumers.

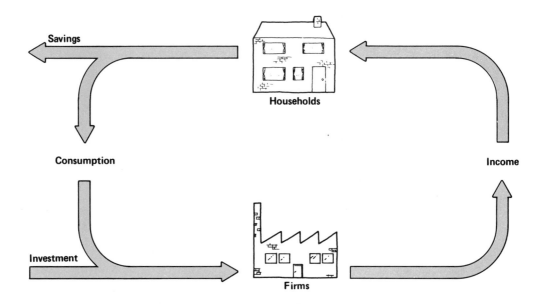

(a) In the diagram, what can households do with their income? **(2 marks)**

(b) Which item in the diagram would include:

    (i) spending by a company on a car; **(1 mark)**
    (ii) spending by a family on a car? **(1 mark)**

(c) Are each of the following included in the diagram as part of income? Explain your answer:

    (i) dividends paid to shareholders in a company; **(2 marks)**
    (ii) social security benefit paid to a full-time student; **(2 marks)**
    (iii) the output of housewives. **(2 marks)**

(d) Use the diagram to explain the likely effects of a £50 million increase in investment on income, savings and consumption. **(6 marks)**

Solution 10.1

(a) Households can use their money either to buy goods or to save.
(b) (i) Spending by a firm on a car is an example of investment.
    (ii) Spending by a family on a car is an example of consumption.

(c) (i) Shareholders supply capital to the firm and are entitled to a reward in the form of dividends. Dividends are included as income in the diagram.
    (ii) A full-time student receiving benefits does not help to produce a good. His income is an example of a transfer payment and is not included.
    (iii) Housewives provide essential services for their families but receive no income for their effort. They are not included.

(d)

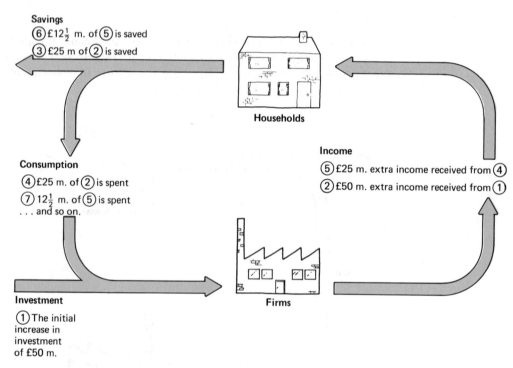

Savings
⑥ £12½ m. of ⑤ is saved
③ £25 m of ② is saved

Households

Income
⑤ £25 m. extra income received from ④
② £50 m. extra income received from ①

Consumption
④ £25 m. of ② is spent
⑦ 12½ m. of ⑤ is spent
. . . and so on.

Investment
① The initial increase in investment of £50 m.

Firms

Looking at the diagram you can see that the initial increase in investment (1) is received as income (2). Households save part of the extra income (3) and spend part (4). The extra spending (4) results in a further increase in income (5), part of which is saved (6) and part spent (7), and so on.

The diagram shows the multiplier effect of an initial increase in investment.

Example 10.2

(a) What do you understand by the term 'national income'? **(2 marks)**
(b) Explain briefly how national income is calculated using:

    (i)   the income method; **(3 marks)**
    (ii)   the expenditure method. **(3 marks)**

(c) What problems do each of the following cause when calculating national income? Explain your answer:

     (i)   social security benefits;   **(2 marks)**
    (ii)   indirect taxes;   **(2 marks)**
    (iii) inflation.   **(4 marks)**

Solution 10.2

(a) National income is the money value of all the goods and services produced by an economy in a given time period, usually one year.

(b) (i) The income method adds up the earnings of everyone who has contributed to the production of goods and services in the current time period. Account is taken of income received from owning assets abroad to arrive at a value for gross national product.

    (ii) The expenditure method adds up all the money spent by households, firms, the government and overseas customers in buying this year's output. The government ignores any money spent buying second-hand goods as these were produced in previous time periods. The amount of revenue raised from indirect taxation is deducted.

(c) (i) Social security benefits are received by people who are in need and are not a reward for helping to produce commodities. People in work pay taxes to the government which then transfers that money as benefit payments. Such payments are not included in national income.

    (ii) Indirect taxes are a tax on spending. This means that a seller does not keep all the money received from the sale of a good. The amount of indirect tax must be subtracted from the market price to give a true expenditure valuation.

    (iii) Inflation occurs when the price of goods is continually increasing. The value of national income equals the quantity of goods made multiplied by their selling price. In times of inflation it is quite possible for national income to be rising even though the amount of goods made remains fixed.

       For example, assume that, in 1986, 400 goods costing £5 each are made. A year later output stays constant at 400 units while price rises to £6 per item. The value of goods in 1986 is £2000, while the value of the same goods one year later is £2400. National income figures must be adjusted to take account of price changes if they are to give a true value for current output.

Example 10.3

The standard of living is the amount of goods and services consumed by the average person each year. Study the information in the table on the next page about UK living standards.

(a) Give one example of a consumer durable given in the information.   **(1 mark)**
(b) What was national income in 1984?   **(1 mark)**
(c) Calculate the percentage increase between 1974 and 1984 in:
    (i) national income, and   (ii) the retail price index.   **(2 marks)**
(d) What does your answer to (c) suggest about changes in real national income over the period?   **(2 marks)**

	1974	1984
National income	£68 000 million	£240 000 million
Percentage of households owning:		
Central heating	43%	65%
Telephone	50%	80%
Time worked to pay for:		
A long-playing record	3 hours	1½ hours
A cinema ticket	30 minutes	35 minutes
Retail price index	100	350

(e) What evidence is there in the information for believing the standard of living increased between 1974 and 1984? **(3 marks)**

(f) Why do you think the length of time necessary to pay for a cinema ticket went up? **(2 marks)**

(g) Does an increase in the standard of living always mean people are better off? **(5 marks)**

Solution 10.3

(a) Central heating is an example of a consumer durable.

(b) National income was £240 000 million in 1984.

(c)   (i) National income increased $\dfrac{240\ 000 - 68\ 000}{68\ 000} \times 100 = 253$ per cent.

    (ii) The retail price index increased $\dfrac{350 - 100}{100} \times 100 = 250$ per cent.

(d) Since the percentage increase in national income is greater than the percentage increase in prices, (c) suggests that real national income increased between 1974 and 1984.

(e) The number of people owning luxury items such as central heating and a telephone increased over the period, indicating that in 1984 people had a higher standard of living. The time taken to work for a record fell, which also suggests an increase in living standards.

(f) The time taken to earn enough money to pay for a cinema ticket increased over the period because the price of a cinema ticket went up by more than average earnings.

(g) The standard of living is an average. It is possible for an increase in the supply of goods to be used by only a small number of very wealthy people while the majority live in poverty.

The increase in the standard of living may result in an increase in pollution and damage done to the environment.

The production of extra goods may result in a loss of leisure time or an increase in the amount of stress and anxiety associated with work.

10.5 Questions

1 What type of income is included in the circular flow of income?
2 What can households do with their income?
3 To which economic groups do firms sell their output?
4 Which of the following is a withdrawal from the circular flow of income?
  A imports   **B** exports   **C** investment   **D** wealth
5 Which of the following is most likely to reduce the circular flow of income?
  A an increase in government spending **B** a decrease in personal savings
  C reduced export spending   **D** reduced import spending
6 Which of the following is an injection into the circular flow of income? An increase in:
  A savings   **B** investment   **C** taxation   **D** imports
7 Which one of the following is most likely to increase the circular flow of income?
  A a fall in personal savings   **B** a fall in government expenditure
  C an increase in import expenditure **D** an increase in taxation
8 Define national income.
9 What is meant by 'national income accounting'?
10 Adding together the total earnings of all the factors of production in one year, is known as the .... method.
11 The total of all wages, salaries, profits, interest and dividends is called the national ....
12 An example of a transfer payment is:
  A a student's grant   **B** a shareholder's dividend
  C a doctor's wage   **D** a landlord's rent
13 Which of the following is a transfer payment?
  A profit from the sale of a house   **B** interest received from a building society
  C income received from an old-age **D** the repayment of a bank loan pension
14 Adding together all the money spent buying this year's output is called the .... method.
15 Adding together the total value of all goods and services produced in a country in one year is called the .... method.
16 Which of the following would be regarded by economists as productive workers?:
  A students   **B** housewives   **C** pensioners   **D** actors
17 What is the difference between money national income and real national income? income?
18 Changes in a country's standard of living are most commonly measured by changes in:
  A real national income   **B** real national income per head
  C money national income   **D** money national income per head
19 Which of the following is most likely to be found in a country with a high standard of living?:
  A a low life expectancy   **B** a low infant death rate
  C a low literacy rate   **D** a low investment rate
20 State two reasons why an increase in the standard of living may not mean a better life style.

10.6 Answers

1 Income earned from helping to produce goods and services.
2 Households can use their income to buy commodities, to save, or to pay taxes.
3 Firms sell to consumers, other firms, the government and overseas.
4 A   5 C   6 B   7 A
8 National income is the value of this year's output.

9 National income accounting is the method used to calculate the value of this year's output.

10	Income	11	Income	12	A	13	C
14	Expenditure	15	Output	16	D		
17	See section 10.3(a).			18	B	19	B
20	See section 10.3(b).						

11 Money and Banking

11.1 Features of Money

(a) Functions of Money

Money is something which people generally accept in exchange for a good or a service. Money performs four main functions:

 (i) a *medium of exchange* for buying goods and services;
 (ii) a *unit of account* for placing a value on goods and services;
(iii) a *store of value* when saving;
(iv) a *standard for deferred payment* when calculating loans.

(b) Properties or Characteristics of Money

Any item which is going to serve as money must be:

 (i) *acceptable* to people as payment;
 (ii) *scarce* and in controlled supply;
(iii) *stable* and able to keep its value;
(iv) *divisible* without any loss of value;
 (v) *portable* and not too heavy to carry.

(c) Origins of Money

The earliest method of exchange was *barter* in which goods were exchanged directly for other goods. Problems arose when either someone did not want what was being offered in exchange for the other good, or if no agreement could be reached over how much one good was worth in terms of the other.

Valuable metals such as gold and silver began acting as a medium of exchange. Governments then decided to melt down these metals into coins.

By the seventeenth century people were leaving gold with the local goldsmith for safe keeping. Receipts of £1 and £5 were issued which could then be converted back into gold at any time. Soon these receipts were recognised as being 'as good as gold' and were readily taken in exchange for goods. Goldsmiths became the first specialist bankers and their receipts began to circulate as *banknotes*.

Only the Bank of England can now issue banknotes in England and Wales. However, notes are not usually used to buy expensive items such as cars. The buyer is more likely to write out a *cheque*, which instructs his bank to transfer money from his account into the account of the seller. Hence bank deposits act as money.

11.2 Commercial Banks

Banks are *licensed deposit takers* and perform four functions. They accept deposits, make loans, arrange payment of bills and provide a number of customer services. The four main high street or *clearing banks* in the UK are Barclays, Lloyds, Midland and National Westminster.

(a) Types of Bank Account

Banks provide different types of account for different needs. Customers can open:

  (i) A *current account* which provides a cheque book but pays no interest. Current accounts are mainly used to pay bills.
 (ii) A *deposit account* which does pay interest but money can only be taken out by visiting the bank. Deposit accounts are mainly used for short term saving.
(iii) An *investment or savings account* which pays a higher rate of interest but written notice of withdrawal must be given. Accounts of this type are used mainly for long-term saving.

(b) Types of Bank Loan

  (i) An *overdraft* is when the bank allows a customer to take out more money than is in his account. Overdrafts are up to an agreed limit, and must be paid off whenever the bank asks. Interest is charged daily on any outstanding balance.
 (ii) A *loan account* is when a customer borrows a fixed sum of money to be repaid in monthly instalments over a number of years. A fixed rate of interest is charged.

(c) Methods of Payment

These include:
  (i) *Cheques* when the bank is ordered to pay money to someone else. The people involved in writing a cheque are:

  (1) The person writing out the cheque (*drawer*).
  (2) The bank ordered to pay money (*drawee*).
  (3) The person receiving the money (*payee*).

A *cheque card* is issued to trusted customers which guarantees payment by the bank of any cheque up to the sum of £50.
 (ii) *Standing orders* when a fixed sum is paid out on set dates.
(iii) *Direct debits* when a variable sum is paid out on set dates.
(iv) *Credit cards* when customers have a special card (e.g. Visa or Access) which can be used to buy goods.
      Cardholders receive a statement every month and no interest is charged if the account is settled in full. Interest is charged monthly on any outstanding balance.

(d) Other Services

Banks have cash points; exchange foreign currency and issue travellers' cheques; provide night safes and store valuables; *execute* (carry out) wills and trusts; and *factor* (collect) debts.

11.3 Commercial Bank Balance Sheet

A *balance sheet* shows the present position of a company. One for a commercial bank is shown here.

The balance sheet of a commercial bank

Liabilities		Assets	
(a) Current a/c	£100	(e) Cash in tills	£20
(b) Deposit a/c	£200	(f) Money at the Bank of England	£40
(c) Savings a/c	£100	(g) Money at call and short notice	£40
		(h) 91-day bills	£50
		(i) Government securities with less than 1 year to maturity	£50
		(j) Investments	£50
		(k) Loans	£150
(d) Total liabilities	£400	(l) Total assets	£400

In the balance sheet the *liabilities* column shows the origin of the money held by the bank. Items (a) to (c) show the amount of money held in each type of account. Item (d) states the total value of deposits held by the bank.

The *assets* column shows what the bank has done with the money. Note that only a small percentage of total liabilities is kept as cash in tills (item (e)). Item (f) is the bank's own current account for settling debts. Item (g) is money lent out to discount houses (see section 12.4(c)) for a few days. Items (i) and (j) are IOUs issued mainly by the government (see section 14.3). Items (e) to (i) are the bank's *liquid* or *reserve assets* and can easily be turned into cash.

Items (j) and (k) are *illiquid* (not easily turned into cash) but highly profitable. By definition, the amount of total assets (item (l)) must equal total liabilities.

11.4 Credit Creation

Some customers leave money in the bank earning interest. A bank can use these *idle* deposits to make loans to people who then buy goods. Shopkeepers receive extra money which they *redeposit* with the bank. Some of this redeposited money is left to earn interest and can be re-lent. Figure 11.1 on the next page illustrates the process of credit creation.

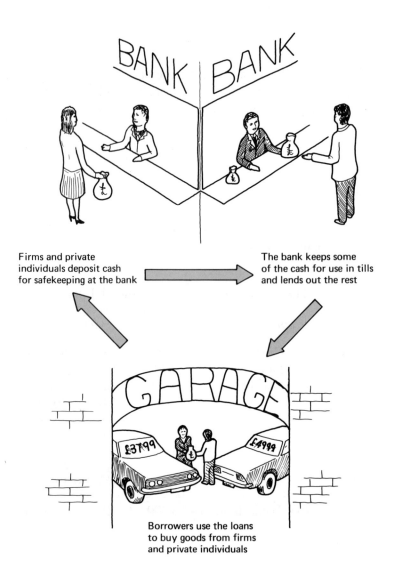

Figure 11.1 Credit creation

11.5 Money Supply

(a) Definition

The *money supply* is the total amount of assets in circulation which are acceptable in exchange for goods. In modern economies people accept either notes and coins or an increase in their current account as payment. Hence the money supply is made up of cash and bank deposits. There are five main measures of the money supply:

  (i) *M0* made up of notes and coins in circulation.
 (ii) *M1* made up of M0 and current accounts.
(iii) *£M3 ('sterling M3')* made up of M1 and deposit accounts.
(iv) *M3* made up of £M3 and deposits held overseas.
 (v) *PSL2* made up of M3 plus all building society and Post Office accounts.

(b) Control of the Money Supply

The Bank of England is responsible for controlling the money supply and this involves limiting the amount of cash, and bank deposits in circulation.

As the Bank of England actually issues notes and coins, it can easily control the amount of cash in the money supply.

However, the major part of the money supply is not created by the Bank of England. Commercial banks decide the amount of bank deposits in circulation using the equation:

$$D = 1/\phi \times A_L$$

where D = total deposits,
$\quad A_L$ = liquid assets,
and ϕ = the percentage of deposits held in liquid form.
The Bank of England can:

(i) Place a limit on the amount of deposits a bank can have.
(ii) Force up interest rates to discourage customers from taking out loans.
(iii) Reduce the amount of liquid assets held by a bank by selling bills to the public. The public then write out cheques to the government and money leaves the bank.

11.6 Worked Examples

Example 11.1

Baker and Brewer live in a simple economy which does *not* use money. Instead, goods are brought to market each week and exchanged by barter. The diagram shows Baker and Brewer trying to trade their surplus produce.

(a) From the diagram:

    (i) How many loaves has Baker to trade? **(1 mark)**
    (ii) How does Brewer calculate the value of his beer? **(2 marks)**

(b) How will Brewer get some bread if Baker does not want his beer? **(3 marks)**
(c) Can Baker use his surplus bread as a method of long-term saving? **(1 mark)**
(d) Explain carefully how money could be used by Baker as a method of exchange. **(3 marks)**
(e) Assess how suitable each of the following might be if used as money:

    (i) cattle, and   (ii) iron. **(5 marks)**

Solution 11.1

(a) (i) Baker has thirteen loaves to trade.
    (ii) Brewer calculates the value of his beer using other goods. If the beer can be exchanged for thirteen loaves then that is its value.

(b) Brewer will have to exchange his beer for another good which Baker does want, e.g. milk. Brewer can then offer milk in exchange for bread.
(c) Bread is unsuitable as a method of long-term saving because loaves go stale after a day or two.
(d) Baker could sell his surplus bread for an asset everyone accepts as payment—money. The money he receives from the sale of his bread is used to buy many of the things he has not had time to make.
(e) (i) Any asset which is going to act as money must have certain characteristics. Some people would not be prepared to accept a cow as payment. The cow could not be used to buy a small item such as a chicken unless it was killed and split up. While cows are scarce and in limited supply they are not very portable.
    (ii) In many ways iron is a better form of money than cows. Unlike cows, iron can be split up into smaller units without any loss of value, and iron does not lose its value after a few years. However iron can rust and is rather heavy to carry. Some people may not accept iron in exchange for their goods.

Example 11.2

(a) Money can be deposited at a bank in a current or deposit account. Which type of account would you use if you were saving for a house? Explain your answer. **(3 marks)**
(b) Cheques, standing orders and direct debits are types of payment. Select one of these methods of payment which is the most convenient for each of the following situations. Explain your choice:

    (i) making monthly hire purchase payments; **(2 marks)**
    (ii) payment of a 10 000-mile car service bill; **(2 marks)**
    (iii) payment of quarterly gas bills. **(2 marks)**

(c) How can customers avoid paying bank charges? **(2 marks)**
(d) What are the main types of money found in the UK? **(5 marks)**

Solution 11.2

(a) A current account allows the use of cheque books which can be used to pay bills conveniently but does not normally pay any interest. A deposit account does pay interest but has no cheque book. When saving for a house a cheque book is not so important as earning interest. Therefore a deposit account would be better means of saving for a house.

(b) (i) The hire purchase payment is for a fixed amount paid at regular intervals. A standing order is used to pay fixed-amount regular bills and is the best method of payment.

(ii) 10 000-mile services do not take place at the same time each year. Since the date of payment is not fixed, standing orders and direct debits are inappropriate methods of payment. The best method is to use a cheque.

(iii) A gas bill is paid every three months but varies in amount according to the time of the year. A direct debit is used to pay regular bills of a variable amount and is the best method of payment.

(c) Banks offer free banking to anyone who keeps their account in credit. Customers can avoid paying bank charges by not getting overdrawn.

(d) Money is any asset people accept as payment. The main types of money in the UK are notes, coins and bank deposits.

Notes and coins issued by the Bank of England or Scotland, are legal tender and must be accepted as payment in the UK.

Bank deposits are created by commercial banks. Customers use the money held in their current account to settle bills. They write out a cheque and the bank arranges for a deposit to be moved to the account of the payee.

There are several different definitions of money. Some economists only count cash (M0), while others count cash and current accounts M1). £M3 includes M1 and deposit accounts. The widest definition of money (PSL2) includes cash and all deposits held in banks, in building societies and in Post Office accounts.

Example 11.3

Read the following passage and answer all the questions which follow.

Banks are financial institutions which act as links between savers and borrowers. Customers who deposit money for safekeeping are paid 12 per cent interest each year. Idle funds are then lent out to clients who are short of cash, either as a temporary overdraft or as a longer-term loan. The bank makes a profit by charging an annual rate of interest of 20 per cent on all accounts which are in debt.

Loan applications are usually decided at a meeting between the manager and a client. The manager will want to know the purpose of the loan and what security can be offered should the money not be repaid.

Some customers do find they are unable to keep up with repayments. The manager will often allow a breathing space by collecting interest payments only. However, if the borrower falls further behind with his repayments then the bank may be forced to sell the borrower's collateral.

(a) From the passage, give briefly the meaning of:

(i) financial institution;   **(1 mark)**
(ii) rate of interest.   **(2 marks)**

(b) Name the two types of bank loan given in the passage.   **(2 marks)**

(c) Which type of loan would be given by a bank to pay for:

     (i) an extension to the factory; **(2 marks)**
     (ii) purchase of raw materials. **(2 marks)**

(d) The bank receives a deposit of £500 which it lends out to a small firm. Using the information given in the passage calculate after one year:

     (i) the amount of interest received by the depositer; **(1 mark)**
     (ii) the amount of interest paid by the small firm; **(1 mark)**
     (iii) the profit made by the bank on the loan. **(1 mark)**

(e) Why do banks require borrowers to offer *collateral* (security)? **(2 marks)**
(f) What will a bank accept as collateral for a £500 loan? **(2 marks)**

Solution 11.3

(a)   (i) A financial institution accepts deposits from savers and lends out these deposits to borrowers.
     (ii) The rate of interest is the charge made each year by a lender calculated as a percentage.

(b) The two types of bank loan mentioned are overdrafts and long-term loans.

(c)   (i) A factory extension is a long-term project and the firm will use future profits to pay back the loan. The bank will offer a long-term bank loan.
     (ii) Raw materials are turned into finished goods and then sold within a few months. The loan is needed only in the short term and will be financed by an overdraft.

(d)   (i) The depositer earns 12 per cent interest on money left with the bank, i.e.

$$£500 \times \frac{12}{100} = £60.$$

     (ii) The small firm pays 20 per cent interest on the money borrowed from the bank, i.e.

$$£500 \times \frac{20}{100} = £100.$$

     (iii) The bank pays £60 out to the depositor and charges the small firm £100. Hence the bank's profit is £40.

(e) Collateral is an asset such as the ownership deeds to a house which the borrower leaves with the bank to guarantee repayment of a loan. If the customer is unable to pay back a loan then the bank can sell the house and keep the proceeds up to the amount of the loan plus interest.
(f) A bank will accept as security any certificate of ownership for a financial asset. A customer can offer share certificates or a life assurance policy as collateral.

Example 11.4

(a) Study the names of various banks given here. Give the names of two commercial (clearing) banks.   (1 mark)

(b) With specific reference to banking:

    (i) What are cleared?   (1 mark)
    (ii) How are they cleared?   (1 mark)

(c) Study the bank advertisement on page 124.
    Give three ways in which commercial banks help businesses to grow.
                                     (3 marks)

(d) How are commercial banks able to arrange and manage business transactions by using very little cash?   (3 marks)

(e) (i) When banks use the term 'liquid assets', what does the word 'liquid' mean?
                                                    (1 mark)

    (ii) Why do commercial banks have some of their assets in liquid form?
                                                    (2 marks)

    (iii) Explain fully why commercial banks try to satisfy their need to be both liquid and profitable.   (4 marks)

                                  (LEAEG specimen GCSE)

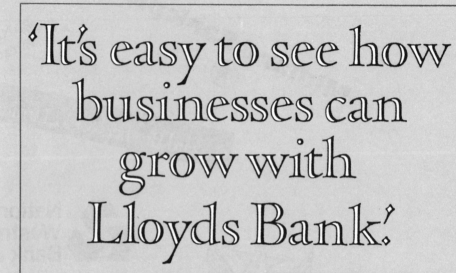

A THOROUGHBRED AMONGST BANKS

Published by Lloyds Bank Plc, 71 Lombard Street, London EC3P 3BS

Printed by Quicksilver Offset Ltd., London SE14 CMP9 (12.85.)

(Reproduced by permission of Lloyds Bank)

Solution 11.4

(a) National Westminster and Barclays are examples of commercial banks.

(b) (i) Cheques drawn on current accounts are cleared.
(ii) The account of the drawer is debited and the account of the payee is credited.

(c) A business needs capital if it is to grow. One source of capital is a bank loan. The money borrowed can be used to buy raw materials or machinery.

A commercial bank helps businesses to grow by paying interest on any profit left in a deposit account. This interest can be used for investment.

A company may be owed money by a number of firms. This money can be used for expansion. A bank can help by offering a factoring service where the bank purchases the company's debts for up to 90 per cent of their value. While the company loses 10 per cent, the cash raised can be used for expansion.

(d) There are two reasons why banks manage business transactions using little cash:

(i) Most customers do not use cash to settle debts. Instead, they write out cheques ordering their bank to transfer bank deposits from their account to the payee's account.

(ii) Customers who do draw out cash from their accounts make purchases from shops which then redeposit the cash with the bank. At any one time customers will be queuing up not only to take cash out but to pay cash back in.

(e) (i) Liquid means the ability of an asset to be turned into cash.

(ii) Some assets are kept in liquid form in case an unusually large number of customers want to withdraw some of their deposits in cash. For example, if the bank is running low on cash in tills it can recall money lent overnight to discount houses.

(iii) Banks have to make sure that they have sufficient liquid assets to meet everyday cash claims. If the bank cannot pay out cash to customers on demand then there will be a loss of confidence. There may even be a 'run on the bank' when all depositors try to close their bank accounts, and the bank collapses.

The bank must also be sure that it is making sufficient profit to pay the interest due on deposit accounts. The bank makes a profit by lending out cash not needed as liquid assets. The bank covers its costs by charging a high rate of interest to borrowers.

Example 11.5

Imagine an economy in which there is only one bank! Soon after beginning business it finds that individuals and firms have placed £10 000 with it for safekeeping.
(a) Construct a balance sheet for the bank and explain why liabilities equal assets.

(2 marks)

(b) Study the balance sheet below:

Balance Sheet 1

Liabilities		Assets	
Customers' deposits	£11 000	Cash in hand	£10 000
		Loans to customers	1000
Total	£11 000	Total	£11 000

(i) Why have both liabilities and assets increased by £1000 compared with the first balance sheet? **(4 marks)**
(ii) If the bank discovers that cash withdrawals by customers amount to 10 per cent of the total original deposits (i.e. £10 000), how much credit can be created by this bank?
   Illustrate this on a balance sheet. **(6 marks)**
(iii) What factors limit the ability of banks to create credit? **(8 marks)**

(NISEC specimen GCSE)

Solution 11.5

(a)

Balance Sheet 2

Liabilities		Assets	
Customer's deposits	£10 000	Cash in hand	£10 000

A balance sheet shows the present financial position of the bank. The liabilities column shows the source of the money held by the bank. The asset column shows what the bank has done with that money. Hence liabilities always equal assets.

(b) (i) Liabilities and assets have increased by £1000 because the bank has created a £1000 loan to customers. The loan enters the asset column because the borrower owes the bank £1000. The loan enters the liability column because the borrower has £1000 which will be used to pay for goods.

(ii) The relationship between a bank's liabilities (D) and its liquid assets (A_L) is given by the equation:

$$D = 1/\phi \times A_L$$

where ϕ is the percentage of liabilities held as cash.

If cash withdrawals by customers amount to 10 per cent then 10 per cent is the value of φ.

$$D = \frac{1}{10/100} \times £10\,000 = 10 \times £10\,000 = £100\,000.$$

If £100 000 of deposits requires £10 000 worth of liquid assets to meet customers' everyday demands for cash then the bank can lend out £90 000. The final balance sheet of the bank is given below:

Balance Sheet 3

Liabilities		Assets	
Customers' deposits	£100 000	Cash in hand	£ 10 000
		Loans to customers	£ 90 000
Total	£100 000	Total	£100 000

(iii) Commercial banks' ability to create credit is largely determined by the Bank of England. The Bank of England is the central bank of the United Kingdom and is responsible for carrying out government monetary policy.

The Bank of England may set a limit on the total amount of deposits a bank can have. Banks which create too much credit and exceed these limits may be fined.

Commercial banks may find that high interest rates discourage customers from taking out loans. If banks are unable to make loans then they are unable to create credit.

The Bank of England can limit the ability of banks to create credit by changing the percentage of deposits banks must hold in liquid form (φ). An increase in the value of φ reduces the ability of banks to create credit.

A fall in the amount of liquid assets held by commercial banks reduces their ability to create credit. If the Bank of England sells treasury bills to the general public then funds will be transferred to the government. Banks' liquid assets will fall, causing a multiple contraction in the volume of overall deposits equal to $1/\phi$ multiplied by the fall in liquid assets.

11.7 Questions

1 Define money.
2 Money helps the exchange of goods and services because it:

  A avoids the need for a double coincidence of wants
  B can be earned
  C can be saved
  D keeps its value

3 State two major functions of money.

4 Which of the following is *not* a desirable characteristic of money:

    A it should be perishable   **B** it should be scarce
    C it should be divisible   **D** it should be acceptable

5 Barter is not an efficient means of exchange because it requires:
    A factors of production   **B** a choice of goods
    C unlimited wants   **D** a double coincidence of wants

6 What is meant by legal tender?

7 The two mediums of exchange in a modern economy are ....

8 What is meant by a commercial bank?

9 State two services which commercial banks provide for individuals.

10 You write out a cheque for £60. The cheque is drawn on your:
    A investment account   **B** current account
    C savings account   **D** deposit account

11 What is the difference between a cheque card and a credit card?

12 Interest on an overdraft is charged:
    A daily   **B** weekly
    C monthly   **D** at a fixed rate

For each of questions (13) to (17) select from the list A to D the most appropriate method of payment.
    A cheque   **B** standing order
    C direct debit   **D** bank giro credit transfer

13 Paying a quarterly gas bill conveniently.

14 Paying your rent each month conveniently.

15 Paying for a single car service conveniently.

16 Paying a telephone bill without using your current account.

17 What are assets called that can easily be turned into money?

For each of questions 18 to 21 select the most appropriate descriptions from the list **A** to **D**.
    A advances to customers   **B** cash
    C customer's deposit account   **D** money at call

18 The bank's most liquid asset is ....

19 The bank's most profitable asset is ....

20 Money lent out overnight is ....

21 One of the bank's liabilities is ....

22 Define the money supply.

23 Which one of the following banks is responsible for the other three:
    A Bank of England   **B** Trustees Savings Bank
    C Midland Bank   **D** Royal Bank of Scotland

24 The bulk of the money supply is created by ....
....

25 When a clearing bank makes a loan it:
    A raises the rate of interest   **B** lowers the rate of interest
    C increases the money supply   **D** lowers the money supply

26 State two methods the Bank of England can use to reduce the supply of money.

11.8 Answers

1 Any asset accepted in exchange for goods and services or a method of payment or a medium of exchange.

2 **A**   3 See section 11.1(a)   4 **A**   5 **D**

6 Notes and coins issued by the Bank of England and the Bank of Scotland which must be accepted in exchange for goods and services in the UK.

7 Notes and coins, and bank deposits.

8 A financial institution which accepts deposits and lends money, or a licensed deposit taker.

9 Any two of: accepts deposits; makes loans; makes payments; or any of section 11.2(d). **10 B**

11 Credit cards are used to buy goods while cheque cards guarantee payment of a cheque.

12	**A**	13	**C**	14	**B**	15	**A**
16	**D**	17	Liquid assets	18	**B**	19	**A**
20	**D**	21	**C**				

22 The total amount of assets generally accepted as payment, or any of the definitions given in section 11.5(a).

23 **A**

24 Commercial banks, by creating deposits.

25 **C**   26 See section 11.5(b)

12 Financial Institutions

12.1 The Bank of England

The *Bank of England* is the *central bank* of the United Kingdom and is therefore responsible for supervising the workings of all other financial institutions in the country. It was established in 1694 and nationalised in 1946.

(a) Functions of the Bank of England

(i) The Bank of England is the sole issuer of notes and coins through the Royal Mint.

(ii) The Bank of England is the government's banker.

(iii) The Bank of England is the banker for commercial banks.

(iv) The Bank of England has close links with foreign central banks and the IMF (see section 17.4(c)).

(v) The Bank of England holds the UK gold and foreign currency reserves in the *exchange equalisation account* which it uses to help stabilise sterling.

(vi) The Bank of England issues treasury bills, government securities (see section 13.4(a)) and pays interest to the holders. It also arranges the eventual repayment of loans.

(vii) Discount houses borrow money from commercial banks and buy bills. If the discount house is temporarily unable to pay back a loan it can, in the last resort, turn to the Bank of England which will buy back (rediscount) the bills.

(viii) The government announces monetary policy for the next few years in the *medium term financial strategy*. The Bank of England is responsible for keeping M0, £M3, etc., within the target range.

12.2 The Money Market

The *money market* arranges large-scale short-term loans (up to three months) and is mainly used by commercial banks and discount houses.

12.3 The Stock Exchange

The *London stock exchange* is the centre of the *capital market* and provides large-scale long-term loans for companies and the government.

(a) New Share Issues

Firms can raise money for expansion by reinvesting profits or arranging a loan through a bank. However, a company wanting to raise millions of pounds' worth of capital may consider going public, i.e. becoming a public limited company. The firm prepares a prospectus stating the history and aims of the company and inviting the public to buy shares.

A public limited company can raise further capital through a *rights issue* when shareholders are invited to buy new shares at a discount on the current stock market price.

An alternative method of raising money is to issue debentures. A *debenture* is a loan to a company paying a fixed rate of interest. Second-hand debentures can be bought and sold on the stock exchange.

Table 12.1 Types of share

Type	Dividend	Vote	Order of dividend payment
Ordinary or equities	Depends on size of profits	1 per share	Paid last
Preference	Fixed but no profit means no dividend	None	Paid first
Cumulative preference	Fixed but lost dividends made up	None	Paid first

(b) Organisation of the Stock Exchange

In 1986 the stock exchange underwent a radical change in organisation (the 'big bang'):

(i) *Market makers* buy and sell shares.
(ii) *Brokers* or *dealers* represent the client but may be part of the same firm as the market maker.
(iii) Market makers and brokers are linked by a new computer system, *SEAQS* (Stock Exchange Automated Quotation System).
(iv) The stock exchange has been enlarged to include a number of high street banks and foreign financial institutions.
(v) The *Stock Exchange Council* (a committee of elected dealers) is directly responsible for policing the market. The council itself is under the supervision of the *Securities and Investment Board*.

(c) Changes in Share Prices

An increase in the demand for a share will raise its price. This may be the result of a possible takeover bid, increased profits or because the economy is booming.

A *speculator* buys or sells shares hoping to make a quick profit. There are three sorts:

(i) A *bull* buys shares now expecting share prices to rise.
(ii) A *bear* sells shares now expecting share prices to fall.
(iii) A *stag* buys new share issues expecting their price to rise.

(d) Functions of the Stock Exchange

   (i) An organised market for the purchase and sale of second-hand shares.

  (ii) The stock exchange gives people confidence to buy new shares issued by companies since they know there is an organised market for their resale.

 (iii) The stock exchange allows institutions collecting money for small investors such as trade unions, insurance and pension funds to make large purchases of shares in UK companies.

12.4 Other Financial Institutions

A number of specialist institutions lend for special purposes:

(a) *Building societies* assist house buyers by collecting money from many small savers and lending large long-term loans.

(b) *Merchant banks* specialise in lending directly to firms, and in giving advice to companies involved in takeover deals.

(c) *Discount houses* borrow money from commercial banks and buy treasury bills.

(d) *Finance houses* specialise in leasing and hire purchase agreements.

(e) *Pension funds* collect contributions which are then used to buy stocks and shares.

(f) *Unit trusts* allow small investors to buy a spread of shares in different companies. The money raised from selling units is used to buy stocks and shares in a large number of companies. Units can only be bought and sold from the trust.

(g) *Insurance companies* collect premiums from policy holders. Some of this money is used to buy stocks and shares.

There is an increasing trend for financial institutions to extend the scope of their business. For example, banks now offer mortgages while building societies will soon be able to offer personal loans for non-house-buying purposes.

12.5 Worked Examples

Example 12.1

Read the following passage which describes the workings of the Bank of England and answer all the questions which follow.

The Bank of England is the UK central bank and has responsibility for controlling the activities of other UK financial institutions. For example, the Bank of England checks the balance sheets of high-street banks and building societies to make sure they each have sufficient money in hand to meet customers' everyday demands for cash.

The Bank of England is also responsible for carrying out the government's monetary policy. The government asks the Bank of England to limit the increase in the money supply. In particular, the Bank of England has to control the amount of money created by commercial banks.

One method of monetary control is to sell government securities (IOUs) to the general public. The public use their bank accounts to pay for the stocks, which results in a reduction in commercial banks' cash reserves. The amount they can then lend out is severely reduced.

The Bank of England has an international role to play. In 1985 British tourists in America found that £1 bought only $1. A year later £1 bought $1½. The Bank of England can influence the sterling exchange rate by using pounds held in the exchange equalisation account to buy or sell dollars.

(a) Name three types of financial institution mentioned in the passage. **(2 marks)**

(b) Using the information given in the passage briefly explain the meaning of the following terms:

 (i) central bank; **(1 mark)**
 (ii) monetary policy; **(2 marks)**
 (iii) sterling exchange rate. **(2 marks)**

(c) From the passage calculate:

 (i) the number of pounds an American tourist could buy with $500 in 1985; **(1 mark)**
 (ii) the number of dollars a British tourist could buy with £500 in 1986; **(1 mark)**
 (iii) the percentage increase in the value of sterling between 1985 and 1986. **(1 mark)**

(d) Use the information provided to explain:

 (i) how the Bank of England can increase the money supply; **(3 marks)**
 (ii) how the Bank of England can encourage a fall in the value of sterling. **(3 marks)**

Solution 12.1

(a) The Bank of England, high-street banks and building societies are three financial institutions mentioned in the passage.

(b) (i) A central bank is the most important financial institution in a country and is responsible for checking the workings of other financial institutions.
 (ii) Monetary policy refers to the control of the amount of money in circulation.
 (iii) The sterling exchange rate is the amount of foreign currency, e.g. dollars ($), one pound (£) can buy. The passage quotes the number of dollars one pound can buy, i.e. $/£.

(c) (i) In 1985 the exchange rate was $1/£. An American tourist with $500 could buy 500 × £1 = £500.
 (ii) In 1986 the exchange rate was $1.5/£. A British tourist with £500 could buy 500 × $1.5 = $750.
 (iii) The percentage increase in sterling between 1985 and 1986 equals

$$\frac{\text{The change in } \$/£}{\text{The original } \$/£} \times 100 = \frac{0.5}{1} \times 100 = 50 \text{ per cent.}$$

(d) (i) The Bank of England can increase the money supply by purchasing government securities owned by the general public. The owners of government securities receive cheques from the Bank which are paid into current accounts. Commercial banks experience an increase in their cash reserves which they use to create credit.
 (ii) A fall in the value of sterling means a fall in the number of dollars one pound can buy. The Bank of England can encourage a fall in the value

of sterling by selling pounds held in the exchange equalisation account for dollars. The increase in the supply of pounds reduces the dollar value of sterling.

Example 12.2

Study the information given in the following report on the stock exchange 'big bang' and answer all the questions which follow.

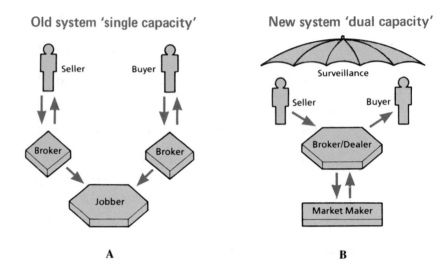

The stock exchange has revolutionised its trading system. Membership of the exchange has been thrown open to outside bodies such as foreign banks. The old single-capacity system has been swept away. Dual capacity allows a firm to act as both buyer and seller.

Change is certainly necessary if London is to meet the challenge of increased overseas stock exchange competition. The abolition of minimum commissions once charged by all brokers now encourages firms to be more competitive.

The stock exchange has to ensure the new system gives investors the protection they need. A computer network called SEAQS (stock exchange automated quotation system) transmits details of each market maker's buying and selling prices to brokers by means of television screens. Brokers will then be able to contact the market maker offering the best deal for his client's needs. Details of share purchases will be stored on computer disks and will be available for investigation in case of a complaint.

Source: Adapted from *Stock Exchange Spectrum*, No. 1, 1985

(a) From the passage, who represents the seller of shares in:

    (i) the single-capacity system;   **(1 mark)**
    (ii) the dual-capacity system?   **(1 mark)**

(b) What evidence is there in the passage for believing that in the new system:

    (i) the charge made by the stock exchange for buying shares will fall;

                                                       (3 marks)
    (ii) clients will buy shares at the lowest price available?   **(2 marks)**

(c) How will investors be protected in the new system?   **(2 marks)**
(d) Using the information given in the passage comment briefly on how the new system will affect:

    (i) the number of dealers;   **(2 marks)**
    (ii) the number of people using the stock exchange;   **(2 marks)**
    (iii) the balance of payments.   **(3 marks)**

Solution 12.2

(a) (i) From diagram A, the broker represents the seller in the single-capacity system.
    (ii) From diagram B, the broker-dealer represents the seller in the dual-capacity system.

(b) (i) Minimum commissions have been abolished which means that each firm is now free to charge a competitive rate.

    Moreover, there has been an increase in the number of firms belonging to the stock exchange. New firms will be prepared to reduce commissions to attract new clients.

    (ii) Brokers representing clients are connected up to a computer network which displays each firm's selling price. In a matter of seconds the dealer can contact the market maker with the lowest quote and buy shares for his client.

(c) The new stock exchange computer system protects investors by keeping a record of all transactions. This allows the stock exchange to check any investor's complaint.

(d) (i) The new system has introduced banks and other financial institutions to the London stock exchange. Customers are now able to choose from a larger number of dealers.

    (ii) The new system reduces the cost of dealing in stocks and shares. This will encourage more people to use the stock exchange. Moreover, many banks are now also members of the stock exchange and are more able to help their customers buy and sell shares.

    (iii) The London stock exchange is an international centre for finance. Profits made from representing foreign investors make a large contribution to the balance on invisibles. If the new system succeeds in attracting more foreign investors then the London stock exchange will earn higher profits and the balance on invisibles will improve. Moreover, there will be an increase in capital inflows. The overall balance of payments improves.

Example 12.3

The data in the table show the price of a number of shares of public limited companies listed on the London stock exchange in June 1986.

Stores

1986 high	1986 low	Company name	Current price (pence)	Change	Yield (% each year)
650	387	Body shop	620	+ 1	0.5%
289	220	Boots	247	− 2	4.1%
438	216	Dixons	354	+ 2	1.2%
231	163	Marks & Spencer	197	− 4	2.8%
297	189	Next	247	− 1	2.3%
364	234	Smith (W. H.)	278	. . .	3.0%
925	430	Woolworth	825	−15	1.7%

(a) What type of company has its shares listed on the stock exchange? **(1 mark)**

(b) Using the information in the table:

    (i) Name the company with the highest current share price. **(1 mark)**
    (ii) What is the lowest price they have been in 1986? **(1 mark)**
    (iii) Which share lost 2p on the previous day's trading? **(1 mark)**
    (iv) Which share had no price change on the day's trading? **(1 mark)**
    (v) Which share has shown the greatest percentage change in value in 1986?

        (2 marks)
    (vi) How much would an investor owning £500 of W.H. Smith shares currently receive each year in dividends? **(2 marks)**

(c) Assess the likely effect on the price of Boots shares of:

    (i) a takeover bid; **(2 marks)**
    (ii) a fall in profits; **(2 marks)**
    (iii) a rights issue. **(3 marks)**

Solution 12.3

(a) Public limited companies have their share listed on the stock exchange.

(b)   (i) Woolworth have the highest share price at 825 pence.
    (ii) The lowest price of Woolworth shares in 1986 is 430 pence.
    (iii) Boots lost 2p on the previous day's trading.
    (iv) W.H. Smith had no price change on the day's trading.
    (v) Woolworth shares changed by the largest percentage amount in 1986. The change in value equals

$$\frac{\text{Current price} - \text{Lowest price}}{\text{Lowest price}} \times 100 = \frac{825 - 430}{430} \times 100 = \frac{395}{430} \times 100 = 92\%.$$

    (vi) Yield refers to the amount of money received each year for every £100 of shares held. W.H. Smith yield £3 on every £100. An investor owning £500 worth of shares receives:

$$\text{£500} \times \frac{3}{100} = \text{£15 in dividends each year.}$$

(c)   (i) A takeover bid by another company involves offering Boots shareholders more than the current market price for their equities. The price of Boots shares will rise.
    (ii) A fall in profits reduces the ability of Boots to pay out a dividend to shareholders. A lower dividend reduces the price of Boots shares.
    (iii) A rights issue occurs when a company wants to raise capital for expansion by selling shares to existing shareholders. To encourage sales, the shares are offered at a discount. The increase in the supply of shares, and the discount on offer, will result in a fall in the price of Boots shares.

Example 12.4

A company manufacturing ties wishes to raise £50 000 capital to buy a new machine. Once operating costs have been considered, the machine will earn the company £8000 profit each year. The managing director finds that there are three sources of finance:

Type of loan	Annual interest
Bank loan	20%
Finance house	15%
Debenture	10%

(a) Which is the cheapest method of raising capital given in the table?   **(1 mark)**
(b) How much interest does the finance house charge each year for a £50 000 loan?
    (1 mark)
(c) How much profit is left after interest is paid to the finance house?   **(2 marks)**
(d) Ignoring interest charges, after how many years does the machine pay for itself?
    (2 marks)
(e) What is the economic term for the company's purchase of the machine?
    (1 mark)
(f) A rights issue occurs when existing shareholders are invited to buy new shares in the company. What would be the advantages to the company of raising the capital through a rights issue?   **(3 marks)**
(g) Assess the likely effect on the company's plan if:

    (i) the annual wage bill for operating the tie machine increases by £2000;
    (3 marks)
    (ii) a major competitor leaves the industry.   **(3 marks)**

Solution 12.4

(a) The cheapest method of raising capital is the one with the lowest rate of interest. Issuing debentures is the cheapest method.

(b) A finance house charges £50 000 × 15 per cent = £50 000 × $\frac{15}{100}$ = £7500.

(c) The profit from the machine is £8000 and interest charges to the finance house are £7500, leaving a £500 profit.
(d) Dividing the cost of the machine by its expected yearly profit will tell you the number of years the machine takes to pay for itself. £50 000/£8000 = 6.25 years.
(e) The purchase of a new machine is called investment.
(f) A rights issue allows the company to raise money now with no immediate interest payments to be met. Once the money raised has been invested and is returning a profit, part of that profit will be returned to the shareholders as dividends. However, if the investment is a failure, the company does not have to return the shareholders' money

(g) (i) If the wage bill for operating the tie machine increases by £2000, then expected profit falls from £8000 to £6000. The lowest annual interest charge is £50 000 × 10 per cent = £5000. The machine is still profitable and will be bought.

(ii) If a major competitor leaves the industry then many consumers will switch to buying this firm's products. Price will increase following the increase in demand, which will make the company's plan even more attractive than before.

Example 12.5

Study carefully the following information which appeared in a report in 1986.

The Case for Wider Share Ownership

Shareholders in UK companies (%)		
	1963	1981
Persons	54.0	28.2
Pension funds	6.4	26.7
Insurance companies	10.0	20.5
Investment and unit trusts	12.6	10.4
Industrial and commercial companies	5.1	5.1
Other	11.9	9.1

The number of individual investors directly involved in the stock market has steadily declined since the Second World War. In 1986, there are some 2.75 million individual investors who between them own just 25 per cent of UK companies quoted shares.

The decline in individual share ownership has seen the emergence of huge shareholdings by the 'institutions'—the pension funds and insurance companies. Such institutions, of course, provide millions of people with an indirect link to the stock market. However, wider share ownership would provide industry with more sources of fund-raising, and individuals with a share in growing company profits.

It has been suggested that more shares in the hands of a greater number of small shareholders would mean:

  (i) a more equal distribution of wealth;
 (ii) greater public interest in the running of companies;
(iii) improved relations in the workplace.

Source: Adapted from Stock Exchange Spectrum, No. 2, 1986

(a) How many people owned shares in companies in 1986? **(1 mark)**
(b) What percentage of shares were owned by people in 1963? **(1 mark)**
(c) Describe the trends in share ownership after 1963, as shown by the table.
    (4 marks)
(d) Explain how people can have an indirect link with the stock exchange.
    (2 marks)
(e) Using the information given in the passage, explain briefly how a wider share ownership might:

    (i) improve industrial relations; **(4 marks)**
    (ii) improve the distribution of income. **(3 marks)**

Solution 12.5

(a) Some 2.75 million people owned shares in companies in 1986.
(b) The percentage of shares owned by people in 1963 was 54 per cent.

(c) There was a large fall in the percentage of ordinary people owning shares. The figure almost halved after 1963. However, there was a large increase in the number of institutional investors such as pension funds and insurance companies. Surprisingly, the percentage of shares companies held in other companies remained the same over the period in question.

(d) Millions of people make contributions to trade unions, insurance and pension funds. Institutions use money received from customers to invest on their behalf in companies quoted on the stock exchange, thus providing an indirect link.

(e)   (i) If more workers begin to own shares they will take a greater interest in the running of the company. Moreover, part of any profits will be returned to the worker in the form of higher dividends. If the company does particularly well then the value of the workers' shareholding will rise. For these reasons industrial relations might improve.

  (ii) Share owners receive dividends. If there are more shareholders then more people will receive part of the profits made by companies. This will mean a fairer spread of incomes.

12.6   Questions

1 The Bank of England is the UK:
  A stock exchange   **B** joint stock bank
  C central bank   **D** commercial bank

2 State two major functions of the Bank of England.

3 Lender of last resort refers to the lending of which financial institution?

4 Future government monetary policy is set out in the ....

5 Which one of the following is an example of a short-term loan bought and sold in the money market?
  A shares   **B** bills   **C** commodities   **D** futures

6 What is the name of the market that mainly deals in existing shares?

7 What is a new issue?

8 Which of the following are usually known as equities?:
  A ordinary shares   **B** preference shares
  C debentures   **D** treasury bills

9 Shares which have no fixed income are known as ....

10 State a type of share which has a fixed rate of dividend.

11 Calculate from the following information the amount the company pays out to preference shareholders. A company has issued £20 000 worth 10 per cent £1 preference shares and 4000 ordinary 25p shares. A profit of £6000 is to be distributed in full.

12 Calculate from the information in question 11 the dividend per ordinary share.

13 Members of the public buying shares in the stock exchange could use the services of:
  A a stag   **B** an equity
  C an underwriter   **D** a market maker

14 Which of the following can be bought on the stock exchange?:
  A shares in private companies   **B** insurance policies
  C existing shares in public companies **D** government stock

15 A speculator who buys shares hoping to sell at a higher price is known as a ....

16 A speculator in new issues is called a ....

17 The speculator on the stock exchange who expects the price to fall is called a....... ....

18 State two reasons why the price of a share might fall.

19 State two functions of the stock exchange.
20 Finance houses specialise in:
    A mortgages **B** insurance **C** factoring **D** hire purchase
21 What is a merchant bank?
22 Which of the following will *not* provide a mortgage:
    A commercial banks **B** building societies
    C insurance companies **D** unit trusts
24 What is the main difference between the money market and the capital market?

12.7 Answers

1 C 2 See section 12.1(a).
3 Bank of England 4 Medium-term financial strategy
5 B 6 Stock exchange
7 A public limited company issuing shares for the first time.
8 A 9 Ordinary shares
10 Preference shares
11 The firm has issued 20 000 £1 preference shares, i.e. a total of £20 000. 10 per cent of £20 000 = £2000 will be paid out to preference shareholders.
12 The company has made a £6000 profit and £2000 of this goes to preference shareholders. Ordinary shareholders get what is left over, i.e. £6000 − £2000 = £4000. Each share will receive a £1 dividend.
13 D 14 C 15 Bull 16 Stag
17 Bear 18 See section 12.3(c).
19 See section 12.1(a). 20 D
21 See section 12.4(b). 22 D
23 The money market deals with short-term loans. The capital market deals with long-term loans.

13 Government Income

13.1 Sources of Government Income

The government needs money to pay for public expenditure (see section 14.1. Revenue can be raised through taxation, national insurance contributions, borrowing, charging for services or by selling off state-owned assets.

13.2 Taxation

(a) Aims of Taxation

(i) To raise money to pay for government spending.
(ii) To discourage people from buying harmful goods such as cigarettes.
(iii) To influence the level of total demand in the economy.
(iv) To redistribute income from the rich to the poor.

(b) Principles of Taxation

(i) A tax should be *certain* so that everyone knows the amount, method and time of tax payment.
(i) a tax should be *convenient* so that tax collection is at a time and in a form suitable to the payer.
(iii) A tax should be *economical* with the cost of collection representing only a small part of the revenue raised.
(iv) A tax should be *equitable* (fair) so that wealthy people pay more than poor people.
(v) A tax should not act as a *disincentive* and stop people from working.
(vi) A tax should be *flexible* so that the government can use tax changes to help control the level of demand in the economy.

(c) Main Types of Taxation

(i) *Income tax.* Everyone is given a tax-free *personal allowance* (amount) above which additional earnings are taxed at an increasing rate.
(ii) *Value added tax (VAT)* is a tax on spending. 15 per cent is added onto the selling price of most non-essential goods and services.
(iii) *Duties* are taxes on the sale of luxury goods. A fixed amount is added to the selling price.
(iv) *Rates* are a local tax on property. Within a particular local authority area, people living in larger houses pay higher rates.
(v) *Corporation tax* is a tax on company profits.
(vi) *Petroleum revenue tax* is a tax on oil taken from the North Sea.
(vii) *Inheritance tax* is a tax on the transfer of money and property.

(d) Method of Collection

(i) *Direct taxes* are paid straight to the Inland Revenue.
(ii) *Indirect taxes* are first collected by the seller and then passed on to Customs and Excise.

(e) Tax Burden

Some taxes are fairer than others. A tax can be:

(i) *Progressive*, where the percentage of income taken in tax rises as income rises. Income tax is an example of progressive taxation.
(ii) *Regressive*, where the percentage of income taken in tax falls as income rises. Rates are an example of regressive taxation.
(iii) *Proportional*, where the percentage of income taken in tax stays the same as income rises. VAT is an example of proportional taxation.

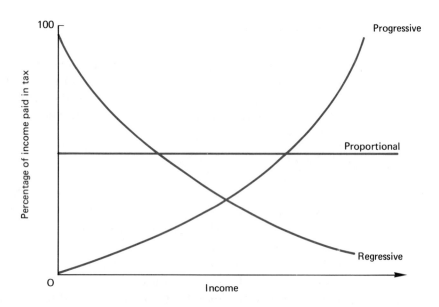

Figure 13.1   Tax burden

(f) Advantages and Disadvantages of Different Taxes

See Table 13.1 on the opposite page.

13.3 **Budgets**

(a) Calculation of the Budget

The *Chancellor of the Exchequer* is the minister of finance in charge of the Treasury. The Chancellor announces how much the government is going to spend over the next twelve months, sometime in February.

The government states how it is going to raise the money to pay for its expenditure each spring in the Budget.

Table 13.1   Advantages and disadvantages of various taxes

Tax	Collection	Burden	Advantages	Disadvantages
Income	Direct	Progressive	Fair Certain Economical Convenient (PAYE) Large revenue raiser	Disincentive to work Disincentive to save Reduces demand
VAT	Indirect	Proportional	Economical Convenient Avoidable	Inflationary Discourages consumption
Duties	Indirect	Regressive	Economical Convenient Avoidable	Inflationary Regressive therefore unfair
Rates	Direct	Regressive	Economical Certain Unavoidable	Regressive
Corporation	Direct	Progressive	Economical Certain	Disincentive to invest

(b) Types of Budget

(i) A *reflationary or deficit budget* where government spending is greater than government income. Reflationary budgets increase total demand within the economy.

(ii) A *deflationary or surplus budget* where government income exceeds expenditure and total demand is falling within the economy.

(iii) A *neutral or balanced budget* where government income and spending are the same and total demand in the economy remains constant.

The part that different types of budget play in overall government economic policy is discussed in section 14.2(e).

13.4 Government Borrowing

(a) Public Sector Borrowing Requirement

If the government spends more than its received income it will have to borrow the difference. The amount the government needs to borrow in a given time period is called the *public sector borrowing requirement (PSBR)*. The PSBR is met by:

(i) Selling National Savings certificates and Premium Bonds.

(ii) Selling *Treasury bills* which are IOUs which will be bought back in ninety-one days' time.

(iii) Selling *securities*, which are IOUs paying interest yearly which will be bought back sometime in the future. Securities are sometimes called *gilts, stocks or bonds*.

(b) National Debt

The total amount owed by the government to UK citizens and foreigners at a particular moment in time is called the *national debt*. The money raised may have been spent on capital goods which increase our ability to produce goods. Interest has to be paid on the debt. A large national debt is a problem if:

(i) Interest has to be paid to overseas citizens, so that the balance of payments suffers.

(ii) Taxes have to be increased to meet interest payments.

13.5 Worked Examples

Example 13.1

(a) Give two reasons why government levy taxes.   **(4 marks)**

(b) Explain the main differences between income tax and value added tax.

                                                                            (6 marks)

(c) Assess the economic effects of a cut in income tax on:

  (i) the availability of jobs;
  (ii) public expenditure in Wales;
  (iii) the rate of inflation.   **(6 marks)**

(WJEC specimen GCSE)

Solution 13.1

(a) Taxes raise money to pay for services provided by the government such as education. Taxes can also be used to increase the price of harmful goods such as alcohol and so reduce consumption.

(b) Income tax is a direct tax on earnings collected by the Inland Revenue, while VAT is an indirect tax on spending collected by the seller.

   Income tax is fairer because it is progressive. People on high incomes pay a greater percentage in tax than the less well off. VAT is proportional and takes a standard 15 per cent of income when a good is bought.

   Income tax can act as a disincentive to work while VAT can act as a disincentive to spend.

(c) (i) A cut in income tax increases workers' take-home pay and so results in an increase in the demand for goods and services. Part of this extra spending will go on imports. However there will be some increase in the demand for UK-made goods.

      Even so, some firms may not take on new workers but instead may sell off existing stocks of unsold goods. Alternatively, they may ask existing employees to work overtime. However, if firms are certain that the cut in income tax has increased demand permanently then they may well make more jobs available.

   (ii) A cut in income tax reduces the income of government. Current public expenditure in Wales can be maintained only if the government is prepared to borrow. Alternatively, the reduction in income tax will be financed by cutting back on public expenditure in Wales.

   (iii) If the extra spending caused by the income tax cut is met by an increase in output there will be no inflationary effect. If however the extra demand is chasing the same amount of goods then prices will tend to rise.

Example 13.2

The graph shows the percentage of total income taken in tax as income increases for three alternative types of taxation.

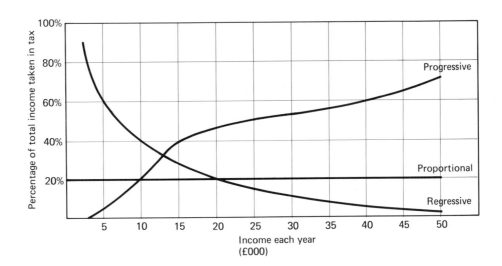

(a) From the graph describe the main difference between regressive and progressive taxation. **(2 marks)**

(b) Give one example of (i) a regressive tax and (ii) a progressive tax. **(2 marks)**

(c) At what level of income would a worker start paying progressive taxation? **(1 mark)**

(d) At what level of income would the percentage taken in tax by regressive or progressive taxation be the same? **(1 mark)**

(e) Work out for a person earning £30 000 the percentage of income taken in tax by:
(i) regressive taxation, and (ii) progressive taxation. **(2 marks)**

(f) Your yearly income is £25 000. Calculate the amount of tax to be paid for each alternative type of taxation. **(3 marks)**

(g) Which of the three types of taxation shown on the graph would you use as a basis for income tax? Explain your answer. **(6 marks)**

Solution 13.2

(a) As income increases regressive taxation takes a smaller percentage of total income while progressive taxation takes a larger percentage.

(b) Rates is an example of a regressive tax and income tax is an example of progressive tax.

(c) Looking at the graph, the progressive taxation line does not start until annual income is £3 000. Hence workers start paying progressive taxation at £3 000.

(d) The regressive and progressive taxation lines cross at income level £13 000. Hence £13 000 is the level of income where the percentage taken in tax by progressive or regressive taxation is the same.

(e) (i) Moving up from income level £30 000 on the *x*-axis until you touch the regressive line and then moving across to the *y*-axis indicates that 10 per cent is taken in tax.

(ii) From the graph, 53 per cent of the income of someone earning £30 000 is taken by progressive taxation.

(f) Progressive taxation takes 50 per cent, i.e. £25 000 × 50/100 = £12 500.
Proportional taxation takes 20 per cent, i.e. £25 000 × 20/100 = £5 000.
Regressive taxation takes 14 per cent, i.e. £25 000 × 14/100 = £3 500.

(g) Regressive taxation is unsuitable because it places a greater burden on the less well-off than on the rich. Progressive taxation is fairer because people with higher incomes can afford to pay a high percentage of their income in tax.

The disadvantage of progressive taxation is that it may put high earners off working overtime. For every extra pound earned only a few pence are kept by the worker. Proportional taxation has the advantage of not acting as a disincentive to extra work.

It would be better to use a progressive system of income tax which does not have very high rates of taxation for high income earners.

Example 13.3

Here is a simplified version of the Budget statement by the Chancellor of the Exchequer:

Income (£bn.)		Planned expenditure (£bn.)	
Income tax and other direct taxes	£25	Social security	£28
VAT	£30	Defence	£13
		Health and personal social services	£12
Customs and excise, etc.	£10	Education, science and libraries	£10
		Housing	£3
		Industry, energy, trade and employment	£4
		Other	£3

From the information given in the above statement:
(a) Calculate
    (i) the total income available to the Chancellor, **(1 mark)**
    (ii) the total planned expenditure. **(1 mark)**
(b) Has the Chancellor enough income for planned expenditure? **(1 mark)**
(c) Write down the term to describe this type of budget. **(1 mark)**
(d) What might be the purpose of such a budget? **(2 marks)**
(e) Identify two economic problems which might result from this type of budgeting. **(4 marks)**

(NISEC specimen GCSE)

Solution 13.3

(a)   (i) Adding together income received from direct taxes (£25bn.), VAT (£30bn.) and customs duties (£10bn.) gives a total of £65bn.
    (ii) Adding together the items shown in the expenditure column gives a total of £73bn.
(b) Planned expenditure is £73bn. while income is only £65bn. Income falls short of expenditure by £8bn.
(c) This is a deficit budget.

(d) Deficit budgets increase overall demand in the economy for goods and services. To increase output firms take on more workers so that the level of unemployment falls.

(e) The extra spending generated by a deficit budget may result in demand-pull inflation if there is no increase in output.

Some of the extra spending will go on imports thus causing balance of payment problems.

Example 13.4

Read the following passage and study the diagram.

The Treasury's Balancing Act

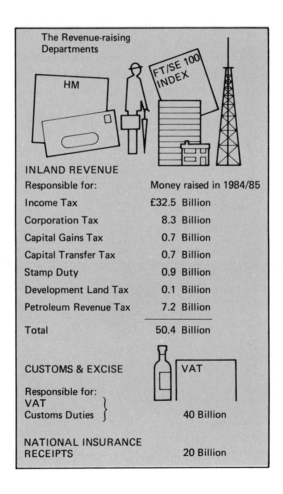

While the spending departments are working out their plans, the Treasury (the Chancellor's department) is busy making its forecasts and plans. It will be looking at the likely trends of *economic activity* and estimating the likely rate of inflation.

All this will give the Treasury some idea of how much income it may expect to receive in the coming year, what its expenditure might be and how it will *balance the books*.

On the basis of its forecasts the Treasury may decide it will not have enough income to carry out the overall *spending plans* for the following year. It must decide what to do about it.

The Treasury will try to cut down on the amount the other departments want to spend but this makes it unpopular with the spenders. The Treasury may want to increase taxes, which makes it unpopular with everyone else. Alternatively, overspending can be financed by borrowing.

Source: Adapted from *Stock Exchange Spectrum*, No. 2, 1986

(a) From the diagram:

    (i) list from highest to lowest the four types of tax collected by the Inland Revenue which raise the most revenue; **(2 marks)**
    (ii) calculate the amount of money raised from expenditure taxes; **(1 mark)**
    (iii) calculate the total amount of money raised from all sources by the Treasury; **(1 mark)**
    (iv) calculate the percentage of money raised from all sources as income tax. **(2 marks)**

(b) State one source of revenue given in the diagram which does *not come from taxation*. **(1 mark)**

(c) Give briefly the meaning of the following terms:

    (i) economic activity; **(1 mark)**
    (ii) balance the books. **(1 mark)**

(d) The government decides in its budget to increase taxation and maintain current spending at its present level. Advise the Chancellor on the likely effects of the proposed budget on unemployment. **(5 marks)**
(e) How could the Chancellor change the proposed budget to make income equal expenditure? **(2 marks)**
(f) Explain the difference between the national debt and the public sector borrowing requirement (PSBR). **(4 marks)**

Solution 13.4

(a)   (i) Income tax (£32.5bn.); corporation tax (£8.3bn.); petroleum revenue tax (£7.2bn.); and stamp duty (£0.9bn.).
    (ii) Expenditure taxes are collected by the Customs and Excise and amounted to £40bn.
    (iii) Adding together, the money raised by the Inland Revenue (£50.4bn.), customs (£40bn.) and national insurance (£20bn.) means the Treasury raised £110.4bn.

    (iv) Income tax accounted for $\dfrac{32.5 \times 100}{110.4} = 29.4$ per cent.

(b) National insurance is not a tax but a scheme which helps employees if they become unemployed and when they become pensioners.

(c)   (i) 'Economic activity' refers to the production and consumption of commodities.
    (ii) 'Balance the books' refers to the procedure of matching income with expenditure.

(d) When the government raises more money than it spends there is a surplus budget. An increase in taxation reduces spending. A fall in spending reduces the number of goods sold, and some workers are no longer required. Total income falls, creating a multiplier effect in reverse. This process is shown in the accompanying diagram.

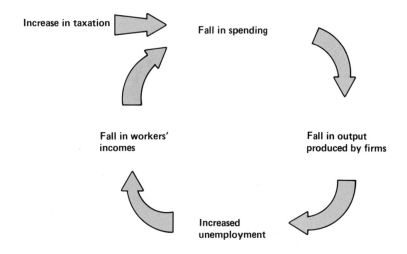

Reverse multiplier effect

The downward spiral of reduced spending causing reduced income means firms need fewer workers. Unemployment rises.

(e) A surplus budget can be turned into a balanced budget if the government increases its own spending or reduces taxation.

(f) The PSBR is the amount the government needs to borrow each year to balance its income and expenditure and is a flow value. The national debt is the overall amount of money the government owes at a particular moment in time and is a stock value.

Example 13.5

Study the following information sent out to all ratepayers by Oxfordshire County Council explaining why the tax they pay for living in a house (rates) is going up.

> The County Council has agreed an increase of 10 per cent in its budget for 1986–7 which will allow a 5.5 per cent improvement to services. However, rates will increase by 25 per cent. Why?
> A quarter of the County Council's expenditure is financed by a central government block grant. In spite of inflation the block grant has been cut by £10.7m. Hence, a large element of the rate increase results directly from a loss of central government grant.
> The council has tried, without success, to prevent this by representations to the government.
> Source: Adapted from circular issued by Oxfordshire County Council in February 1986

(a) What is the percentage increase in rates given in the passage? **(1 mark)**
(b) State three reasons given by the council for the increase in rates. **(3 marks)**
(c) From the information given in the figure on the next page calculate:

    (i) the rate increase in pence; **(1 mark)**
    (ii) the amount of rates paid in 1986–7 by someone living in a house with a rateable value of £500; **(2 marks)**
    (iii) the amount of extra revenue raised in 1986–7 by an increase in rates of 5 pence. **(2 marks)**

(d) What are the likely effects of the council's budget on:

    (i) local businesses; **(3 marks)**
    (ii) local employment? **(4 marks)**

(e) What are the economic arguments for and against replacing rates with a tax on the number of adults living in a house (a community charge)? **(5 marks)**

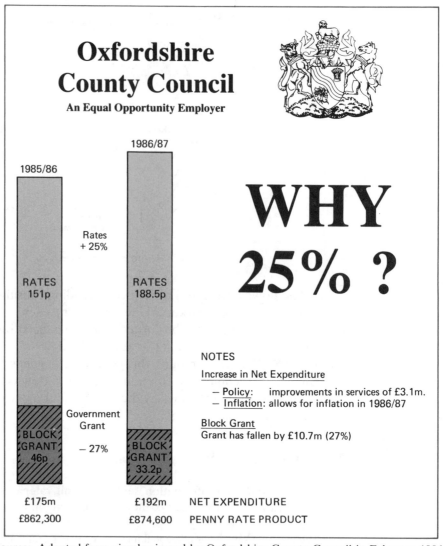

Oxfordshire County Council
An Equal Opportunity Employer

WHY 25% ?

1986/87

1985/86

Rates + 25%

RATES 151p

RATES 188.5p

NOTES

Increase in Net Expenditure

— <u>Policy</u>: improvements in services of £3.1m.
— <u>Inflation</u>: allows for inflation in 1986/87

Block Grant
Grant has fallen by £10.7m (27%)

Government Grant
− 27%

BLOCK GRANT 46p

BLOCK GRANT 33.2p

| £175m | £192m | NET EXPENDITURE |
| £862,300 | £874,600 | PENNY RATE PRODUCT |

Source: Adapted from circular issued by Oxfordshire County Council in February 1986

Solution 13.5

(a) The percentage increase in rates is 25 per cent.
(b) Rates were increased to pay for improved services and to meet extra costs caused by inflation. The reduction in the block grant also meant rates had to be increased.

(c) (i) Rates were 151p in 1985–6 and increased to 188.5p in 1986–7, an increase of 37.5 pence.
  (ii) Rates paid = rateable poundage × rateable value. Rates are now 188.5p and the rateable value of the house is £500. Rates paid = £1.88½ × £500 = £942.5.
  (iii) The notes to the diagram indicate that in 1986–7 each extra penny on the rates (penny rate product) raises £874 600. Therefore 5p on the rates would raise:

$$£874\ 600 \times 5 = £4\ 373\ 000$$

(d) (i) Local businesses gain and lose from the council's budget. On the one hand, extra spending by the council may go to local firms, thus increasing their turnover and profits.

However, local businesses will be faced with a large increase in their rate bill. This has the effect of increasing fixed costs and reducing profits.

(ii) Oxfordshire Council hope to improve services. Many services provided by the Council are labour-intensive and will create many jobs for local people.

However, the increase in rates will reduce the amount of money local people have to spend and Oxfordshire firms will sell fewer goods. Businesses may reduce the number of people they employ as a result of falling sales and the increase in rates they themselves have to pay.

In short, the number of people employed by the Council will probably rise while the number employed by local firms will fall.

(e) A fair system of taxation makes sure that those people who are better off pay more tax than the less well off. At present, two identical houses in the same area pay the same rates even though one property may have four wage earners under the same roof. A community charge would overcome this unfairness. Moreover, each adult would then make a bigger contribution to paying for the council services they consume.

However, it may be that adults living in a house do not have paid employment. Households where one person is a student, is retired or looks after the house will be faced with a large community tax bill even though there is only one breadwinner.

13.6 Questions

1 Apart from taxation, state three different methods by which the government can raise money.

2 For what purposes other than raising revenue may a government make changes in taxation?

3 Which of the following is *not* a principle of taxation?
   A a tax is acceptable to everyone   B a tax is convenient to pay
   C a tax is economic to collect   D a tax is based on ability to pay

4 Pair each of the following:
   A income tax   B value added tax   C duties
   D rates   E corporation tax
   (a) tax on property   (b) tax on earnings
   (c) fixed tax on the sale of goods   (d) percentage tax on the sale of goods
   (e) tax on company profits

5 Your gross income is £10 000. Your tax allowance is £3 000. If tax is charged at a standard rate of 25p in the pound then total tax paid is:
   A £1500   B £1750   C £2000   D £2250.

6 An increase in taxpayers' personal allowance would result in a/an .... in the amount of tax-free income.

7 What is the name of the system where tax is collected by your employer before you receive your pay?

8 From which tax do local authorities directly receive most of their revenue?:
   A VAT   B duties   C rates   D income tax

9 VAT is an example of:
   A an indirect tax   B a direct tax
   C a proportional tax   D both A and C

10 Which one of the following is free from value added tax?
   A beer   B sweets   C milk   D petrol

11 Explain the difference between an indirect tax and a direct tax.

12 Give an example of an indirect tax and a direct tax.

13 In the tax year 1984–5 the government collected:

Income tax	£32 000 000 000
VAT	£23 000 000 000
National insurance receipts	£20 000 000 000
Duties	£17 000 000 000
Company profits tax	£ 8 000 000 000

  Calculate: (a) the total direct tax collected;
  (b) the total indirect tax collected;
  (c) the total amount of money raised.

14 A progressive tax means that the rate of tax .... as income increases.

15 A tax is said to be .... if the rate of tax remains the same as income rises.

16 What is a regressive tax?

17 The replacement of a progressive tax by a regressive tax means:
  A increased taxes for the well off   **B** income becomes more equal
  C most people pay the same tax   **D** increased taxes for the less well off

18 Jean earns £30 000 each year and pays £3000 in income tax. Derek earns £10 000 each year and pays £1000 in income tax. This type of income tax system is:
  A progressive   **B** proportional   **C** regressive   **D** fair

19 State two examples of taxes on spending and two examples of taxes on income.

20 The government announces its proposals for raising revenue in the ....

21 A budget .... occurs when a government spends more than its revenue.

22 The amount the government needs to borrow to balance the budget is known as the ....

23 State two methods the government can use to borrow money.

24 The total amount of money the central government has borrowed is known as the ....

25 When can the national debt be a problem?

13.7 Answers

1 National insurance contributions; borrowing; charging for services; income from assets; selling assets.

2 Stop the consumption of harmful goods; to redistribute income; to influence aggregate demand; to reduce the money supply; to pay for public services.

3 **A**   4 **A (b) B (d) C (c) D (a) E (e)**   5 **B**

6 Increase   7 Pay as you earn (PAYE).

8 **C**   9 **D**

10 **C**—all the other goods are luxuries.

11 Indirect taxes are collected by the seller. Indirect taxes are a tax on expenditure. Direct taxes are paid straight to the Inland Revenue. Direct taxation is on income.

12 See Table 13.1.

13 (a) 60 billion   (b) 40 billion   (c) 100 billion

14 Increases   15 Proportional   16 See section 13.2(e)

17 **D**   18 **B**

19 VAT and duties are taxes on spending. Income tax and corporation tax are taxes on income.

20 Budget   21 Deficit

22 The public sector borrowing requirement.

23 See section 13.4(a)   24 The national debt.

25 See section 13.4(b).

14 Government Spending

14.1 Public Expenditure

(a) Structure of Public Expenditure

Public expenditure is spending by central government, local government, and nationalised industries. For every pound of public spending in 1986:

(i) Central government spends 73p.
(ii) Local authorities spend 25p.
(iii) Nationalised industries spend 2p.

Table 14.1 The main government spending departments

Name of department	Responsibility
Health and Social Security	National Health Service; pensions
	Unemployment and welfare benefits
Defence	Navy, Army and Air Force
Education and Science	Schools; universities; the arts
Environment	Roads; housing; local authorities
Home Office	Courts; police; prisons; fire service
Employment	Training schemes; jobcentres
Agriculture, Fisheries and Food	Agricultural policy
Trade and Industry	Regional and Industrial policy
Foreign Office	Embassies
Energy	Electricity; gas; oil; atomic energy

(b) Public and Merit Goods

A *public good* is an item which cannot be withheld from one consumer without withholding the good from all customers. Since public goods, such as street lighting, can be used free of charge, they will not be supplied by private-sector firms. Public goods are therefore supplied by central and local government.

A *merit good* is a useful item, such as education, which some people are unwilling to buy. Merit goods are supplied by the public authorities either free or for a minimal charge.

(c) Aims of Government Spending

(i) To provide public goods and services.
(ii) To encourage the consumption of merit goods.
(iii) To relieve poverty.
(iv) To influence the level of total demand in the economy.

14.2 Macroeconomics

(a) Macroeconomic Problems

Macroeconomics is concerned with the study of the whole economy. Problems arise when the economy suffers from high unemployment, inflation, or a balance of payments deficit. Therefore the government sets itself certain macroeconomic objectives:

  (i) low unemployment;
  (ii) low inflation;
  (iii) a balance of payments surplus;
  (vi) economic growth;
  (v) a fair share of income between different groups.

(b) Booms in the Economy

A *boom* is when output and employment in the economy are rising (Fig.14.1).

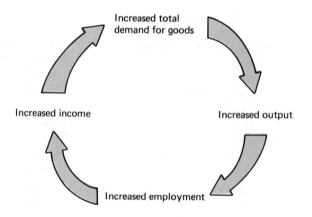

Increased total demand for goods

Increased income

Increased output

Increased employment

Figure 14.1   A boom

However:

  (i) A boom increases spending on imports, causing balance of payments problems.
  (ii) Once high levels of employment have been reached, output cannot be increased any further and the boom causes inflation.

(c) Slumps in the Economy

A *slump* is when output and employment in the economy are falling (Fig. 14.2).
  However:

  (i) A slump reduces spending on imports, thus improving the balance of payments.
  (ii) Reduced total spending lowers inflationary pressure.

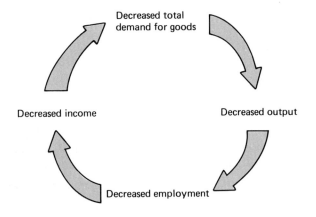

Figure 14.2 A slump

(d) Trade Cycles

The *trade or business cycle* refers to regular movements in the economy between booms and slumps (Fig. 14.3).

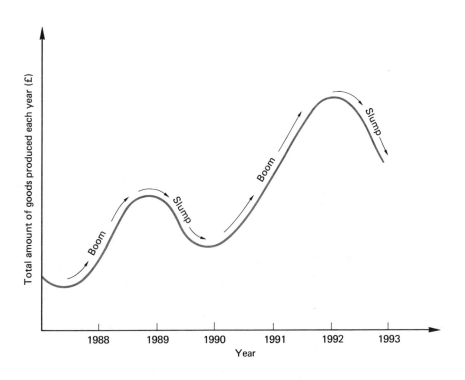

Figure 14.3 Trade cycles

(e) Government Macroeconomic Policies

Table 14.2 on the next page shows some of the policies the government can use to try to get full employment, stable prices, etc.

Table 14.2   Macroeconomic policies

Policy	Description
Fiscal	Changes in government expenditure and taxation
Monetary	Changes in the money supply and interest rates
Prices and incomes	Legal or voluntary limits on price and wage increases
Regional	Measures to help depressed areas
Industrial	Government planning of industry
Commercial	Quotas, tariffs, exchange controls or free trade
Exchange rate	Encouraging a depreciation or appreciation of sterling

14.3   Worked Examples

Example 14.1

Study the following photographs here which show some of the services provided by the government and answer the questions that follow.

(a) Which of the photographs shows:
  (i) a public good;
  (ii) a merit good;
  (iii) a transfer payment?   **(3 marks)**

(b) For what economic reasons does the government provide each of the services shown in photographs A, B and C?   **(5 marks)**

(c) Give two main methods of raising money to provide the services shown in the photographs.   **(2 marks)**

(d) Are any of the services shown in the photographs also provided by the private sector?   **(1 mark)**

(e) What would be the effect of an ageing population on each of the services shown in photographs A, B and C?   **(5 marks)**

A   Senior citizens collecting their pensions

B   The British army on exercise

C   Children in a state primary school

Solution 14.1

(a) (i) Photograph B shows a public good.
    (ii) Photograph C shows a merit good.
    (iii) Photograph A shows a transfer payment.
(b) One of the aims of government spending is to make income more equal. State pensions to people over 60 (women) or 65 (men) ensure a basic income level for retired people.

   Private firms would not supply public goods such as defence, because once provided they can be consumed by anyone, even non-payers. Private firms have no way of forcing the whole community to pay and cannot exclude non-payers from using the good. Only governments can collect taxes to finance the provision of public goods.

   Some goods such as education are undervalued by private consumers and would not be bought in large enough quantities. To ensure an adequate supply, education is supplied by the government free of charge.
(c) The government can provide the services shown in the pictures by raising taxes or by borrowing.
(d) Education is provided by the private sector. Some private firms offer pension schemes to the public.
(e) An ageing population means that the average age of the population is rising. This will result in an increase in the number of people able to claim pensions and this sector will expand.

   An increase in average age suggests a fall in the number of people of working age. The number of people able and willing to enter the army will fall and there may be a problem in recruiting soldiers.

   An ageing population also suggests a fall in the number of young people going to school. There will be a fall in the number of primary schools needed.

Example 14.2

(a) Explain the difference between central government expenditure and central government revenue. **(2 marks)**
(b) (i) Identify the major source of central government income. **(3 marks)**
    (ii) Indicate the major items of central government expenditure. **(3 marks)**
(c) How does central government taxation and expenditure policy:

   (i) affect/influence the distribution of personal income in the United Kingdom; **(4 marks)**
   (ii) reduce inequalities in the living standards of various sections of the United Kingdom population? **(4 marks)**
(d) Suggest ways in which spending on education could be on

   (i) consumer goods,
   (ii) capital goods. **(4 marks)**

(NISEC specimen GCSE)

Solution 14.2

(a) Central government expenditure refers to state spending while revenue refers to state income from taxation.
(b) (i) The major sources of central government income are direct taxes such as income tax collected by the inland revenue; indirect taxes such

as VAT collected by customs and excise; and national insurance contributions.

(ii) The major items of central government expenditure are public goods such as street lighting; merit goods such as the health service; and social security services such as pensions and unemployment benefits.

(c) (i) Government taxation takes money away from the rich through progressive taxation. Some of the money raised is then paid out in benefits to low-income groups such as pensioners and the unemployed. This makes personal income more equal.

(ii) The government provides a number of welfare services, such as dental treatment, at little or no cost. Low-income groups are then able to consume goods and services they could not have afforded to buy themselves. This makes the standard of living of different people more equal.

(d) (i) Consumer goods are items used to satisfy household wants and needs. Education involves the use of consumer goods such as books and televisions.

(ii) Capital goods are items used to produce other goods and services. The school building is an example of a capital good.

Example 14.3

The following report is based on information given to Chichester District Council (18 December 1984) about a decision to build a new sports centre. Read it carefully then answer the questions which follow.

The Council has already approved the spending of £1.6 million on a new sports hall. It now has to decide if a new swimming pool should be included in the building plans. Enough land is available for both. The extra cost of the new swimming pool would be £650 000 if the sale of the Council's existing pool is taken into account. The Council has money available for both projects. However, it is important to remember that the money could be used on other projects. It could be used to repay existing debts, kept to earn interest or spent on other projects which might not otherwise go ahead. The money used for the sports hall could earn £170 000 a year in interest. The funds for the combined sports hall and swimming pool could earn £240 000 a year in interest.

The table here shows the estimated annual running costs and expected income from

(i) the existing swimming pool and a new sports hall, and
(ii) a new sports centre, made up of a new sports hall and a new swimming pool.

	Existing swimming pool and new sports hall	New sports centre (combined sports hall and swimming pool)
Total running cost	£390 000	£330 000
Total expected income	£170 000	£170 000
Expected loss	£220 000	£160 000

(a) (i) Give two alternative ways in which the money set aside for the sports centre could be spent. **(2 marks)**

(ii) What term do economists use to describe the cost of something in terms of the next best alternative forgone? **(1 mark)**

(b) When comparing the different schemes, why is it important to take into account the sale of the existing swimming pool? **(2 marks)**

(c) The annual running cost of a new sports hall with the existing swimming pool is given as £390 000. Give three reasons why a combined sports hall and swimming pool is likely to be cheaper than the present swimming pool and a new sports hall. **(3 marks)**

(d) If you were advising the Council, which decision should it take? Should it:

  (i) not go ahead with the new project,
  (ii) only build a new sports hall, or
  (iii) build a new sports centre with swimming pool and sports hall combined?

  Using the information contained in this report, explain the reasons for your answer. **(6 marks)**

(e) Explain why Chichester District Council might be prepared to build a sports centre even though it expects to start losing money when the centre is open. **(6 marks)**

(SEG specimen GCSE)

Solution 14.3

(a) (i) The money set aside for the sports centre could be spent on some alternative project such as new housing or it could be used to repay a loan.

  (ii) The term used is opportunity cost.

(b) The sale of the existing swimming pool will raise money which can be used to pay for part of the new building, and must be included if the council's costings are to be accurate.

(c) Operating a swimming pool and sports centre on the same site allows the council to make a number of savings. One hall requires fewer managers and assistants than two sites. Only one pay desk needs to be manned. There will also be a considerable saving on heating and lighting costs.

(d) The initial decision by the council to improve sporting facilities by building a new sports hall suggests that existing facilities are inadequate. Therefore option (i) is not advisable.

  Maintaining the existing swimming pool and building a separate sports hall involves high running costs and is not a good use of council staff. Option (iii) is the most expensive option in the short term but it has a lower annual expected loss than option (ii). I advise that option (iii) is put into action.

(e) One of the aims of local government spending is to improve the standard of living of the less well off by providing services such as leisure facilities at little or no cost.

  The sports centre allows people the opportunity of improving their fitness and health. A healthier population reduces the demand for medical care and the council will be able to save money on local health services to offset the loss made by the centre. Society will also benefit from a fall in the number of days people take off work.

  The council may feel that the sports centre will have the effect of keeping people off the street, thereby reducing the amount of vandalism.

  In short the council may feel that the benefits to society as a whole are greater than the private loss to the council of running the centre.

Example 14.4

The following passage is an extract from the *Economic Progress Report* and gives the Treasury's view on public expenditure plans.

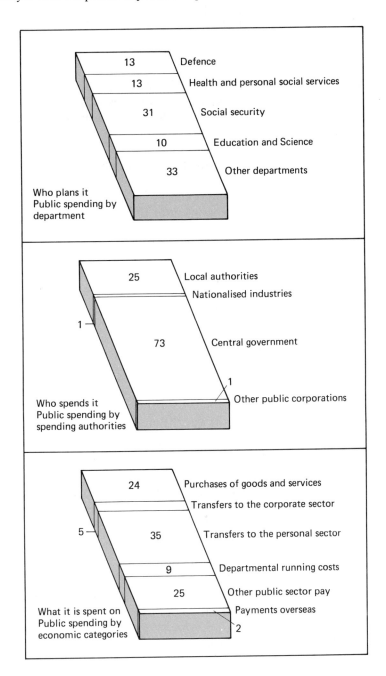

Public spending in 1986–7: percentages of planning total (excluding reserve, central privatisation proceeds and adjustments)

Planned public spending will amount to £139.2 billion in 1986–7. The government's overall economic strategy is bringing about low inflation and sustained growth. Central government spending as a percentage of gross domestic product has been falling since 1982–3. As public expenditure over the next three years is expected to be stable while the economy continues to grow, this trend should continue.

Within the spending totals extra funds have been found for the Health Service and capital spending on housing and roads. In other areas spending is being held back, for example in defence.

The success of the expenditure programme depends not just on the amount of funds provided but also on how effectively and efficiently the funds are used.

Source: Adapted from *Economic Progress Report*, No. 182, Jan.–Feb. 1986

(a) Give the amount of central government spending planned for 1986–7.

(1 mark)

(b) From the passage, name an item of public spending that is likely to: (i) increase, and   (ii) decrease.

(1 mark)

(c) What reasons are given by the Treasury for believing that future inflation will be low?

(2 marks)

(d) From the diagram give:

    (i) the largest public spending authority;

(1 mark)

    (ii) the largest category of public spending;

(1 mark)

    (iii) the percentage share of education and science in total public spending.

(1 mark)

(e) Calculate the total amount of planned expenditure by:

    (i) local authorities;

(2 marks)

    (ii) the Department of Education and Science.

(2 marks)

(f) What would be the effect of a fall in the number of unemployed on public spending?

(5 marks)

Solution 14.4

(a) Central government plan to spend £139.1bn. in 1986–7.

(b) (i) Spending on the Health Service is likely to increase.

    (ii) Spending on defence is likely to decrease.

(c) The Treasury suggests that stable future government spending and likely increases in output should mean low inflation.

(d) (i) Central government is the largest public spending authority.

    (ii) The largest category of public spending is on transfers to the public sector.

    (iii) Education and science account for 10 per cent of public spending.

(e) (i) Local authorities plan to spend 25 per cent of public spending, i.e. £139.1bn. × 25/100 = £34.775bn.

    (ii) The Department of Education and Science plans to spend 10 per cent of total public spending i.e. £139.1bn. × 10/100 = £13.91bn.

(f) A fall in the number of unemployed will reduce the amount spent on benefits. The current percentage of public spending going on transfers to the personal sector is 35 per cent, i.e. some £48.7bn. Some government transfers to the personal sector are unrelated to unemployment, e.g. pensions. However, a large fall in the number of unemployed will free many billions of pounds for alternative uses.

    The government can use benefit savings (and the extra tax revenue paid by the newly employed) either to reduce overall taxation or to increase the spending of other departments. Public spending on goods and services may increase.

Example 14.5

(a) What is meant by (i) monetary policy and (ii) fiscal policy? **(4 marks)**

(b) The government wishes to raise the level of total demand in the economy. Explain briefly how fiscal policy could be used to do this. **(2 marks)**

(c) Direct controls can also be used by the government to control the economy.
   (i) State two direct controls which are available to the government. **(2 marks)**
   (ii) For each of these two controls, give an example of a situation in which they would be of use to a government. **(2 marks)**
(d) (i) Draw a graph showing a normal demand curve and a normal supply curve. Label the curves. **(2 marks)**
   (ii) On your graph, label the axes so that the graph shows the market for labour in the United Kingdom. **(2 marks)**
   (iii) On your graph, draw the likely effect of the government raising the level of total demand in the economy, on the market for labour. Show clearly how it will affect the market. **(3 marks)**
   (vi) Using the information on the graph, explain the likely effect on unemployment of the government raising the level of total demand in the economy.
   (3 marks)
(SEG specimen GCSE)

Solution 14.5

(a) (i) Monetary policy means government control of the amount of money in circulation in the economy and interest rates.
   (ii) Fiscal policy means government control of its own spending and taxation.
(b) One method is to increase government spending, which raises the level of total demand in the economy. Alternatively, the government can reduce taxation, which increases the amount of disposable income of workers. Higher income increases total demand.
(c) (i) Direct controls occur when the government intervenes in the economy, for example by imposing import quotas or by freezing wages through a prices and incomes policy.
   (ii) Quotas reduce the volume of imports allowed into a country and would help to correct a balance of payments deficit. (See section 17.3(b)).
   A prices and incomes policy is when the government bans pay and price increases beyond a set level, e.g. 3 per cent, and is useful if the government wants to reduce short-term inflation.
(d) (i) to (iii) See the graph.

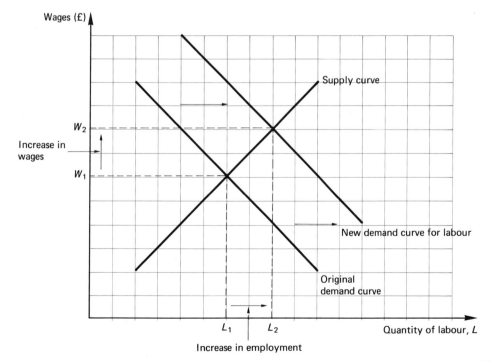

163

(iv) The demand for labour is derived from the demand for finished goods and services. An increase in total demand increases the demand for labour so that the original demand curve on the graph shifts to the right. Firms take on more workers, with the result that the number of unemployed falls.

14.4 Questions

1 Which of the following is a public good?:
   A a school   B a park
   C a public limited company   D a public corporation
2 Which of the following is a merit good?:
   A taxes   B insurance
   C dental care   D defence
3 State two reasons for government spending.
4 State two items of government spending.
5 Which of the following are items of public spending?
   A social security benefits   B value added tax   C customs duties
   D defence   E education   F income tax
6 Which of the following is/are examples of public expenditure in the United Kingdom?:
   A household spending   B central government spending
   C local government spending   D public corporation spending
7 Which of the following is *not* an example of public expenditure?:
   A public enterprises' purchase of machines
   B public purchases of goods produced by public corporations
   C social security benefits paid to the unemployed
   D spending by local authorities on goods and services
8 Which item of public spending is most likely to increase during an economic depression?
9 What is meant by macroeconomics?
10 An economic boom occurs when there is:
   A a fall in inflation   B an increase in total demand
   C an increase in unemployment   D a balance of payments surplus
11 A slump in the economy may result in:
   A a current account deficit   B a budget surplus
   C a fall in inflation   D immigration
12 Draw a graph to illustrate the trade cycle.
13 State two macroeconomic objectives.
14 Changes in government expenditure and taxation to influence the level of demand is:
   A incomes policy   B fiscal policy
   C commercial policy   D monetary policy
15 The government carries out its fiscal policy by altering ....
   and/or ....
16 Which of the following leads to an increase in the level of demand in the economy?
   A an increase in the rate of interest   B an increase in indirect taxation
   C a decrease in government spending D a decrease in direct taxation
17 An example of government carrying out monetary policy is:
   A a change in the rate of VAT
   B a change in the value of sterling
   C a change in the rate support grant to local authorities
   D a change in the rate of interest
18 Which of the following policies aims to increase aggregate demand in the economy?
   A reflation   B disinflation   C depreciation   D deflation

19 A balanced budget is one which:
   A ensures that the balance of payments is in balance
   B ensures that public spending equals public revenue
   C ensures that all taxes are equitable
   D ensures economic growth in all sections of the economy

20 In the year after a balanced budget the government then increases taxation and reduces its own expenditure. The result will be a budget ....

14.5 Answers

1	**B**	2	**C**	3	See section 14.1(b).	
4	See Table 14.1.			5	**A, D, E**	
6	**B C D**			7	**B**	

8 Spending on social security payments to the newly unemployed.

9 The study of the economy as a whole.

10	**B**	11	**C**	12	See Fig. 14.3.			
13	See section 14.2(a)			14	**B**			
15	taxes and government expenditure			16	**D**			
17	**D**	18	**A**	19	**B**		20	surplus

15 Unemployment

15.1 Working Population

(a) Structure of the Working Population

Figure 15.1 divides the UK population into two sections:

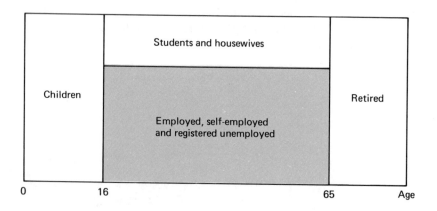

Figure 15.1 The working population and dependants

(i) The *working population* is made up of the groups shown in the shaded area. All those people employed or self-employed make up the labour force.
(ii) *Dependants* make up the groups shown in the unshaded area.

(b) Employment Trends

There has been a radical change in the structure of occupational employment. Before the industrial revolution over 80 per cent of the labour force were employed in agricultural production. Now the figure is less than 3 per cent. As recently as 1951, over half the labour force were employed in manufacturing. Since then there has been a period of rapid decline, particularly in the heavy-engineering sector. The complexity of modern society has increased the number of administrators. This trend has been accelerated by the spread of information technology.

15.2 Measurement of Unemployment

When calculating the level of unemployment the government only counts those people who register as unemployed and claim benefit. A large number of people seeking work either do not register or do not claim benefit and are now excluded from official figures.

The *unemployment rate* is the percentage of the labour force officially jobless. *Full employment* occurs when the number of notified job vacancies exceeds the number of registered unemployed.

15.3 Costs of Unemployment

(a) Lost Output

The opportunity cost of each unemployed person is their foregone output. Since average annual output per worker is £12 000, unemployment of $3\frac{1}{3}$ million costs the UK £40 billion a year in lost goods.

(b) Increased Benefit Payments

Each extra person who becomes unemployed stops paying tax (£2500) and starts receiving benefit (£3000). The government has to raise an extra £15 billion to finance unemployment benefits.

(c) Human Costs of Unemployment

The long-term and youth unemployed feel increasingly isolated and removed (*alienated*) from society.

15.4 Types, Causes, and Remedies for Unemployment

Table 15.1 summarises the main causes and remedies for different types of unemployment.

The Thatcher administration (1979 to date) believes that the current high level of unemployment cannot be reduced by more government spending. The government argues that extra spending only increases inflation and UK imports. The government does offer a number of employment and training schemes summarised in table 15.2.

15.5 Unemployment Trends

Figure 15.2 shows the types of unemployment inflows (people becoming unemployed) and outflows (people ceasing to be unemployed).

All inflows are rising. All outflows except training are falling. Therefore overall unemployment is rising. Young people, women, the over-fifties and ethnic minorities are hardest hit. Inner cities and manufacturing areas have above-average unemployment. The average length of time workers remain unemployed is rising.

167

Table 15.1 Causes and remedies of unemployment

Type	Description	Cause	Remedy
Frictional	Workers temporarily between jobs	Delays in applying interviewing and accepting jobs	Improve job information, e.g. computerised job centres
Structural	Workers have the wrong skills in the wrong place	Declining industries and the immobility of labour	Subsidies and improve the mobility of labour
Cyclical	All firms need fewer workers	Low total demand in the economy	Increased government spending or lower taxes
Technological	Firms replace workers with machines	Automation and information technology	Retraining
International	Overseas firms replace UK producers	High-priced/low-quality UK goods	Tariffs quotas or sterling depreciation
Regional	High unemployment in one area	Local concentration of declining industries	Regional aid, e.g. relocation grants
Seasonal	Unemployment for part of the year	Seasonal variation in demand	Retraining
Voluntary	Workers choose to remain unemployed	More money 'on the dole' than from working	Remove the low-paid from the liability to pay income tax

Table 15.2 Employment and training schemes

Scheme	Description
Restart Programme	Interviews and training for the long-term unemployed
Community Programme	Local projects for the long-term unemployed
New Workers Scheme	A subsidy to employers taking on youth unemployed
Job Search Scheme	Return fare and allowances for job interviews
Job Release Scheme	Older workers retire early with an allowance and are replaced by an unemployed person
Job Splitting Scheme	A subsidy to employers who encourage job sharing
Youth Training Scheme	Two-year work experience and training for school leavers
Job Training Scheme	Retraining scheme for unemployed adults

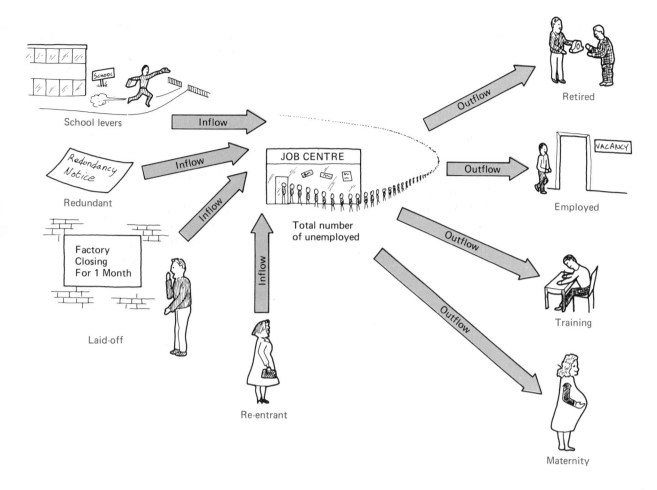

Figure 15.2 Unemployment inflows and outflows

15.6 Worked Examples

Example 15.1

The diagram shows the distribution of employment in the UK.

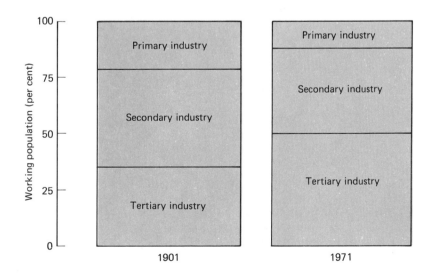

(a) Give two examples of 'tertiary industry'. **(2 marks)**
(b) Explain the meaning of the term 'working population'. **(4 marks)**
(c) Give reasons for the change in the distribution of the population between the two years. **(6 marks)**

(SREB 1983)

Solution 15.1

(a) The tertiary sector is made up of industries supplying services such as banking or retailing.

(b) The working population is made up of people with paid jobs (sometimes called the labour force) and anyone registered as unemployed. This government definition excludes students, the retired and housewives doing unpaid work. Anyone looking for work but not actually drawing social security is also not a member of the working population.

(c) The primary sector consists of the agricultural, fishing and mining industries, each of which has gone into decline over the last eighty years. Alternative energy sources such as oil and electricity have reduced the demand for coal while at the same time many pits have become exhausted. Agriculture has seen the increasing application of new labour-saving machines such as combine harvesters.

Manufacturing has also been in decline with imports sometimes outcompeting industries such as motor cars and motor cycles. The remaining companies have gone over to automation with resultant job losses.

At the same time there has been a growth in services which has drawn extra labour. Today there are more people employed in producing a service than producing a good. This in part reflects the rise of the Welfare State with governments needing more civil servants and employees to provide improved health and education services. Moreover, as living standards rise, so more people demand more leisure services. The result is an increase in the percentage of the working population employed in the tertiary sector.

Example 15.2

Answer all the questions which follow the passage below:

It is quite possible for the number of registered unemployed to fall while the seasonally adjusted figure rises. Traditionally, the spring is a time of relatively low unemployment as a number of outdoor workers take up employment. However, poor weather may keep some labourers on the dole. Many indoor vacancies appearing in spring may be taken up by officially unemployed groups such as housewives. The result is a record level of unemployment with over one in seven people without a job. At the same time there is a record level of output and standard of living.

(a) Name two industries where employment levels change according to the season of the year. **(2 marks)**
(b) Why do these two industries have different levels of employment according to the time of year? **(2 marks)**
(c) How can there be a fall in registered unemployment and yet a rise in the seasonally adjusted figure for the same month? **(4 marks)**
(d) Who does the government define as 'the unemployed'? **(2 marks)**
(e) How is the present rate of unemployment calculated in the UK? **(2 marks)**
(f) Is it possible for output, standards of living and unemployment all to be rising at the same time? **(4 marks)**

Solution 15.2

(a) Tourism and farming have different levels of demand for workers according to the time of the year.

(b) The tourist industry uses more labour in the traditional summer season than in the winter when there are fewer visitors to holiday centres. Farming makes intensive use of labour in the late summer and autumn so as to bring in the harvest.

(c) Unemployment figures are adjusted to take account of regular seasonal changes such as outside workers taking up employment in the spring. Normally February would see a large fall in unemployment of, say, 50 000. A lower fall of only 30 000 would mean a seasonally adjusted rise of 20 000.

(d) The government defines as unemployed all those people registered as jobless and receiving benefit.

(e) The government calculates the number of people employed and registered as unemployed and uses the equation

$$\text{Unemployment rate} = \frac{\text{Number registered unemployed}}{\text{Number employed and registered unemployed}} \times 100.$$

(f) Labour is only one of the factors of production used to produce output. An improvement in the efficiency of enterprise or capital can raise output but generate unemployment. Electronically controlled printing presses have cost the jobs of thousands of Fleet Street workers. Even though a small number of workers may lose their jobs as the result of automation those still in work benefit from lower-priced and better-quality products. This has the effect of raising the standard of living of the majority at the expense of the minority.

Example 15.3

Answer all the questions which follow the table.

Region of the UK	Percentage unemployed	
	1974	*1984*
North	4.6	18.3
Yorks and Humber	2.5	14.4
East Midlands	2.2	12.2
East Anglia	1.9	10.1
South East	1.5	9.5
South West	2.6	11.4
West Midlands	2.1	15.3
North West	3.4	15.9
Wales	3.7	16.3
Scotland	3.8	15.1
Northern Ireland	5.4	20.9
United Kingdom	2.6	13.1
Working population	25.7 million	27 million

Source: Adapted from *Annual Abstract of Statistics*, No. 122, HMSO, 1986

(a) Name the region with the most severe problems of long-term unemployment.

(2 marks)

(b) Name the region with the lowest rate of unemployment in 1984.　(1 mark)

(c) Calculate how many more people were unemployed in the UK in 1984 than 1974.

(3 marks)

(d) Name the region which experienced the most rapid increase in the rate of unemployment between 1974 and 1984.　(3 marks)

(e) Use the data to comment briefly on the impact of the recession on manufacturing regions compared with rural areas.　(3 marks)

(f) What do you consider to be the 'costs' to society of high unemployment?

(4 marks)

Solution 15.3

(a) From the table Northern Ireland has the most chronic unemployment at 20.9 per cent.

(b) The South East has the lowest rate of unemployment at 9.5 per cent.

(c) In 1974 2.6 per cent of the 25 700 000 were unemployed, i.e.

$$\frac{2.6}{100} \times 25\,000\,000 = 668\,200.$$

In 1984 12.5 per cent of 27 000 000 were unemployed, i.e. 3 375 000. Therefore unemployment rose by 2 706 800 between 1974–84.

(d) The rate of increase in the rate of unemployment can be calculated using the formula

$$\frac{1984 \text{ unemployment rate minus } 1974 \text{ unemployment rate}}{1974 \text{ unemployment rate}} \times 100.$$

For the West Midlands this was

$$\frac{15.3 - 2.1}{2.1} \times 100 = 629 \text{ per cent}$$

which was the most rapid increase of any region over the period.

(e) While unemployment has gone up in rural areas such as East Anglia, the largest increases have been recorded in areas where there is a large concentration of manufacturing industries. Areas such as the West Midlands have suffered particularly badly.

(f) Society loses the value of the goods and services that an unemployed person could have made. Average annual output of each worker in the UK is over £12 000, implying an overall loss in excess of 40 billion pounds. In addition, those with jobs have to pay additional taxes which may act as a disincentive to work.

Many unemployed, especially the young and disadvantaged, feel outside and apart from society, which can result in hooliganism or even rioting.

Example 15.4

Study the diagram which shows the trends in employment between 1975 and 1985.

(a) Define was term 'working population'.　(2 marks)

(b) What was the approximate level of registered unemployed at the beginning of 1984?　(1 mark)

Employment trends between 1975 and 1985.

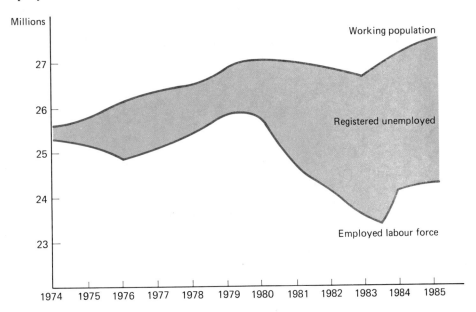

(c) What is meant by the term 'employed labour force'? **(1 mark)**
(d) Describe the main features of the trends in registered unemployed as shown in the chart. **(3 marks)**
(e) Why do you think that the supply of labour increased in later years? **(3 marks)**
(f) What is the likely effect on the level of unemployment of:
   (i) a slump in the economy; **(2 marks)**
   (ii) an increase in the use of robot arms in production? **(2 marks)**
(g) Would the numbers of unemployed fall if there were to be an increase in the number of job vacancies? **(6 marks)**

Solution 15.4

(a) The working population is made up of the employed, the self-employed and the registered unemployed.
(b) There were 2 900 000 unemployed at the beginning of 1984. This is found by measuring the vertical distance between the working-population and employed-labour-force lines.
(c) The employed labour force is made up of people with paid work.
(d) There was a steady increase in the number of registered unemployed throughout the period except between 1977 and 1979. From 1979 to 1983 the number employed and the number in the working population both fell but the fall in employment was greater. Hence unemployment rose. From 1983 to 1985 the growth of the working population exceeded the increase in the employed labour force, so that overall unemployment again rose.
(e) As the postwar 'baby boom' generation reached employment age there was a significant rise in the number of school leavers available for work. Social attitudes to the role of women in society have changed so that more married women are competing for job vacancies.
(f) (i) The demand for labour is derived from the demand for finished goods. A slump means a fall in the demand for all goods which reduces the demand for labour. Wages fall, which in turn reduces still further the demand for products. The slump results in an increase in joblessness through cyclical unemployment.
   (ii) Automation and information technology (IT) can cause technological unemployment in some industries if machines are used to replace

labour. However, the effect on unemployment levels is uncertain. New machinery can reduce prices and so raise demand by so much that no one loses their job.

(g) There will be some delay before increased vacancies reduce the level of unemployment. This is because time is taken looking and applying for jobs and in interview procedures. Applicants do not necessarily accept the first job they are offered as unemployment benefits allow time to find better work.

In the long term there may be a fundamental mismatch between the unemployed and the new vacancies, causing structural unemployment. Labour is said to be 'immobile'. The unemployed may be unable to fill the vacancies if they are in alternative trades because they do not possess the required skills (occupational immobility).

If the new vacancies are in other areas then the unemployed may be unable to move because of local family ties, lack of rented accommodation or the high cost of moving (geographical immobility).

Example 15.5

Look at the advertisement opposite for the government youth training scheme (YTS) which appeared in national newspapers in June 1986.
(a) According to the passage:

    (i) what period of training is offered by the YTS to sixteen-year-olds;
            (1 mark)
    (ii) what percentage of sixteen-year-olds go on to further education or job training in Japan;   **(1 mark)**
    (iii) what do firms have to offer before being accepted on the YTS?   **(2 marks)**

(b) State *one* advantage given in the advertisement of the YTS to:

    (i) school leavers;   **(1 mark)**
    (ii) employers;   **(1 mark)**

(c) Many of the goods owned by the man in the photograph are foreign made. How does this affect:

    (i) UK employment;   **(2 marks)**
    (ii) the UK balance of payments?   **(2 marks)**

(d) Advise the government on the measures it should take to reduce unemployment.
            (6 marks)

Solution 15.5

(a)   (i) Sixteen-year-olds are offered two years' training.
     (ii) 95 per cent of Japanese sixteen-year-olds go on to further education or training.
    (iii) To be accepted, firms have to have a proper training scheme which has set aims, and which is regularly inspected.
(b)   (i) Young people following the YTS acquire work experience.
    (ii) Employers who use the YTS end up with skilled workers.
(c)   (i) Many traditional domestic manufacturing industries have found increasing difficulty in matching foreign competitors on price or quality.

TRAIN THE BIT THAT'S BRITISH AND YOU'LL CHANGE THE WHOLE PICTURE.

You can see what happens when a country doesn't do enough about training its school leavers.

Its young people end up buying other nations' goods instead of making them for themselves.

And whilst Britain has never been short on talent, we have tended to be rather short-sighted on training. We've lagged a long way behind West Germany and Japan for instance, where around 95% of 16 year olds go on to further education or job training.

(Ahem. No need to mention how their economies have been doing lately.)

All is not lost, however. This April, the new 2 Year YTS was born. And now every 16 year old school leaver in Britain can get two years of first class training – just for the asking. (17 year olds can still train for a year.) Not only that, over 100,000 of Britain's far-sighted employers are waiting to be asked.

The list includes the cream of British business . . . names like Marks and Spencer, ICI, B.P. and Allied-Lyons.

(It also excludes hundreds of companies who have so far failed to convince us that they have set up a proper training scheme.)

Every YTS trainee will have to be given both work experi-ence and off-the-job training. Definite goals have to be set and met and every training programme will be monitored regularly.

But whilst it's not easy for a company to succeed in getting on the new 2 Year YTS, life will soon be a lot harder for the ones who aren't accepted. Because before long they'll lack the skills they need for the future.

Fortunately, enough em-ployers have realised there is a skill crisis in Britain and over 400,000 training places have been promised for this year. It seems that our school leavers finally have a chance to come up with the goods.

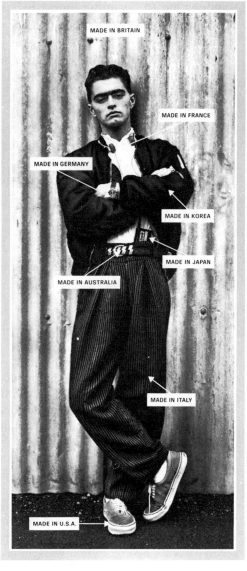

THE NEW 2 YEAR YTS. TRAINING FOR SKILLS.

Reduced UK market share has lowered output and increased unemployment.

(ii) The goods shown in the photograph are visibles imported into the UK and this will worsen the balance of trade and therefore the balance of payments.

(d) Any measure which either reduces the number of people registering as unemployed or increases the number finding work will reduce unemploy-ment. Raising the school leaving age or lowering the retirement age would counteract recent increases in the labour supply. The YTS has the advantage of equipping school leavers with modern skills as well as reducing the labour supply.

Any measure which increases the mobility of labour reduces structural unemployment. Retraining schemes such as Restart and JTS give unemployed specialists greater occupational mobility. Grants towards removal expenses (job search) and supplying more rented accommodation improve geographical mobility. Industrial immobility can be overcome by giving aid to declining industries or to firms who move to the same areas.

Cyclical unemployment can be reduced through additional government spending or lower taxation (fiscal policy). However, the government must be careful to ensure that the extra demand does not simply raise imports and inflation rates. It is better to adopt labour-intensive projects such as new motorways or the Channel Tunnel if extra spending is to reduce unemployment.

Unemployment can be also be reduced by improving the price and quality of UK goods. The government can improve our trading position through measures such as a depreciation of sterling or quotas. However, these policies can be effective only if foreign governments do not retaliate.

15.7 Questions

1 The supply of labour would increase following a *reduction* in
    A   the retirement age   B   the school leaving age
    C   unemployment   D   the working week

For each of questions 2 to 5 select from the list **A** to **D** the unemployment term described.
    A seasonal   **B** structural   **C** cyclical   **D** frictional
2 A new set of nuclear reactors reduces the demand for British coal.
3 The government announces a deflationary budget.
4 A painter remains unemployed while deciding which of two jobs to take.
5 The end of summer leads to a fall in the demand for strawberries.

For each of questions 6 to 9 select from the list **A** to **D** the term described.
    A geographical immobility   **B** economically inactive
    C occupational immobility   **D** industrial immobility
6 A worker unable to fill a vacancy in an alternative trade.
7 A worker unable to fill a vacancy in another location.
8 A worker unwilling to fill any vacancy.
9 A worker unable to find work in his current trade.

For each of questions 10 to 13 select from the list **A** to **D** the most appropriate unemployment policy.
    A retraining   **B** improved job centres
    C assisted areas   **D** increased government deficit
10 Frictional unemployment is best tackled by........
11 Cyclical unemployment is best tackled by........
12 Regional unemployment is best tackled by........
13 Structural unemployment is best tackled by........
14 Which type of unemployment is usually regarded as *least* serious?
    A regional   **B** cyclical   **C** frictional   **D** structural
15 Which region of the UK has the lowest rate of unemployment?
    A North   **B** South East   **C** West Midlands **D** North West
16 State three reasons why unemployment is a problem.
17 Give three examples of unemployment inflows.
18 State one reason why official figures may underestimate the true level of unemployment.
19 Vacancies will be unfilled at a time of high unemployment because of
    A automation   **B** the immobility of labour
    C training schemes   **D** an ageing population

20 Give two examples of groups which experience above-average levels of unemployment.
21 State three reasons for the recent increase in UK employment.
22 Explain briefly the term 'full employment'.
23 If inflows exceed outflows then the level of unemployment is ....

15.8 Answers

1	B	2	B	3	C	4	D	5	A
6	C	7	A	8	B	9	D	10	B
11	D	12	C	13	A	14	C	15	B

16 See section 15.3   17 See Figure 15.2.
18 See section 15.2.   19 B   20 See section 15.5
21 Manufacturing decline, new technology, more school leavers, more women in the labour force, or a world recession.
22 See section 15.2   23 Rising

16 Inflation

16.1 Measurement of Inflation

(a) Definition of Inflation

Inflation refers to the continual increase in prices. The *value* or *purchasing power* of money refers to the amount of goods and services one pound can buy. Inflation means the value of money is falling because prices keep rising.

(b) Calculating the Retail Price Index

The *retail price index (RPI)* is a monthly survey carried out by the government which measures price changes. The following procedure is used:

(i) A *basket of goods* and services consumed by the average family is listed. For example, food, clothing and transport are included in the basket.
(ii) The price of items in the basket in the *base* (first) year is noted.
(iii) Each item in the basket is given a number value (*weighted*) to reflect its importance to the average family. For example, food has a higher weighting than transport.
(iv) The price of goods in the basket is recorded every month and compared with the base year as a percentage (*price relative*) using the equation:

$$\text{Price relative} = \frac{\text{Current price}}{\text{Base price}} \times 100.$$

(v) The price relative of each item is then multiplied by its weighting.
(vi) The new RPI is found using the equation:

$$\text{RPI} = \frac{\text{Total weightings} \times \text{Price relative}}{\text{Total weightings}}.$$

The value of the RPI in the base year is always 100. After twelve months the price of food items in the basket may have risen by 25 per cent and that of housing by 20 per cent while the cost of transport is unchanged. Table 16.1 shows how the RPI for year two might then be calculated.

$$\text{The RPI} = \frac{\text{Total weightings} \times \text{Price relative}}{\text{Total weightings}} = \frac{12\ 100}{100} = 121.$$

Table 16.1 Calculation of the retail price index

Basket	Weighting	Price relative	Weightings × price relative
Food	60	125	7 500
Housing	30	120	3 600
Transport	10	100	1 000
Total	100		12 100

The *rate of inflation* is the percentage change in the RPI over the last twelve months and is calculated using the equation:

$$\text{Rate of inflation} = \frac{(\text{Current RPI} - \text{Last RPI})}{\text{Last RPI}} \times 100.$$

At the beginning of year two the rate of inflation is:

$$\frac{(121 - 100)}{100} \times 100 = 21 \text{ per cent.}$$

(c) Problems in Using the Retail Price Index

(i) Which items should be included in or excluded from the basket of goods?
(ii) Different families have different tastes hence different weightings. How is an average family found?
(iii) Not all regions in the country experience identical price changes.
(iv) For a while new products (e.g. videos and microwaves) may not be included in the index.

16.2 Effects of Inflation

(a) Advantages of Inflation

Not everyone suffers from inflation. Some parts of society actually benefit:

(i) The government finds that people earn more and so pay more income tax.
(ii) Firms are able to increase prices and profits before they pay out higher wages.
(iii) Debtors (borrowers) gain because they have use of money now, when its purchasing power is greater.

(b) Disadvantages of Inflation

(i) People on fixed incomes are unable to buy so many goods.
(ii) Creditors (savers) lose because the loan will have reduced purchasing power when it is repaid.
(iii) UK goods may become more expensive than foreign-made products so the balance of payments suffers.

(iv) Industrial disputes may occur if workers are unable to secure wage increases to restore their standard of living.

16.3 Causes of Inflation

(a) Cost-push Inflation

Cost-push inflation occurs when a firm passes on an increase in production costs to the consumer. Figure 16.1 shows the inflationary effect of increased costs, which can be the result of:

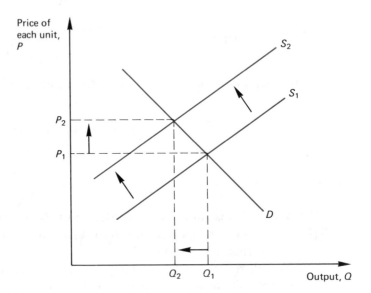

Figure 16.1   Cost-push inflation

(i) Increased wages, leading to

(1) a *wage–price spiral* (Fig. 16.2), which occurs when price increases spark off a series of wage demands which lead to further price increases and so on;

(2) a *wage–wage spiral* (Fig. 16.3), which occurs when one group of workers receive a wage increase which sparks off a series of wage demands from other workers.

(ii) Increased import prices which can be the result of:

(1) a rise in world prices for imported raw materials;
(2) a depreciation of sterling (see section 18.3(c)).

(iii) Increased indirect taxation (see Fig. 7.6).

(b) Demand-pull Inflation

Demand-pull inflation occurs when there is 'too much money chasing too few goods' because the demand for current output exceeds supply.

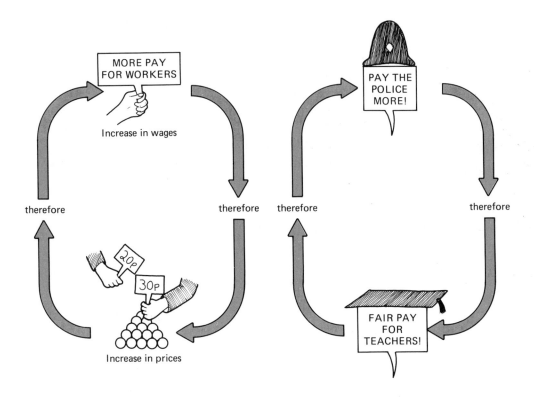

Figure 16.2 Wage–price spiral **Figure 16.3** Wage–wage spiral

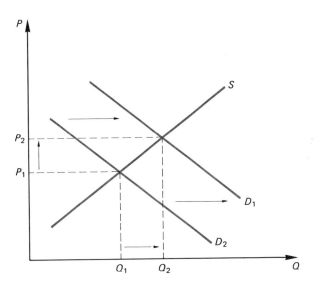

Figure 16.4 Demand-pull inflation

Figure 16.4 shows increased demand and increased prices as consumers compete to buy up goods still available.

A major source of inflationary pressure is the government which can print money to buy goods. The *monetarist* view of inflation can be stated in the equation:

$$MV = PT$$

where M = the money supply,
   V = the number of times each pound changes hands (the *velocity of circulation*),
   P = the average price of goods, and
   T = the number of goods bought (*transactions*).

Monetarists believe that the values of V and T are fixed so that any increase in M, the money supply, must raise P, the level of prices, i.e. be inflationary.

16.4 Remedies for Inflation

(a) Cost-push Remedies

(i) Introduce a prices and incomes policy to freeze price and wage increases.
(ii) Encourage an appreciation of sterling.
(iii) Reduce indirect taxation.

(b) Demand-pull Remedies

(i) Reduce government spending.
(ii) Increase income tax to reduce consumer spending.
(iii) Reduce people's ability to borrow money by increasing interest rates and tightening credit regulations.
(iv) Control the supply of money.

16.5 Worked Examples

Example 16.1

Read the following article and answer all the questions which follow.

Weighing up the Level of Inflation

by Joanna Slaughter
In 1986 the annual rate of inflation has fallen to 3 per cent, its lowest figure for 18 years—or has it?

Many people doubt the accuracy of the retail price index (RPI). The weightings given to various goods in the RPI seldom match most household budgeting. It is odd that the weighting for petrol is only just higher than for eating out.

Britons spend an average of £291 each on holidays and yet this item is not included in the RPI. The RPI ignores any capital gains from owning your own house when estimating housing costs.

Higher prices can result from improved quality but this fact is overlooked by the RPI.

The RPI disguises different inflation rates for different households. A number of goods such as coal and electricity mainly consumed by the poor have risen by 8 per cent more than the average.

Source: Adapted from *The Observer*, 18 May 1986

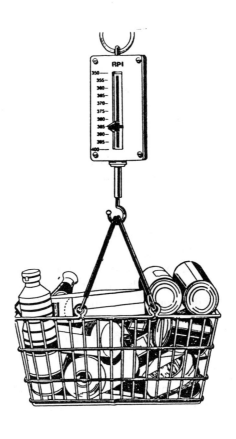

(a) For what reason is the RPI calculated? **(1 mark)**

(b) Explain briefly the meaning of the following terms:
   (i) 'retail', and   (ii) 'annual rate of inflation'. **(3 marks)**

(c) From the report work out:

   (i) the 1986 inflation rate; **(1 mark)**
   (ii) the year when inflation was previously at this level. **(1 mark)**

(d) The base year of the current RPI is 1974. Calculate the percentage increase in the RPI between 1974 and 1986. **(1 mark)**

(e) From the passage;
   (i) state two items not included in the RPI; **(2 marks)**
   (ii) when is a price increase not necessarily inflationary? **(2 marks)**

(f) The following table states two major items included in the RPI and gives their weightings:

Item	Weighting (%)
Food	18.5
Fuel and light	6.25

Would you expect the weightings for these items be the same for:
(i) old-age pensioners and   (ii) a young family?
Explain your answer. **(5 marks)**

Solution 16.1

(a) The RPI is calculated so that inflation can be measured.
(b) (i) Retail means goods sold in shops.

183

(ii) The annual rate of inflation means the percentage increase in the RPI over the last twelve months.

(c) (i) The passage states that the 1986 inflation rate is 3 per cent.

(ii) Inflation was previously at this level eighteen years earlier, i.e. 1968.

(d) The diagram indicates that the current RPI is 385. The percentage increase in the RPI equals:

$$\frac{\text{Current RPI} - \text{Last RPI}}{\text{Last RPI}} \times 100 = \frac{385 - 100}{100} \times 100 = 285 \text{ per cent.}$$

(e) (i) The passage states that both the money made from buying and selling a house (capital gains) and the money spent on holidays are ignored by the RPI.

(ii) A price increase is not inflationary if it occurs because of an improvement in the quality of the good.

(f) Weightings reflect the importance the average household gives to various items. A young growing family is likely to spend a far greater proportion of their income on food than are pensioners. I would expect the weighting for food for a young family to be about 25 per cent, and for a pensioner around 15 per cent.

Pensioners, however, place far greater weight (e.g. 20 per cent) on heating because older people feel the cold. I would expect a young family to have the same weighting for fuel as the average given.

Example 16.2

The graph shows the percentage change in retail prices on a year earlier. Study the graph and then answer the questions which follow.

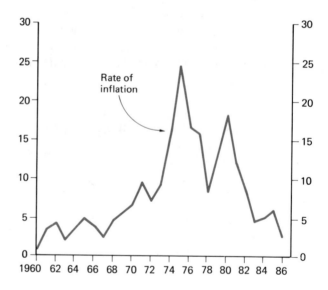

General index of retail prices 1960–1986: percentage change on a year earlier

Source: *Economic Progress Report*, No. 184, May–June 1986

(a) From the graph estimate:

(i) the rate of inflation in 1983;   **(1 mark)**
(ii) the year when inflation was highest;   **(1 mark)**
(iii) the rate of inflation during that year.   **(1 mark)**

(b) What do you understand by the term 'general index of retail prices'?   **(2 marks)**
(c) In which years after 1975 did the rate of inflation increase?   **(2 marks)**
(d) How would you account for an increase in inflation?   **(5 marks)**
(e) Advise the government on the policies it should adopt to reduce inflation.
    (5 marks)

Solution 16.2

(a) (i) Reading up from 1983 on the *x*-axis to the inflation line indicates that the rate of inflation was 5 per cent.

(ii) The inflation line on the graph is at its highest point in 1975.

(iii) Reading across from the highest point on the inflation line to the *y*-axis indicates that inflation was almost 25 per cent in 1975.

(b) The general index of retail prices measures the prices at a particular moment in time of a list of goods consumed by the average household.

(c) Where the inflation line is rising, the rate of inflation has increased. After 1975 this occurred during 1978–80 and 1983–5.

(d) An increase in the rate of inflation can be caused by an increase in firms' costs of production (cost-push inflation). For example, firms may grant wage increases or may have to pay more for raw materials. If the increases in costs are passed on to the consumer then inflation will increase.

An increase in total demand in the economy can cause an increase in inflation if existing resources are fully employed. Output cannot be increased. The extra demand is chasing the same quantity of goods, which results in demand-pull inflation. Demand-pull inflation is often the result of increases in the money supply.

(e) Any measure which reduces costs of production will reduce cost-push inflation. A reduction in expenditure taxes such as VAT means lower costs. An increase in the value of sterling against foreign currencies will reduce the price of imported raw materials.

Any measure which reduces total demand in the economy reduces demand-pull inflation. Increasing taxes and lowering government spending (deflationary fiscal policy) help to reduce total spending in the economy.

Decreasing the amount of money in circulation increases interest rates and reduces the demand for credit. Saving is encouraged so that overall demand for goods and services falls.

Example 16.3

Study the extracts on the next page taken from the front pages of different newspapers on the same day in 1986, and then answer the questions that follow.

Each of the extracts refers to inflation.

(a) What do you understand by the term 'inflation'?   **(2 marks)**
(b) During a period of inflation which group of people may:

(i) benefit,   **(1 mark)**
(ii) suffer?   **(1 mark)**

Inflation set to hit 3% by summer

The rate of inflation fell to 5.1 per cent last month, its lowest level for over a year, from 5.5 per cent in January. A sharp fall to 3 per cent is expected by the summer.

Jobs boost as inflation drops

A FALL in price inflation from 5.7 to 5.5 per cent, last month was acclaimed by the Government yesterday as 'good news for everyone.'

INFLATION EASES TO 5.5p.c.

CHEAPER petrol is helping the Government win its battle against inflation, official figures out yesterday show.

According to the Department of Employment, the annual inflation rate fell to 5.5 per cent in January after touching 5.7 per cent in December. Rail fares, bread, vegetables and alcoholic drinks all went up in price during the month, but this was offset by a fall in petrol prices and a large number of bargains in the shops for household goods and clothing.

(c) Give reasons for 'Jobs boost as inflation drops'. **(3 marks)**

(d) Comment on the accuracy of measuring inflation as a percentage. **(3 marks)**

(e) (i) Give two methods by which a government might attempt to control inflation.
(2 marks)

(ii) Examine both the advantages and the disadvantages of using one of these methods. **(4 marks)**

(LEAG specimen GCSE)

Solution 16.3

(a) Inflation refers to the continual increase in prices over a number of years.

(b) (i) The government benefits from inflation because people are paid more and so pay more income tax. (See also section 16.2(a)).

(ii) People on fixed incomes are unable to buy so many goods. (See also section 16.2(b).)

(c) Lower inflation means our exports become cheaper and our imports more expensive. This increases the competitiveness of UK goods so that more UK goods are sold. Increased output requires more workers which boosts the number of jobs available.

(d) The inflation rate is the percentage change in the retail price index over the last twelve months. The RPI is an average. Different families have different items in their 'shopping basket' and will give different weightings to each item. Different regions experience different price changes. (See also section 16.1(c).)

(e) (i) A prices and incomes policy (direct controls), and reduced government expenditure/increased direct taxation (fiscal policy), can be used to control inflation.

(ii) The government might try freezing prices and pay. A prices and incomes policy can be carried out either by passing laws limiting increases or by voluntary agreement with the unions.

Initially workers are prepared to accept lower wage settlements and inflation falls without the need for reduced government spending.

186

Eventually, workers find themselves able to buy fewer and fewer goods and they then ask for massive pay increases to restore previous living standards.

Prices and incomes policies are effective in the short run but break down in the long run.

Example 16.4

Table 16.2 compares the 1986 price of some everyday items with the prices faced by consumers in 1968.

Table 16.2 Comparison of prices, 1968 and 1986

Item	1968 price	1986 price	Increase from 1968 to 1986
Average house	£4 500	£36 000	× 8
Family car	£1 000	£ 5 000	× ?
Television	£?	£250	× 2½
Fridge	£60	£?	× 3
Average wage	£20	£190	× 9½
Income tax	41 pence in the pound	29 pence in the pound	

(a) What happened to prices after 1968?   (1 mark)

(b) What term would an economist use to describe your answer to question (a)?
                                                                        (1 mark)

(c) From the data state:

    (i) the 1968 price of a house;   (1 mark)
    (ii) how much more it cost to buy the same house in 1986;   (1 mark)
    (iii) by how many times the price of a family car increased from 1968 to 1986;
                                                                        (1 mark)
    (iv) the 1968 price of a television;   (1 mark)
    (v) the 1986 price of a fridge.   (1 mark)

(d) Complete the following table:

Item	Increase	Rank order
House	× 8	Largest
?	× ?	2nd largest
?	× ?	3rd largest
?	× ?	Smallest

(e) How many weeks' wages did it take to buy a family car in:

    (i) 1968, and   (ii) 1986?   (2 marks)

(f) What evidence is there in the data for believing that living standards improved?
                                                                        (5 marks)

Solution 16.4

(a) Prices increased after 1968.

(b) Economists call continual increases in prices 'inflation'.

(c)   (i) A 1968 house cost £4500

    (ii) By 1986 the average house price had risen to £36 000.
Therefore it cost £36 000 − £4500 = £31 500 more to buy a house than in 1968.

    (iii) A family car increased from £1000 to £500, i.e. a 5 times increase.

    (iv) Between 1968 and 1986 the price of a television went up 2½ times.
Therefore the price of a television in 1968 was £250 ÷ 2½ = £100.

    (v) Between 1968 and 1986 the price of a fridge went up 3 times. Therefore the 1986 price of a fridge was £60 × 3 = £180.

(d)

Item	Increase	Rank order
House	× 8	Largest
Car	× 5	2nd largest
Fridge	× 3	3rd largest
Television	× 2½	Smallest

(e) Dividing price by average weekly wage gives the number of weeks taken to pay for a family car.

    (i) In 1968 it took £1000/£20 = 50 weeks to buy a car.

    (ii) In 1986 it took £5000/£190 = 26.3 weeks to buy a car.

(f) The standard of living refers to the amount of goods and services that wages can buy. In the data, the price of all goods rose. However, there was an even greater increase in the average weekly wage.

The amount of time taken to work and to pay for all items in the data fell. This was particularly true of electrical goods such as televisions.

Moreover, the rate of income tax fell from 41p in the pound to 29p in the pound. Workers in 1986 not only earned more but also paid less of their income in tax.

Example 16.5

Study the two photographs which show queues of potential shoppers.

(a) For each of photographs A and B:

    (i) state one good shoppers are likely to be waiting to buy;   **(2 marks)**

    (ii) give possible reasons why people have been queuing since dawn for the goods on sale.   **(4 marks)**

(b) In which photograph are prices:

    (i) likely to have fallen, and   (ii) likely to have risen?

    Explain your answers.   **(2 marks)**

(c) What terms would an economist use to describe your answers to (b)? **(2 marks)**

(d) Does an increase in wages always mean an increase in prices?   **(5 marks)**

A A sale at Harrods department store, London

B Outside a butchers shop in Torun, Poland.

Solution 16.5

(a) (i) The shoppers in photograph A are waiting to buy luxury goods such as bone china. The shoppers in photograph B are waiting to buy an everyday good such as meat.

189

(ii) The shoppers in photograph A are hoping to buy goods they could not usually afford. Because of low prices the goods are likely to be sold out very quickly. Shoppers anxious to snap up a bargain are prepared to queue for a long time.

In photograph B shoppers are queuing even though there is no sale. This suggests a shortage of meat. People are prepared to queue all day in the hope that the shop will have some meat left or that some will soon be delivered.

(b) (i) Because a sale is when a shop reduces the selling price of goods, prices are likely to have fallen in photograph A.

(ii) Because demand exceeds supply some consumers will be prepared to pay more for meat rather than go without. Therefore prices are likely to have risen in photograph B.

(c) Economists call a continual fall in prices disinflation. Economists call a continual increase in prices inflation.

(d) An increase in wages is not inflationary if it is payment for extra output. However, an increase in wages without any corresponding increase in productivity increases a firm's costs of production. Firms may decide to pass on this increase in the form of higher prices which will cause cost-push inflation.

An increase in wages also allows workers to buy more goods and services. If the resultant increase in demand is not matched by an increase in output then demand–pull inflation will result.

16.6 Questions

1 What is the name given to the economic situation in which prices are continually rising?
2 What term do economists use to describe a situation in which a rise in the value of money occurs?
3 What is the monthly official list which measures changes in consumer prices called?
4 Changes in the value of money are measured by:
   A the standard of living   B the cost of living
   C the retail price index   D the *Financial Times* share index
5 The index of retail prices measures changes in:
   A costs   B prices
   C wages   D the balance of payments
6 A rise in the retail price index suggests that the cost of living is ....
7 Which of the following would *not* be necessary in constructing a retail price index?:
   A the selection of a base year   B the calculation of average wages
   C the selection of items consumed   D the weighting of each item
8 Calculate from the following figures the annual rate of inflation in
   (a) January 1981;   (b) January 1986:

Year	RPI
January 1980	246
January 1981	277
January 1985	361
January 1986	380

9 What is the difference between the retail price index and the rate of inflation?

10 State two problems found in constructing a retail price index.
11 Which one of the following is most likely to benefit from inflation?
    A exporters   **B** debtors   **C** creditors   **D** pensioners
12 Why is inflation harmful to people with fixed incomes?
13 How does a fall in the value of money affect creditors?
14 How can inflation make it more difficult to sell UK goods and services overseas?
15 What is meant by cost-push inflation?
16 Draw a graph to illustrate the effect of cost-push inflation.
17 Cost-push inflation is caused by:
    A an increase in the money supply   **B** a government surplus budget
    C a prices and incomes policy   **D** a depreciation of sterling
18 Draw a graph showing the effect of demand-pull inflation.
19 Which of the following may cause demand-pull inflation?
    A a decrease in wages   **B** a fall in the number unemployed
    C an increase in income tax   **D** a decrease in income tax
20 Which of the following is most likely to lead to higher prices?:
    A decreasing production and lowering indirect taxation
    B increasing production and lowering indirect taxation
    C decreasing production and increasing indirect taxation
    D increasing production and increasing indirect taxation
21 If the government wants to reduce cost push inflation it could:
    A lower the rate of income tax   **B** lower the value of sterling
    C reduce the terms of trade   **D** reduce the rate of value added tax
22 Prices and incomes policy reduces inflation:
    A in the short term only   **B** in the long term only
    C in both the short and the long term **D** not at all
23 If a government wants to reduce demand-pull inflation it could:
    A increase direct taxes   **B** increase indirect taxes
    C increase the money supply   **D** increase welfare benefits

16.6 Answers

1 Inflation   2 Disinflation   3 Retail price index
4 **C**   5 **B**   6 increasing   7 **B**

8 (a) $\dfrac{277 - 246}{246} \times 100 = 12.6$ per cent. (b) $\dfrac{380 - 361}{361} \times 100 = 5.3$ per cent.

9 The retail price index measures the price level at a particular moment in time, e.g. January 1988.
    The rate of inflation is the percentage change in the retail price index over one year.
10 Any two of: knowing what goods to exclude from the basket; knowing what weight to give each item included in the basket; regional variations in weightings and prices; frequency of sample.
11 **B**   12 Inflation reduces their ability to buy goods.
13 The loan will have reduced purchasing power when it is repaid.
14 UK inflation makes our exports less competitive and our imports more attractive to UK citizens.
15 An increase in prices because of an increase in unit costs.
16 See Fig. 16.1.
17 **D**. **A** is an incorrect answer because an increase in the money supply causes demand-pull inflation.
18 See Fig. 16.4.   **19** **D**   **20** **C**
21 **D**   **22** **A**
23 **A**. An increase in direct taxes such as income tax reduces the amount of money people have to spend. Inflationary pressure is reduced.

17 International Trade

17.1 Reasons for Trade

(a) Domestic Non-availability

International trade is the exchange of goods and services between countries. An *import* is the UK purchase of a good or service made overseas. An *export* is the sale of a UK-made good or service overseas.

A nation trades because it lacks the raw materials, climate, specialist labour, capital or technology needed to manufacture a particular good.

(b) Principle of Comparative Advantage

The *principle of comparative advantage* states that countries will benefit by concentrating on the production of those goods in which they have a relative advantage.

For instance, France has the climate and the expertise to produce better wine than Brazil. Brazil is better able to produce coffee than France. Each country benefits by specialising in the good it is most suited to making.

France then creates a surplus of wine which it can trade for surplus Brazilian coffee.

17.2 Protectionism

(a) Advantages of Protectionism

Protectionism occurs when one country reduces the level of its imports because of:

  (i) *Infant industries.* If *sunrise firms* producing new-technology goods (e.g. computers) are to survive against established foreign producers then temporary tariffs or quotas may be needed.
 (ii) *Unfair competition.* Foreign firms may receive subsidies or other government benefits. They may be *dumping* (selling goods abroad at below cost price to capture a market).
(iii) *Balance of payments.* Reducing imports improves the balance of trade.
 (iv) *Strategic industries.* To protect the manufacture of essential goods.
  (v) *Declining industries.* To protect declining industries from creating further structural unemployment.

(b) Disadvantages of Protectionism

(i) Prevents countries enjoying the full benefits of international specialisation and trade.
(ii) Invites retaliation from foreign governments.
(iii) Protects inefficient home industries from foreign competition. Consumers pay more for inferior produce.

17.3 Protection Methods

(a) Tariffs

Tariffs (import duties) are surcharges on the price of imports. Figure 17.1 uses a supply-and-demand graph to illustrate the effect of a tariff.

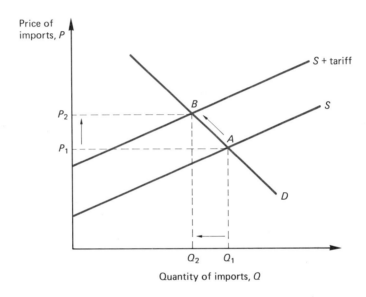

Figure 17.1 A tariff

Note that the tariff

(i) raises the price of the import;
(ii) reduces the demand for imports;
(iii) encourages demand for home-produced substitutes;
(iv) raises revenue for the government.

(b) Quotas

Quotas restrict the actual quantity of an import allowed into a country. Figure 17.2 on the next page illustrates the effect of a quota.

Only Q_2 units of the good are now allowed into the country. Note that a quota:

(i) raises the price of imports;
(ii) reduces the volume of imports;
(iii) encourages demand for domestically made substitutes.

193

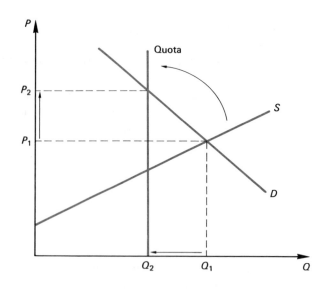

Figure 17.2 A quota

(c) Other Protection Techniques

(i) Administrative practices can discriminate against imports through customs delays or setting specifications met by domestic, but not, foreign producers.
(ii) *Exchange controls* (currency restrictions) prevent domestic residents from acquiring sufficient foreign currency to pay for imports.

17.4 International Institutions

(a) The European Community (EC)

The European Community was established by the Treaty of Rome (1957) and is also called the European Economic Community (EEC) or the Common Market. The twelve members of the EC (Belgium, Denmark, France, Greece, Irish Republic, Italy, Luxembourg, Netherlands, Portugal, Spain, West Germany and the United Kingdom) form a *customs union* which aims for eventual economic and political unity. The EC has:

(i) free movement of capital and labour within member countries;
(ii) free trade between member countries;
(iii) common tariffs against non-members;
(iv) a *Common Agricultural Policy (CAP)* which guarantees minimum prices for farmers' output;
(v) standardised trade and customs procedures, e.g. metric measurements;
(vi) some members who are part of the *European Monetary System (EMS)* which aims to maintain exchange rate stability by concerted government intervention.

(b) The Council for Mutual Economic Aid (Comecon)

Established in 1949, Comecon is a trading bloc of command-planned economies. The eight members of Comecon (Bulgaria, Czechoslovakia, Cuba, East

Germany, Hungary, Poland, Romania and the Soviet Union) aim to develop the structure of each member's economy so that all trade takes place within the group. Comecon will not then need to trade with market economies such as the United States.

(c) The International Monetary Fund (IMF)

Established in 1944 at Bretton Woods, the main aim of the IMF is to stabilise exchange rates and to lend money to countries needing foreign currency. Over 140 member countries pay a sum of their own currency into a pool. The amount paid in depends on the size of their economy. Each country can then borrow foreign currency from the pool according to their contribution to settle temporary balance-of-payments problems. Countries can draw up to 25 per cent of their quota before the IMF begins to set conditions on the loan. In 1967 the IMF created a new international currency called *special drawing rights* (SDRs) which governments use to settle debts with other countries.

(d) The International Bank for Reconstruction and Development (IBRD)

Known as the World Bank, IBRD lends money to developing countries for capital projects such as power stations or roads. Loans are for about thirty years and carry a low rate of interest.

(e) The General Agreement on Tariffs and Trade (GATT)

The interwar years were characterised by competitive trade restrictions. The American and British governments established GATT in 1948 to provide a system of rules governing international trade. Membership has now increased to 122 countries. The main aims of GATT are to ensure that:

(i) GATT members do not place tariffs on each other's produce;
(ii) infant industries are protected by tariffs but not quotas;
(iii) GATT members inform each other about domestic trade restrictions;
(iv) GATT negotiates general tariff cuts between members.

(f) The Organisation for Economic Co-operation and Development (OECD)

The OECD is made up of member countries who send a representative to a council. This offers an opportunity to discuss common policies to help stabilise exchange rates and encourage growth. The OECD also publishes surveys of individual economies.

(g) The Organisation of Petroleum Exporting Countries (OPEC)

This is an international group of many of the largest oil-producing nations which tries to limit world production and so maintain the price of oil. In 1985 the price of a barrel of oil stood at over $30. By mid-1986 members had exceeded set production levels and the price of oil had fallen below $10 for the first time in a decade.

17.5 Worked Examples

Example 17.1

Study the photograph, which shows a busy container terminal mainly for imported goods. The markings on the ground form a grid for computerised container control.

(a) Three items are marked A, B, and C in the photograph. Explaining each of your answers, match letters to the following terms:

  (i) imports;
  (ii) producer goods;
  (iii) infrastructure.   (6 marks)

(b) Describe briefly how the area shown in the photograph helps international trade.
                                                                                  (3 marks)

(c) State two pieces of evidence in the photograph of capital-intensive production.
                                                                                  (2 marks)

(d) Assess the likely effect on the level of economic activity shown in the photograph of:

  (i) the introduction of a tariff on imports;   (2 marks)
  (ii) an increase in the value of sterling (the currency of the UK).   (3 marks)

Solution 17.1

(a) (i) The letter B is pointing to a group of cars which may well have been made overseas, i.e. an import.

196

(ii) The letter C is pointing to a ship. A ship is used to help in the transportation of goods, i.e. a producer good.

(iii) The letter A is pointing to a road which is an item of underlying capital, i.e. infrastructure.

(b) International trade is the exchange of goods between countries. Trade requires some method of transportation. The photograph shows a port which allows goods to leave and enter a country. Without a port it would be almost impossible to move bulky goods between countries.

(c) Capital-intensive production makes great use of machinery, and hardly any use of workers. There are no workers shown in the picture. There are, however, a large number of machines including ships and cranes.

The grid layout suggests that computers are used to run the container port, thereby reducing the need for labour still further.

(d) (i) A tariff is a tax on imports. A tax increases the price of imports and reduces their demand so that the quantity of foreign-made goods entering the country is reduced. There will be a fall in the amount of activity in the port.

(ii) An increase in the value of the pound against other currencies reduces the cost of imports. For example, at an exchange rate of $1/£, a $500 American computer sells for £500 in the UK. If the exchange rate then rises to $2/£, the same $500 American computer now sells for £250 in the UK.

A fall in the price of UK imports increases their demand so that more goods will enter through the port.

Example 17.2

Study the drawings and then answer the questions which follow.

(a) If the price of bananas drops how will this affect the economy in Honduras?

(2 marks)

(b) If the price of the tractors rises at the same time how will this affect the economy in Honduras? **(3 marks)**

(NISEC specimen GCSE)

Solution 17.2

(a) A fall in the price of bananas means that Honduras earns less foreign currency. For example, if Honduras exports 1 million tonnes of bananas and the price of bananas falls from $400 per tonne to $300, then its export earnings fall from

      1m. tonnes × $400 = $400 000 000

to 1m. × $300 = $300 000 000, a reduction of $100 000 000.

(b) A rise in the dollar price of tractors means Honduras will have to reduce the number of tractors it buys. Since tractors are a producer good, Honduras will be unable to plant as large a crop as previously. Output and employment will fall. Export earnings will be further reduced.

Example 17.3

(a) Give two reasons why a country may wish to reduce its imports from other countries. **(4 marks)**

(a) Apart from quotas, describe two methods a country can use to reduce its imports. **(4 marks)**

(c) (i) Draw a graph showing the supply and demand curves for a normal good. Label each curve. **(2 marks)**

  (ii) On your graph, label the axes so that the graph shows the market for imported apples. Show the market price and the amount of apples imported. **(2 marks)**

 (iii) On your graph draw the effect of a quota reducing by half the amount of apples allowed into the country. Show the new market price. **(4 marks)**

(d) What is the likely reaction of an apple-producing country to quotas being put on its exports? **(4 marks)**

Solution 17.3

(a) A country may wish to reduce its imports from other countries if it wants to protect its own emerging industries such as computers.

Alternatively, it may impose import restrictions to protect domestic producers from an overseas competitor who is selling goods unfairly in it at below cost price.

(b) The volume of imports can be reduced by setting standards for foreign manufacturers which are difficult to meet. For example, a country can insist that imported cars are fitted with reinforced door panels or a special type of exhaust system. The importer must then change the standard model to meet these requirements. Special changes are time-consuming and increase the cost of making the car. The price of imported cars rises so that not so many are sold.

A second method of reducing imports is to restrict the amount of foreign currency UK citizens can buy (exchange controls). If firms are unable to buy foreign currency then they are unable to pay for imports.

(c) For answers (i) to (iii) see the accompanying graph.

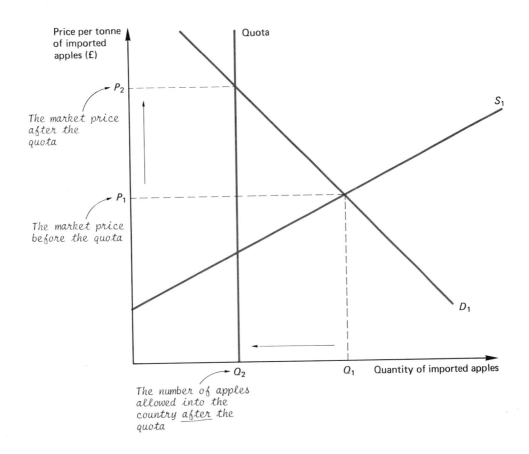

Price per tonne of imported apples (£)

Quota

P_2

The market price after the quota

P_1

The market price before the quota

S_1

D_1

Q_2

Q_1 Quantity of imported apples

The number of apples allowed into the country <u>after</u> the quota

(d) The apple-producing nation may well decide to restrict its imports from the country which has just imposed a quota. By introducing restrictions, the apple-producing nation may hope to exert pressure to remove all trading restrictions between the two nations.

Example 17.4

The EEC Food Mountain
by Richard Owen

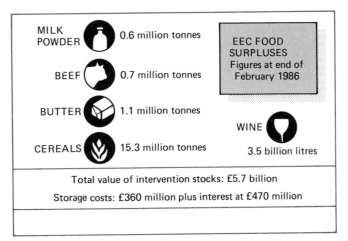

MILK POWDER   0.6 million tonnes

EEC FOOD SURPLUSES
Figures at end of February 1986

BEEF   0.7 million tonnes

BUTTER   1.1 million tonnes

WINE

CEREALS   15.3 million tonnes

3.5 billion litres

Total value of intervention stocks: £5.7 billion

Storage costs: £360 million plus interest at £470 million

Source: EEC Commission and European Parliament Research Division

The EEC last year sold more than seven million tonnes of cereals to Russia for £785 million as well as 162 000 tonnes of butter to a value of £137 million, both at knock-down prices.

But even these large-scale cut-price deals have barely dented the EEC food mountains. The EEC argues that surpluses would be as much as 40 per cent higher but for sales to the Soviet Union.

The Russians paid only £112 per tonne for cereal imports from Europe minus an export subsidy of £30 to £40. Similarly, the Russians paid 38p per pound for EEC butter compared with £1 per pound in the West.

EEC officials point out that grain sold to the Eastern bloc is inferior in quality, and that the butter involved is going off.

The EEC also disposed of thousands of tonnes of grain as food aid last year, including more than 116 000 tonnes to Ethiopia.

Source: Adapted from *The Times*, 21 March 1986

(a) Give one example of a food surplus given in the passage.   **(1 mark)**
(b) What do economists mean by the term 'surplus'?   **(2 marks)**
(c) From the passage find out:

    (i) the number of litres of wine held in storage;   **(1 mark)**
    (ii) the total value of EEC food stocks;   **(1 mark)**
    (iii) the total cost of storing food stocks;   **(1 mark)**
    (iv) the total value of EEC sales to Russia of cereals and butter;   **(1 mark)**
    (v) how much the Soviet Union saved per pound by buying EEC butter.

    (1 mark)

(d) State two reasons given by the EEC for selling surpluses at knock-down prices.
    (2 marks)
(e) Why has the EEC such large food mountains?   **(4 marks)**
(f) Using the information given in the passage, advise the EEC on its future food mountain policy.   **(6 marks)**

Solution 17.4

(a) The EEC has a surplus of beef.
(b) A surplus is the amount of a good or a service that consumers are unwilling to buy at existing prices.
(c) (i) The diagram states that 3.5 billion litres of wine are held in storage.
    (ii) The total value of stocks held is £5.7 billion.
    (iii) Total storage costs consist of storage costs (£360m.) and interest charges (£470m.), making a total of £830m.
    (iv) From the passage, the EEC sold £785m. worth of cereal and £137m. worth of butter, making a total of £922m.
    (v) From the passage, the Russians bought for £0.38 per pound butter retailing in the EEC for £1 per pound—a saving of £0.62 per pound.
(d) Surpluses were sold at knock-down prices to reduce the amount of food held in storage by 40 per cent. Lower food stocks reduce total storage costs.

A second reason for selling surplus stock to the Russians was that the food involved was of poor quality, or nearly rotten.
(e) The EEC guarantees farmers a minimum price for their produce. If there is a good harvest which increases supply then consumers may be unwilling to buy all that has been produced at the minimum price. The EEC steps in and buys up any unsold goods and adds them to existing food surpluses held in storage. A series of excellent harvests will result in large food-mountains.
(f) Existing food stocks can either be stored at great expense or else sold off at a discount. The food can be sold outside the EEC without affecting European agricultural prices. However, the surplus food can be sold cheaply, or even given to low-income householders such as pensioners who are unable to consume large quantities of beef and butter at existing prices.

Alternatively, the surpluses can be given to areas of the world suffering from famine. This saves lives in the short run but may disrupt the local economy. Local farmers will be unable to sell their produce.

A final solution is to do away with minimum prices for farmers. This reduces the income of farmers but eventually removes the surpluses.

Example 17.5

(a) Describe two main features of a customs union such as the European Community.
(4 marks)

(b) Explain the economic reason why the United Kingdom buys

    (i) wine from France;   **(4 marks)**
    (ii) cars from Germany.   **(4 marks)**

(c) Discuss the view that membership of the European Community has produced serious disadvantages for consumers in the United Kingdom.   **(8 marks)**
(SEG specimen GCSE)

Solution 17.5

(a) A customs union is a group of countries within which there are no trade restrictions. One country in the union is unable to tax the imported produce of a second member.

    Members of a union have a common tariff which is used to tax the produce of non-members as it enters the customs union.

(b) (i) France has a natural advantage over the UK in the production of wine. The French climate and soil are well suited to growing vines. As a result, the UK buys French wine of a better quality and at a cheaper price than it could grow itself.

    (ii) The UK is a large manufacturer of cars. However, some consumers prefer to buy foreign-made cars which are of a different or better design than domestically made alternatives.

        If Germany is able to produce more cars than the UK with the same resources then the UK may well buy German cars because they are cheaper.

(c) The EC is a customs union. Prior to entry the UK was free to buy food and other produce on the world market at competitive prices. Membership of a customs union restricts that choice because the produce of non-members is taxed. UK consumers have to pay more for a non-European product.

    The EC also operates a common agricultural policy (CAP) which guarantees farmers a minimum price for their produce. In recent years, the supply of agricultural produce has vastly exceeded the amount consumers want to buy at the minimum guaranteed price set by the EC. The result is so-called food mountains or surpluses of unsold agricultural produce held in warehouses until such time as demand exceeds supply.

    Consumers end up paying more than they need to for their food. Moreover, the cost of storing the food will come partly out of taxes paid by UK consumers. 1 per cent of the total of VAT collected is paid to the EC.

17.6 Questions

1 What is international trade?
2 State three reasons why it is important for a country to trade.
3 Which of the following is *not* an advantage of international trade:
    A an increase in output   **B** a fall in prices
    C an increase in the number of   **D** an increase in employment in all
        goods available   industries
4 Countries benefit by specialising in the production of a few goods because of the
    law of ....
5 Which of the following would result in an increase in international trade?
    A the introduction of tariffs   **B** the introduction of quotas
    C the introduction of exchange   **D** the introduction of a customs union
        controls
6 Free trade occurs when:
    A a country trades without using money
    B goods are exported at below cost price
    C a developed country sends famine relief
    D a government does not interfere with trade
7 State two reasons why a government might seek to restrict international trade.
8 Draw a diagram to illustrate the effect of a tariff on the import of cars.
9 The introduction of tariffs and quotas:
    A encourages home industry to become more efficient
    B reduces the price of imports
    C reduces the price of domestic made goods
    D increases the demand for domestically made goods
10 Dumping occurs when:
    A exports are bartered
    B exports are sold at prices lower than those in the home market
    C exports are sold allowing payment in the future
    D exports are sold to help underdeveloped countries.
11 Restricting trade by raising the price of an import as it enters the country is ....
    ....
12 What is the term used to describe the limit imposed by a country on the number
    of goods which may be imported?
13 Illustrate the effect of such a limit on the number of imported apples.
14 What is a trading bloc?
15 Pair each of the following items:
    A GATT   **B** OPEC   **C** IBRD   **D** EC
    1 cartel   **2** World Bank   **3** customs union   **4** agreement on trade
16 What do the letters IMF mean?
17 Which of the following does *not* belong to the EC?
    A Irish Republic   **B** Denmark   **C** Hungary   **D** West Germany
18 The group which attempts to set the world price of oil is:
    A IMF   **B** GATT   **C** OPEC   **D** OECD

17.7 Answers

1 The exchange of goods between countries.
2 See section 17.1.   **3 D**
4 The law of comparative advantage.   **5 D**   **6 D**
7 See section 17.2(a).   **8** See Fig. 17.1
9 **D.** A is wrong because a tariff results in less competition for home industries.
10 **B**
11 'Protectionism', or tariff or import duties.
12 **A** quota.   **13** See Fig. 17.2
14 A group of countries between which there are no import or export restrictions.
15 **A4; B1; C2; D3**   **16** International Monetary Fund
17 **C**   **18 C**

18 Balance of Payments

18.1 Components of the Balance of Payments

(a) Definition of the Balance of Payments

The *balance of payments* is a record of one country's trade dealings with the rest of the world. Any transaction involving UK and foreign citizens is calculated in *sterling* (UK pounds).

Figure 18.1 shows that dealings which result in money entering the country are *credit* (plus) items while transactions which lead to money leaving the country are *debit* (minus) items.

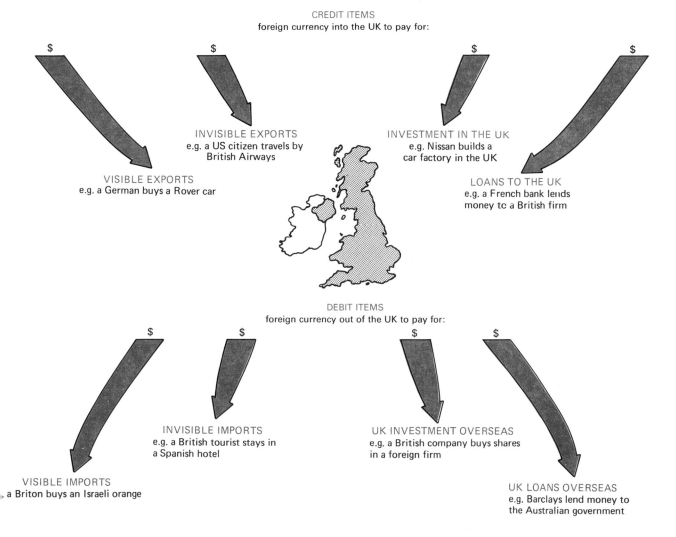

CREDIT ITEMS
foreign currency into the UK to pay for:

INVISIBLE EXPORTS
e.g. a US citizen travels by
British Airways

INVESTMENT IN THE UK
e.g. Nissan builds a
car factory in the UK

VISIBLE EXPORTS
e.g. a German buys a Rover car

LOANS TO THE UK
e.g. a French bank lends
money to a British firm

DEBIT ITEMS
foreign currency out of the UK to pay for:

INVISIBLE IMPORTS
e.g. a British tourist stays in
a Spanish hotel

UK INVESTMENT OVERSEAS
e.g. a British company buys shares
in a foreign firm

VISIBLE IMPORTS
a Briton buys an Israeli orange

UK LOANS OVERSEAS
e.g. Barclays lend money to
the Australian government

Figure 18.1 UK balance of payments transactions

203

The balance of payments can be split up into three sections:

(i) the *current account* which deal with international trade in goods and services;
(ii) the *capital account* which deals with overseas flows of money from international investments and loans;
(iii) *official financing* which deals with changes in a country's foreign currency reserves.

(b) Current Account

The *current account* consists of international dealings in goods (*visible trade*) and services (*invisible trade*).

Invisible trade includes payments for overseas embassies and military bases; interest, profit and dividends from overseas investment; earnings from tourism and transportation.

Table 18.1 The UK current account 1985

Debits	£m.	Credits	£m.	Balance £m.
Visible imports	80 140	Visible exports	78 072	−2 068
Invisible imports	75 007	Invisible exports	80 027	5 020

Source: *CSO Monthly Digest of Stability*, March 1986

By referring to Table 18.1 you can see that in 1985:

(i) The UK bought £80 140 million worth of goods made overseas.
(ii) The UK sold £78 072 million worth of goods overseas.
(iii) The difference between visible exports and imports is known as the *balance of trade* or *visible balance*. This amounted to −£2 068 million.
(iv) The UK bought £75 007 million worth of foreign-produced services.
(v) The UK sold £80 027 million worth of services overseas.
(vi) The difference between invisible exports and imports is called the *invisible balance*. This amounted to £5 020 million.

Adding the balance of trade and balance on invisibles together gives the *balance on the current account*. A *deficit* on the current account means that more goods and services have been imported into the UK than have been sold abroad. A *surplus* on the current account means more goods and services have been exported than imported.

(c) Capital Account

The current account is concerned with items consumed this year. The capital account deals with assets which will earn an income in future years.

UK investment overseas is a *capital outflow* because money leaves the country either to pay for the asset or to be lent. In future years UK-owned foreign assets will earn interest, profits and dividends which will be invisible credit items on the current account.

Overseas investment in the UK brings money into the country and is a *capital inflow*. However, future interest, profit or dividend payments returned to the overseas investor will be invisible debit items on the current account.

The difference between capital inflows and outflows is the *balance on the capital account*. Adding together the balances on the current and capital accounts gives the *balance for official financing*.

(d) Official Financing

If the balance for official financing is positive then UK trading with the rest of the world has created a surplus of foreign currency which can be:

(i) added to foreign currency reserves;
(ii) lent to foreign governments;
(iii) lent to the International Monetary Fund.

A negative balance for official financing means UK trading has resulted in a loss of foreign currency, which must be found either from reserves or by borrowing from foreign governments or the IMF.

18.2 Balance of Payments Problems

(a) Correcting a Balance of Payments Deficit

Strictly speaking, the balance of payments always balances because of official financing. However, a balance of payments deficit means a persistent and large negative balance for official financing. This can be the result of excessive purchases of foreign goods and services or excessive UK investment overseas. In the short term, a balance of payments deficit can be corrected by:

(i) continued borrowing of foreign currency;
(ii) increasing interest rates to attract overseas investors;
(iii) imposing exchange controls;
(iv) imposing tariffs and import quotas.

In the long run, the government can correct a balance of payments deficit by reducing demand in the economy for all goods including imports. Reducing UK inflation rates or encouraging a sterling depreciation will also help.

(b) Correcting a Balance of Payments Surplus

An unwanted balance of payments surplus can be the result of excessive foreign investment in the UK. This will place a future strain on the invisible balance. A reduction in interest rates or restrictive exchange controls will correct the surplus.

18.3 Exchange Rates

An *exchange rate* is the price of one currency in terms of another. For the UK, the dollar exchange rate means the number of dollars ($) one pound (£) can buy. The exchange rate is determined by the supply and demand for *sterling* (pounds) and is $2 per pound in Fig. 18.2 on the next page.

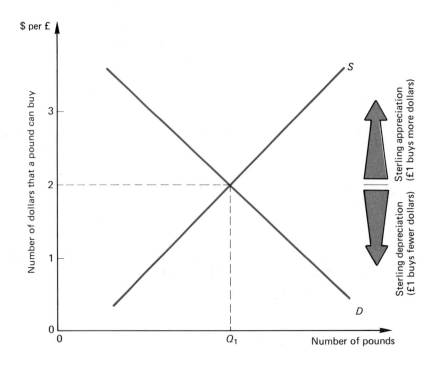

Figure 18.2 Sterling exchange rate

(a) Demand for Sterling

Americans want to exchange dollars for pounds for two reasons:

(i) to buy British goods and services;
(ii) to lend or invest in the UK.

In Fig. 18.2, D shows the number of pounds demanded by Americans at each exchange rate.

(b) Supply of Sterling

Britons want to exchange pounds for dollars for two reasons:

(i) to buy American goods and services;
(ii) to lend or invest in the USA.

In Fig. 18.2, S shows the number of pounds supplied by Britons at each exchange rate.

(c) Changes in the Exchange Rate

A fall in the value of sterling (*depreciation*) means one pound now buys fewer dollars. Sterling depreciates if Americans demand fewer pounds or if UK citizens offer more pounds. UK exports become cheaper and UK imports become dearer. Hence, a sterling depreciation improves the balance of payments.

A rise in the value of sterling (*appreciation*) means one pound now buys more dollars. UK exports become dearer and UK imports become cheaper. Hence a sterling appreciation worsens the balance of payments.

206

18.4 Worked Examples

Example 18.1

The table here shows the quarterly UK balance of payments account on the current account for 1985.

	Balance of trade (visible trade) (£m.)	Invisible balance (£m.)
1st quarter	−1 266	892
2nd quarter	−124	1 457
3rd quarter	−453	1 525
4th quarter	−225	1 146
Annual	?	?

Source: *CSO Monthly Digest of Statistics*, March 1986

(a) Calculate from the above figures in the table:
   (i) the annual visible balance;   **(1 mark)**
   (ii) the annual invisible balance;   **(1 mark)**
   (iii) the annual balance of payments on the current account.   **(1 mark)**

(b) Explain and give an example of:
   (i) a visible export;   **(2 marks)**
   (ii) an invisible import.   **(2 marks)**
(c) Why are imports important to the UK?   **(3 marks)**

Solution 18.1

(a)   (i) Adding up each quarter's visible trade balance gives an annual visible balance of −£2068m.
    (ii) Adding up each quarter's invisible trade balance gives an annual invisible balance of £5020m.
    (iii) Adding together the balance on visibles of −£2068m. and that on invisibles of £5020m. gives the balance on the current account, i.e. £2952m.
(b)   (i) A visible export is the overseas sale of a domestically produced good—for example, the sale of a Jaguar car to an American executive.
    (ii) An invisible import is the domestic purchase of a service supplied by an overseas firm—for example, the purchase of a flight on an American airline by a British tourist.
(c) Imports are important to the UK because they allow the purchase of goods which the country cannot easily manufacture, such as oranges. Imports increase the range and quality of goods for sale in the UK.

Example 18.2

Study the fictitious balance of payments account on the next page and the accompanying description, and then answer each of the questions. (You will be asked to calculate the figures which have been omitted from the account.)

UK Balance of Payments 1988

Current account				
Debits	£m.	*Credits*	£m.
Visible imports	75 000	Visible exports	65 000
Invisible imports	30 000	Invisible exports	35 000
Total debits	105 000	Total credits	100 000
		Current account deficit	?

Investment transactions	£m.
Government and private investment abroad (net)	−1 500

Balance for official financing ('total currency flow')	?

Official financing account	£m.
Borrowing from International Monetary Fund	+2 000
Drawing on currency reserves	

Total official financing	?

In 1988 the value of visible imports exceeded the value of visible exports, and there was a balance of trade deficit. On invisible trade the UK had a favourable balance, though this was not enough to avoid an overall deficit on the current account.

The continued development of UK North Sea Oil was advantageous, as was the recent decision by GATT (General Agreement on Tariffs and Trade) to limit the imports of cheap clothing from the Far East. However, inflation in the UK continued to make it difficult to sell our exports.

(a) Using the figures in the account above, calculate each of the following:

    (i) The balance of visible trade deficit for the United Kingdom in 1988:
       £.......... million   **(1 mark)**
    (ii) The balance on invisible trade surplus for the United Kingdom in 1988:
       £.......... million   **(1 mark)**
    (iii) The current account deficit in 1988.
       £.......... million   **(1 mark)**

(b) Write 'export' or 'import' against each of the following items to show whether it would be included in the export or import totals above.

    (i) German shipowners insure their vessels with Lloyd's in London.   **(1 mark)**
    (ii) Shareholders in France are paid dividends by British Car Auctions.
                                             (1 mark)
    (iii) An American farmer sends a gift to a relative living in Scotland.   **(1 mark)**

(c) Why is a deficit on the current account more serious than a deficit on the balance of visible trade?   **(4 marks)**

(d) The data states: 'the continued development of UK North Sea oil was advantageous. . . .'

    (i) To what was it advantageous?   **(1 mark)**
    (ii) How was it advantageous?   **(3 marks)**

(e) Calculate the balance for official financing ('total currency flow') in 1988. Indicate whether the balance is positive or negative . . .
    £.......... million   **(1 mark)**

(f) Calculate the change in currency reserves in 1988. Indicate whether the change is an increase or a decrease.

£.......... million **(1 mark)**

(g) (i) What do you notice about the amounts for (1) balance for official financing ('total currency flow') and (2) total official financing? **(1 mark)**

(ii) Why is this so? **(3 marks)**

(LEAG specimen GCSE)

Solution 18.2

(a) (i) The balance of visible trade is found by taking visible imports (£75 000m.) from visible exports (£65 000m.). Since visible imports exceed exports by £10 000m., this is the visible trade deficit for 1988.

(ii) Invisible exports (£35 000m.) exceed invisible imports (£30 000m.) by £5000m. which is the amount of surplus on the balance of invisible trade.

(iii) Deducting the total amount of imports (£105 000m.) from the total amount of exports (£100 000m.) gives the balance of payments on the current account i.e. −£5000m.

(b) (i) The purchase by a German of British insurance results in money entering the UK. The transaction is a credit item and would be included as an export.

(ii) Dividend payments to foreign shareholders results in money leaving the country. The transaction is a debit item on the balance of payments and would be included as an import.

(iii) The gift from the American results in money entering the country. The transaction is a credit item and would be included as an export.

(c) A deficit on the balance of visible trade means the UK has imported more goods than it has exported. Traditionally, the UK has always run a visible deficit. However, the UK is a specialist producer of services and exports more invisibles than are imported. A deficit on visible trade is not serious providing there is a larger invisible surplus.

If the current account is in deficit this is always serious because the UK has imported more goods and services than have been exported.

(d) (i) North Sea oil is part of the UK's visible trade and affects the balance of payments on the current account.

(ii) The development of North Sea oil allows the UK to reduce the amount of oil it buys from overseas, thereby reducing visible imports. Once domestic needs have been met then the UK can then sell surplus North Sea oil overseas, thereby increasing visible exports. The balance of trade will improve.

Some of the profits made from North Sea oil can be invested by buying overseas assets. Once these foreign investments begin to make a profit then the UK balance on invisibles will also improve.

(e) Adding together the current account deficit of −£5000m. and investment transactions of −£1500m. gives the balance for official financing, i.e. −£6500m.

(f) Part of the balance for official financing of −£6500m. has been met by borrowing +£2000m. of foreign currency from the IMF. The remaining +£4500m. of foreign currency must come from currency reserves. Therefore +£4500m. of foreign currency has been taken from currency reserves.

(g) (i) Adding together the balance for official financing of (−£6500m. and total official financing of + £6500m. means they 'balance', i.e. equal zero.

(ii) The balance for official financing states the sterling value of foreign currency which the UK has earned or owes as a result of its trade over the last 12 months. If the balance for official financing is positive then the UK has earned foreign currency from trade. Total official financing shows what the UK does with the foreign currency it has earned from trade.

If, as in the example, the balance for official financing is negative then the UK owes foreign currency. Total official financing supplies the necessary foreign currency.

In any event the balance for official financing and total official financing always balance each other and have opposite signs.

Example 18.3

(a) State briefly the broad categories of imports of goods into the United Kingdom indicating recent trends. **(4 marks)**

(b) Examine the balance of payments accounts of the United Kingdom using the following headings:

    (i) the balance of trade;
    (ii) the current account balance;
    (iii) the balance for official financing. **(6 marks)**

(c) Assess the effects on the balance of payments of each of the following trends:

    (i) the rapid contraction of the Welsh coal industry;
    (ii) a major expansion of the tourist industry in Wales;
    (iii) a continuing trend for multinational firms to close branch manufacturing plants in Wales. **(6 marks)**

(WJEC specimen GCSE)

Solution 18.3

(a) One category of imports is raw materials used to manufacture goods. With the decline of UK manufacturing and the arrival of North Sea oil fewer raw materials are now imported. While the UK continues to import fruits such as bananas which it cannot grow itself, imports of other foods have fallen as the UK has become increasingly self-sufficient in agriculture.

The biggest import growth is in manufactures. For the first time since the industrial revolution, the UK now imports more manufactured goods than it exports.

(b) (i) The balance of trade is the difference between the value of foreign goods sold in the UK and the value of British goods sold overseas.

(ii) The current account balance is made up of the balance of trade and the balance on invisibles. If the UK sells more goods and services overseas than it buys then the current account balance will be in surplus.

(iii) The balance for official financing is the balance on the capital account added to the current account balance. The balance for official financing states the total amount of foreign currency leaving or entering the UK as a result of trade.

(c) (i) The sale of Welsh coal represents a visible export. The rapid contraction of the Welsh coal industry means less coal is available for sale overseas. Earnings from the overseas sale of coal will fall. However, the effect on the balance of payments will be small because coal sales form only a small part of overall visible exports.

(ii) The Welsh tourist industry makes a contribution to the balance of invisibles. If the new tourists are from outside the UK then there will be an improvement in the balance of payments.

(iii) A multinational is a foreign-owned company investing in the UK. Closure of one of its branch plants in Wales will result in less foreign investment in the UK and there will be a fall in capital inflows.

However, there will be fewer dividend and profit payments made to the overseas company. The balance on invisibles will improve.

Example 18.4

Study the advertisement on the next page for the Rover Group and answer all the questions which follow.
(a) What term do economists use to describe the overseas sale of UK-made goods?
(2 marks)
(b) From the passage calculate:
  (i) the number of cars per man produced at Longbridge in 1981;   **(1 mark)**
  (ii) the increase in the number of cars per man produced at Longbridge between 1981 and 1985;
  (iii) how many vehicles Rover sold abroad in 1985;   **(1 mark)**

  (iv) Rover's approximate average revenue from the overseas sale of cars in 1985.
  (2 marks)
(c) Using the information given in the passage, how would you explain the increase in Rover's overseas sales?   **(4 marks)**
(d) How would Rover's overseas earnings be affected by:
  (i) the launch of a new executive car;   **(2 marks)**
  (ii) an increase in the value of sterling.   **(4 marks)**

Solution 18.4

(a) The overseas sale of UK-made goods is called visible exports.
(b) (i) Look at the picture of the Longbridge production line. Reading up from 1981 and across to the y-axis indicates that output per man was 7 cars.
  (ii) By 1985 output per man had risen to 13½ cars—an increase of 6½ cars per man.
  (iii) The passage states that Rover exported over 100 000 vehicles in 1985.
  (iv) The passage states that Rover earned over £400 million. Average revenue = Total revenue ($\approx$£400 000 000) divided by the number of vehicles sold ($\approx$100 000). Average revenue was approximately £4000.
(c) Rover have increased their sales by reducing the price and improving the quality of their product. For example, computers have been used at the design stage to help make better cars.

The use of efficient production line techniques using modern robot arms has increased output per worker. Higher productivity reduces unit costs and lowers the final selling price of the cars.
(d) (i) A new executive car can be four times the cost of an ordinary family car. The sale of only a few executive cars would greatly increase overseas earnings.
  (ii) An increase in the value of sterling increases the price of UK exports. For example, if the exchange rate is 10 francs per pound, a £5000 car

211

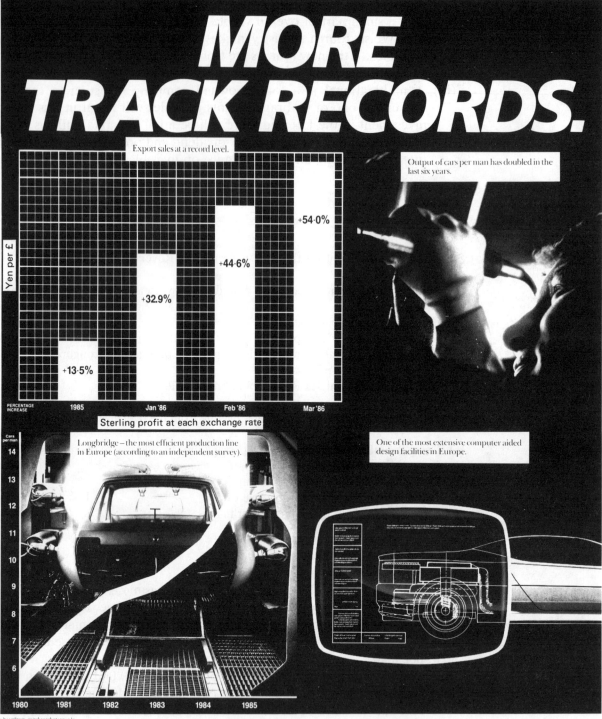

MORE TRACK RECORDS.

Export sales at a record level.

Yen per £

+13·5% — 1985
+32.9% — Jan '86
+44·6% — Feb '86
+54·0% — Mar '86

PERCENTAGE INCREASE

Sterling profit at each exchange rate

Output of cars per man has doubled in the last six years.

Cars per man

14
13
12
11
10
9
8
7
6

Longbridge – the most efficient production line in Europe (according to an independent survey).

One of the most extensive computer aided design facilities in Europe.

1980   1981   1982   1983   1984   1985

According to an independent survey by
The Engineer magazine 'Manufacturer's data

One of the most astonishing industrial turnabouts for generations is gathering speed. It means your next car can be better in every way than the one you drive now.

And it's all happening right here in Britain.

On the track, and on the road, we're breaking records at Austin Rover. Where you'll find Europe's most efficient car production line. Where output per worker has doubled in six short years. Where the benefit of this productivity is reflected in highly competitive prices.

Where advanced technology in design and production ensure performance, quality, comfort, specification and value in the car you buy.

Where rising exports strengthen our place in the market. In 1985 we exported over 100,000 vehicles – earning

over £400 million abroad. For the first three months of 1986 they're even higher.

Achievements that must surely make your patriotic heart beat just a little faster.

Each and every Mini, Metro, Maestro, Montego and Rover is better than ever before. Reassuring and satisfying your motoring needs. And all soundly backed by one of the strongest, most comprehensive after-sales care plans and the strongest dealer network in the country. The people who can get you motoring at an unexpectedly low cost.

Put us to the test – now! Phone, free of charge, on 0800-400-456, any time. We will be delighted to arrange a demonstration. Or simply contact your nearest Austin Rover dealer.

PUT US TO THE TEST
CALL FREE OF CHARGE ON 0800-400-456 ANYTIME—WE'LL ARRANGE A TEST DRIVE

AUSTIN ROVER

NOW WE'RE MOTORING.

212

sells for 50 000 francs. An increase in the value of sterling to 15 francs per pound means the same car sells for 75 000 francs.

If because of the price increase French consumers cut back on the number of Rover cars they buy then export earnings will fall.

Example 18.5

Study the following article by Lynne Bateson which describes some of the goods imported and exported by the UK.

Britain's Imports

Product	Market share
Dishwasher	99%
Iron	84%
Freezer	62%
Colour television	33%

The Japanese do buy consumable goods from Britain. They like our tonic water, biscuits and Scotch. But the Japanese are not interested in British consumer goods like washing machines and fridges. The UK imported £4038 million of Japanese items such as video cameras and cars but sold only £830 million to the Japanese.

Globally, we sell £52 514 million worth of manufactured goods. We import £5774 more than that.

On average a British household spends about £110 a week on consumer goods and services, food and drink. Of this, £30 is spent on imported goods, and the proportion spent on British goods is falling.

If we switched just £5 of the money we each spend on imported goods to British goods some 580 000 jobs could be created.

Source: *Daily Express*, 23 April 1986

(a) From the passage give one type of good that:

    (i) Japan buys from Britain; **(1 mark)**
    (ii) Britain buys from Japan. **(1 mark)**

(b) Calculate the balance of trade deficit between the UK and:

    (i) the rest of the world; **(1 mark)**
    (ii) Japan. **(1 mark)**

(c) Calculate from the article:

    (i) the percentage of dishwashers sold in the UK which are imported;

        (1 mark)
    (ii) the percentage of colour televisions sold in the UK which are home-produced. **(1 mark)**
    (iii) average annual British household expenditure on imports; **(2 marks)**
    (iv) the number of jobs likely to be created in the UK by switching £15 of expenditure from imports to domestically made goods. **(2 marks)**

(d) Advise the government on the policies it should adopt to correct a balance of payments deficit. **(6 marks)**

Solution 18.5

(a) (i) Japan buys scotch whisky from Britain.
    (ii) Britain buys cars from Japan.
(b) (i) The trade deficit is the difference between the amount of goods imported and exported. The UK bought £5774 million more worth of goods from the rest of the world than were exported.
    (ii) The UK bought £4038 million worth of goods from Japan and sold £830 million worth of goods to Japan. The trade deficit was £4038. − £830m. = £3208m.
(c) (i) The table states that 99 per cent of the dishwashers sold in the UK are imported.
    (ii) 33 per cent of colour televisions sold in the UK are imported. The remaining 67 per cent must be produced domestically.
    (iii) Average weekly British household expenditure on imports is £30. Annual average expenditure on imports equals £30 × 52 = £1560.
    (iv) The passage states that £5 switched from imports to UK-made goods would create 580 000 more jobs. £15 of switched expenditure would probably create 580 000 × 3 = 1 740 000.
(d) A balance of payments deficit can be corrected by taking measures which:
    (i) improve the current account by reducing imports and boosting exports;
    (ii) improve the capital account by increasing overseas investment in the UK and reducing UK overseas investment.

Exchange controls limit the amount of foreign currency UK citizens can buy. Both the current account and the capital account are improved because UK citizens are less able to buy foreign goods or to invest in overseas assets.

A depreciation of sterling can improve the current account by increasing the price of imports and reducing the price of exports.

Example 18.6

Read the following extract from an article entitled the 'Japanese Set to Stay Ahead' which appeared in the *Financial Times*. The profit made by a Japanese manufacturer on the sale of a car in the UK depends on the yen against sterling exchange rate. The top graph (opposite) shows different exchange rates. The bottom graph (opposite) shows the effect of exchange rate changes on the sterling cost of production and profit of a Japanese car.

'UK producers might be hoping that the competitive advantage of the Japanese would have been lost because of the rise of the yen. The rise of the yen has meant that a new Japanese car sold for £5111 is earning only £400 for its manufacturer.

The diagram shows that a rise in the yen does reduce profits. However, the Japanese remain one step ahead in terms of cost-effective production and aggressive marketing.

Source: Adapted from *Financial Times*, 21 April 1986

(a) What is the currency of Japan? **(1 mark)**
(b) Give one reason why:
    (i) a Japanese citizen buys pounds. **(1 mark)**
    (ii) A British firm buys yen. **(1 mark)**
(c) How much profit does the passage say a Japanese car manufacturer is currently receiving from the sale of a £5111 car? **(1 mark)**
(d) Use both graphs to calculate the yen-against-sterling exchange rate when a Japanese car manufacturer receives £1000 profit from the sale of a car. **(3 marks)**
(e) Can Japanese manufacturers always sell their cars in the UK at a profit? Explain your answer. **(2 marks)**

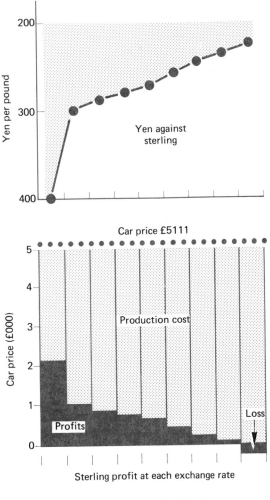

Car price £5111

Japanese cars in Britain

(f) According to the passage, what has happened to the value of the Japanese currency? **(1 mark)**

(g) Give two possible reasons to explain this change. **(6 marks)**

Solution 18.6

(a) The currency of Japan is the yen.

(b) (i) A Japanese citizen might want to buy pounds if he is going on holiday in Scotland.

(ii) A British firm might want yen to pay for imported Japanese goods.

(c) The passage states that a £400 profit is made on the sale of a £5111 car.

(d) The bottom graph shows production costs (lighter shaded area) and the amount of profit (darker shaded areas) made from the sale of a car at different exchange rates. You move along the x-axis until the darker shade profit area equals £1000. This occurs at the second bar. You then move up to the top graph and find the corresponding exchange rate. The second dot is at 300 yen per pound.

(e) The bottom graph indicates that a loss is made at the ninth bar. Moving up to the top graph, the exchange rate is about 220 yen to the pound. If the yen against sterling exchange rate is 220 or less, then a loss is made on the sale of each car.

(f) The value of the yen has risen.

(g) The value of the yen depends on its supply and demand. An increase in the demand for yen, or a fall in the supply of yen increases its value.

Yen are demanded by foreigners wanting to pay for Japanese goods and services. Anything that increases foreign demand for Japanese commodities (e.g. a new range of cameras) encourages a rise in the value of the yen.

Yen are supplied by Japanese citizens wanting pounds to pay for British goods and services. A fall in Japanese demand for UK services (e.g. a fall in the number of Japanese tourists coming to Britain) reduces the supply of yen and encourages a rise in the value of the yen.

18.5 Questions

1 The account which shows a country's trading transactions with the rest of the world over a given period is called ....

2 A good which is sold to an overseas customer by a British company appears on the UK balance of payments as a/an .... export and would be recorded on the .... account.

3 When a service is sold to a person living overseas by a UK company it will appear on the UK balance of payments as a/an........................... export.

4 Which of the following can be considered as an invisible export of the United Kingdom?
   A the sale of Scotch whisky to Japan
   B a British company buying insurance provided by a German company
   C British carpenters working in Spain and sending their wages to the UK
   D the expenditure of British tourists visiting Denmark.

5 UK invisible imports include:
   A the purchase by a UK customer of a Japanese-made computer
   B the purchase by a Japanese citizen of a British-made car
   C purchase by a British customer of a Japanese camera
   D a British travel agent arranges holidays in the USA for Welsh tourists.

6 Visible exports minus .... = balance of trade.

7 Current balance minus balance of trade = ...

8 Visible balance + invisible balance = ...

For each of questions 9 to 12 select from the list A–D the most appropriate term:
   A invisible exports   **B** invisible imports
   C visible exports   **D** visible imports

9 British Coal increases its sales to Italy.

10 Zimbabwe increases its sales of tobacco to the UK.

11 A British shipping company transports cars for an American company.

12 A UK citizen uses an American airline.

Use the following information to answer questions 13 to 15:

UK 1985	£m.
Exports (visible)	78 000
Imports (invisible)	80 000
Invisible credits	80 000
Invisible debits	75 000

13 What is the balance of trade?

14 What is the invisible balance?

15 What is the current balance?

16 The purchase of a German factory by a UK firm is:
   A a visible export   **B** an invisible export
   C a capital inflow   **D** a capital outflow

17   What is the long-run effect of overseas investment in the UK on the UK balance of payments?

18   A balance of payments deficit occurs when:
- A   the visible balance is negative;
- B   the invisible balance is negative;
- C   the current balance is negative;
- D   the current and capital balance is negative

19   State two methods of correcting a persistent balance of payments deficit.

20   What happens to a balance of payments surplus?

21   The value of one currency in terms of another is ....

22   Which one of the following would increase the demand for sterling on the foreign exchange market?
- A   an increase in exports
- B   an increase in imports
- C   a fall in UK interest rates
- D   an increase in UK investment overseas

23   Which of the following would reduce the value of sterling on the foreign exchange market?:
- A   European shipowners insuring their ships in the UK
- B   a surplus on the current balance
- C   a reduction in the American demand for British cars
- D   American pension funds investing in UK property developments

18.6   Answers

1 The balance of payments	2 Visible; current.
3 Invisible.	4 C 5 D
6 Visible imports.	7 Invisible balance.
8 Current balance.	9 C 10 D
11 A	12 B
13 −£2000 million.	14 £5000 million.
15 £3000 million.	16 D

17   Once the foreign-owned factories earn profits these will be returned to the foreign owners. There will be a series of debit items on the invisible balance.

18 D.   19 See section 18.2(a)

20   The foreign currency earned from trade is added to UK reserves, lent to the IMF, or lent to other governments, i.e. there is negative official financing.

21 an exchange rate.   22 A   23 C

19 Economic Growth

19.1   Features of Economic Growth

(a) Definition

Economic growth refers to an increase in a country's ability to produce goods and services. The advantage of economic growth is that an increase in real national income allows more goods for consumption.

(b) Developing Countries

A *developing country* or *less developed country* (LDC) is one which is not yet fully industrialised and tends to have the following features:

  (i) Agriculture is more important than manufacturing.
 (ii) There is limited specialisation and exchange.
(iii) There are not enough savings to finance investment.
 (iv) Population is expanding too rapidly for available resources.
  (v) A low standard of living.

  A *developed country* is more fully industrialised and has a high standard of living.

(c) Barriers to Economic Growth

A country can increase production if it increases the amount of resources used or makes better use of existing factors. Economic growth is more difficult if:

  (i) A country lacks the *infrastructure* (underlying capital) to produce goods more efficiently. There are three types of infrastructure:

    (1) *basic* including electricity, road and telephone networks;
    (2) *social* including schools, hospitals and housing.
    (3) *industrial* including factories and offices.

 (ii) A country lacks the machines or skilled labour needed to manufacture modern goods or services.
(iii) A country lacks the technical knowledge.
 (iv) Workers are not prepared to accept specialisation and the division of labour.
  (v) Population growth is too rapid.
 (vi) A country has too large a foreign debt.

(d) Disadvantages of Economic Growth

(i) Increased noise, congestion and pollution.
(ii) Towns and cities may become overcrowded.
(iii) Extra machines can be produced only by using resources currently involved in making consumer goods.
(iv) A traditional way of life may be lost.
(v) People may experience increased anxiety and stress.

19.2 North *v*. South

(a) The Brandt Commission

The Brandt Report divided the world into rich (North) and poor (South) sectors and found that in developing countries more than 800 million are destitute and 17 million die needlessly before they are five years old. We in the North have 25 per cent of the world's population but consume 80 per cent of all the goods made.

(b) Recommendations of the Brandt Commission

Brandt suggested that the North should help the South by transferring resources and starting a global famine relief programme. The development role of the World Bank should be strengthened. Nations should pay an income tax, and a tax should be put on the sale of military equipment.

19.3 Worked Examples

Example 19.1

Look at the photograph taken in a less developed country (LDC). The woman supports her family by selling ashes for cleaning pots and pans.
(a) How does the woman earn her living?   (1 mark)
(b) Is the woman likely to earn a large income from her occupation? Use the photograph to explain your answer.   (4 marks)
(c) Foreign aid is given by developed countries to LDCs. Say how each of the following types of aid might help the woman in the photograph:

    (i) a shipment of grain to the village;   (2 marks)
    (ii) a grant toward the building of a dam and hydro-electric power station in the region;   (2 marks)
    (iii) a United Nations agricultural advisor staying in the village for one year.
                                                                              (2 marks)
(d) Are there any disadvantages for a LDC in receiving foreign aid?   (5 marks)

Solution 19.1

(a) The woman earns her living by turning rubbish into ashes. The ashes are then sold for cleaning pots and pans.

(b) The woman is unlikely to earn a large income from selling ashes. A large income would allow the woman to buy a large number of consumer goods. However, the family are not wearing expensive clothes. There are no luxury goods shown in the photograph. The children look thin as if they just have enough to eat and no more.

(c) (i) A shipment of grain to the village will increase the amount of food available. The extra food can be used to improve the diet of people in the village—but will soon run out.

(ii) The building of the dam will create work in the area. Local people will have more money to spend on all types of goods including the ashes sold by the woman.

Once the dam is producing electricity new factories can be opened which may offer the woman better-paid employment.

(iii) An advisor may be able to suggest new methods of production to the village which increase output. If the extra output is shared between members of the village the woman and her family will be able to consume more food. Again, the advisor may introduce schemes which offer the woman a better occupation.

(d) Certain types of foreign aid can have disadvantages for the receiving country. The aid may be in the form of a loan that is then repaid with interest. Debt repayments are usually in dollars and this will act as a drain on future reserves of foreign currency. Many Third-World nations are having difficulty repaying their debts.

Continual shipments of food relieve starvation but discourage local farmers from planting crops. Once a famine has been prevented then aid should concentrate on providing local people with the resources to produce their own goods.

Example 19.2

(a) Explain clearly the difference between economic goods and economic growth.
(4 marks)
(b) Why might a country find it difficult to achieve economic growth? **(4 marks)**
(c) How far does an increase in population help a country trying to achieve economic growth? **(6 marks)**
(d) State two possible disadvantages of economic growth. **(4 marks)**

Solution 19.2

(a) Economic goods are items that are in limited supply. Almost all goods are in limited supply and are therefore economic goods. Examples of economic goods are cars and food.

Economic growth is an increase in a country's ability to produce goods and services.

(b) Economic growth requires an increase in the amount or quality of a country's resources. In particular, a country must have sufficient savings to finance investment in new machinery. Economies where there is a low standard of living need all their resources to sustain the current population. There is nothing left over to invest in the capital needed for economic growth.

If economic growth is attempted in new industries then a country may find it lacks the necessary technical knowledge and skilled labour force to make the most efficient use of resources. Maximum output is not reached.

(c) An increase in the population can help or hinder economic growth. If a country is already over-populated then the increase will reduce productivity and hinder economic growth. If a country is under-populated then the increase raises productivity and helps growth.

The composition of the population increase is important. A natural increase in the population caused by a rise in the birth-rate requires more resources in the production of consumer goods. Less resources are then available to produce capital and economic growth is reduced.

If the increase in population is the result of the immigration of skilled workers then the country has more resources to produce goods and services. Output and economic growth increase.

(d) Economic growth may result in an increase in the amount of pollution. The social costs of economic growth are a disadvantage and include increased traffic congestion and polluted rivers.

Economic growth can also destroy traditional ways of life. Modern industrial societies stress the importance of owning consumer goods, which can create a feeling of inferiority in those low-income groups who cannot afford an expensive life style.

Example 19.3

The following photographs show two workers, each producing a table. One is in a developed country, the other in a developing one.

A

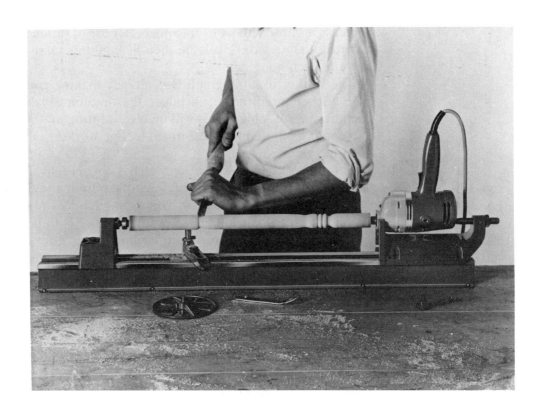

B

(a) Give two examples of capital goods found in each photograph.　　　**(2 marks)**

(b) Explaining each of your answers, which worker is likely to:

　　(i) take longer to produce the table;　　　**(2 marks)**
　　(ii) produce a better table?　　　**(2 marks)**

(c) Suggest a method each of the workers in the photographs could use to increase his output.　　　**(4 marks)**

(d) Why are capital goods important to developing countries?　　　**(5 marks)**

Solution 19.3

(a) A capital good is an item used to help produce another good. Two items of capital shown in photograph A are a saw and a plane. Two items of capital shown in photograph B are a power lathe and a chisel.

(b) (i) The worker in photograph A does not have the advantage of modern items of capital such as a lathe which speed up the process of production. The worker in photograph A is likely to take longer to produce the table.

　　(ii) The worker in photograph B can use the up-to-date equipment to add extra features to the table which are too time-consuming to the worker in photograph A. The photograph shows the worker in B styling a leg to improve the overall quality of the table. He will probably produce a better table.

(c) The worker in photograph A can increase his output by working longer hours. However, he is probably working long hours already. He could increase his productivity by making better use of producer goods. If he could afford to buy a vice or a lathe then he could increase the amount of work done in each hour.

The worker in photograph B is already making good use of machinery. The next step will be to introduce the division-of-labour principle to the manufacture of tables. This will involve splitting up the manufacture of the table into separate tasks performed by one worker. Output per worker will then increase.

(d) A developing country is a nation which is not yet fully industrialised. Capital is important as a means of increasing total output and the standard of living. An increase in the amount of goods and services produced by a country (economic growth) allows more wants and needs to be satisfied.

Capital can be used to sustain economic growth if it is used to produce even more machines. The short-term loss of consumer goods results in a long-term increase in productive capacity.

Without capital a developing country is unable to increase the standard of living of its population.

19.4 Questions

1 Economic growth refers to:
   A integration
   B inflation
   C increases in real national income
   D increases in the size of population

2 Economic growth occurs when there is:
   A an increase in prices
   B an increase in the immobility of labour
   C an increase in migration
   D an increase in output per head.

3 Which of the following indicates economic growth?
   A a balance of payments surplus
   B disinflation
   C full employment
   D the productivity of capital and labour is rising

4 What do the letters LDC stand for?

5 Which of the following is likely to be found in a developing country?
   A high birth rates
   B low death rates
   C low income per head
   D barter

6 Most less developed countries tend to export:
   A tertiary products
   B secondary products
   C primary products
   D oil

7 State three reasons why LDCs are unable to finance investment.

8 What is a developed country?

9 Developed countries are characterised by:
   A large primary sectors
   B large populations
   C low inflation
   D low birth rates

10 In developed countries a lower proportion of income is usually spent on:
   A food   B alcohol   C leisure   D holidays.

	Country A	Country B	Country C
Primary product	80%	3%	10%
Secondary product	15%	40%	50%
Tertiary product	5%	57%	40%

11 The most developed country in the above table is........

12 The least developed country in the above table is ....

13 Which of the following is likely to increase the rate of economic growth?:
   A an increase in interest rates   B an increase in capital investment
   C an increase in inflation   D an increase in exports
14 What is meant by the term 'infrastructure'?
15 Which one of the following is an example of social capital:
   A a motorway   B a university   C a shoe factory   D a lathe
16 State two disadvantages of economic growth.
17 The voluntary transfer of resources from developed countries to less developed countries is known as...........................
18 How can developed countries encourage economic growth in less developed countries?

19.5 Answers

1 C		2 D	3 D		
4 Less developed country.			5 A		6 C

7 See section 19.1(b)(ii) to (v).
8 A country with a high level of industrialisation.
9 D. Not all developed countries have a large agricultural sector, a large population or low inflation. Almost all do have a low birth rate.

10 A	11 C	12 A	13 B

14 A country's underlying capital.

15 B	16 See section 19.1(d).
17 Economic aid.	18 See section 19.2(b).

20 Personal Economics

20.1 Housing

(a) Renting

Many people cannot afford to buy their own homes. *Renting* is when a *tenant* pays money to a *landlord* (owner) for the use of a house.

The landlord is responsible for repairs to the building. The tenant is not allowed to make alterations to the building without the landlord's permission.

A tenant has *security of tenure*, i.e. he cannot be forced out of the house by a landlord. If a tenant thinks his rent is too high then he can go to a *rent tribunal* where a government rent officer will decide a fair rent. The tenant and the landlord have to accept the decision of the rent officer.

Houses can be rented from private landlords but there is a great shortage of rented accommodation. Local authorities provide council housing but there is still not enough to go round. People wanting a council house are put on a waiting list. Priority is given to families in need. Tenants now have the right to buy their council houses from the local authority.

(b) Buying

Houses cost thousands of pounds. Most people buying a house take out a special loan (*mortgage*) from a bank or a building society which they repay usually over twenty-five years. There are two main types of mortgage:

  (i) An *ordinary mortgage* is where the loan is repaid with interest in monthly instalments over twenty five years.
 (ii) An *endowment* mortgage is more expensive than an ordinary mortgage. Every month a premium is paid to an insurance company, and interest is paid on the loan to a building society. After twenty-five years the insurance company pays out enough money to pay for the house and the owner keeps any money left over.

Home ownership is encouraged by the government which reduces the cost of monthly repayments by giving *tax relief* (a reduced tax bill).

People buying their own home have a good choice of property. If house prices go up, they may be able to sell at a profit.

(c) Moving House

The shortage of rented property makes it difficult for tenants to move house. Home owners are faced with various 'hidden' costs when moving. They have to pay for:

(i) An *estate agent* who keeps a list of houses for sale in an area and arranges for potential buyers to see them. The seller pays commission if the agent finds a buyer.

(ii) A *surveyor* who checks the house to see if it is well built and in good repair.

(iii) A *solicitor* who checks the seller actually owns the house and draws up a contract between the buyer and the seller.

(iv) A *removal firm* which transports belongings to the new house.

(v) *Stamp duty* which is a tax on the purchase of a house.

The cost of moving can add up to several thousand pounds.

20.2 Transport

(a) Private Transport

There are two types of cost involved in running a car:

(i) *Fixed or standing costs* which must be paid even if the car if not used. These include the interest lost by not having the money used to buy the car in the bank, depreciation, insurance and car tax.

(ii) *Variable or running costs* for petrol and servicing.

(b) Public Transport

A car is convenient but costs hundreds of pounds a year to run and maintain. Public transport by bus, rail or underground offers a cheaper alternative. An increase in the number of private motorists using public transport would reduce pollution because there would be fewer cars on the road.

20.3 Insurance

(a) Pooling Risks

Insurance is a system where in return for a previous payment a company will give money to repair accidental damage. Insurance is based on the pooling of risks. Thousands of policyholders pay a small sum of money (*premium*) into a central pool. The pool is then large enough to meet the expenses of the small number of people who actually suffer an accident. Insurance companies use the principle of *indemnity* which means that the insured is returned to the same financial position as before the accident. The policyholder is given enough money to repair the damage and no more.

Companies use *data* (information) to calculate a particular risk and the premium to charge.

(b) Main Types of Insurance

(i) *Liability insurance*. See Worked Example 20.4(d).

(ii) *Household insurance* covers damage to the building and the contents.

(iii) *Motor insurance* covers damage to your car, to other people and their property. There are three main types of car insurance:

    (1) *Third party.* You are the first party; the insurance company is the second party; anyone else is a third party. You are covered for damage to other people and their property, only.

    (2) *Third party, fire and theft.* As for (1) plus you are covered for damage to your own car through fire or theft, only.

    (3) *Comprehensive.* You are covered for any damage to your own car, other people and their property.

(iv) *Life assurance* which covers dependants and provides for retirement. There are three main types of life assurance:

    (1) *Term.* Money is paid to dependants if death occurs within a stated period, e.g. twenty-five years.

    (2) *Whole life.* Money is paid to dependants upon your death.

    (3) *Endowment.* Money is paid at death or after a stated period—whichever is the sooner.

(v) *National insurance.* Workers pay 5 per cent or more of their wages into a pool. If they are ill or unemployed they receive *benefits* (money). Once they are over 60 (woman) or 65 (man) they receive a *pension.*

20.4 Leisure

Leisure is free time when someone is not doing paid work, or at school or looking after the house. The average worker spends 45 hours each week on employment and travel. The average worker has 2.6 hours of free time each weekday and 10.2 hours of free time per weekend day.

    The principle of *opportunity cost* is used to value leisure time. For example, the cost of going to the cinema is the cost of the ticket plus any lost overtime payments that could have been earned from working.

20.5 Retailing and Advertising

(a) Types of Retail Outlet

A *retail outlet* is a shop. There are several types:

(i) A *unit or corner shop* is local, convenient, friendly, open long hours and offers credit to known customers but is also expensive and has little choice.

(ii) A *multiple or chain store* is several shops using the same name. Chain stores are cheap and offer a large choice but they are not always local or friendly places to shop.

(iii) A *department store* is several shops under one roof. They are luxurious, stock all types of goods and offer personal service but they are found only in city centres and can be expensive.

(iv) *Supermarkets* have goods on shelves (*open display*) and customers help themselves (*self service*). Payment is made at tills.

(v) *Hypermarkets* are huge supermarkets found on the outskirts of large towns. They have their own car parks.

(b) Advertising

Advertising is the publicising of goods and services. Advertising creates a *brand image* whereby consumers buy more of a good because they believe it is better than substitutes.

There are two types of advertising:

(i) *Informative* which gives details about the use, price, quality, etc. of a product.
(ii) *Persuasive* which gives opinions about a product.

20.6 Consumer Protection

(a) Legislative Protection

Many laws have been passed to protect the consumer when he buys a good. Here are a few:

(i) *Trades Descriptions Act.* Goods must be marked with their country of origin. A good on special offer must have been on sale at a higher price for at least twenty-eight days in the last six months.
(ii) *Weights and Measures Act.* The weight of a good must be shown on a packet. It is an offence to sell under weight goods.
(iii) *Sale of Goods Act.* Goods sold must match their description. Goods sold must be undamaged. Goods sold must live up to their description. For example, a waterproof coat must be waterproof.
(iv) *Goods Act.* If you are sold faulty goods you are allowed your money back or a replacement. Proof of purchase must be given.

(b) Voluntary Protection

The Consumers' Association is an independent watchdog which investigates products and applies pressure on the government on behalf of the ordinary shopper. The Association publishes a monthly magazine called *Which?* giving impartial information about products.

20.7 Personal Budgeting

(a) Making a Budget

Budgeting means making your expenditure less than your income. You draw up a budget plan by:

(i) Making a list of all the money you receive each month (income).
(ii) Making a list of all the money you spend each month (expenditure).

If your expenditure is greater than your income you will have to buy fewer things.

(b) Credit

Credit involves buying a good now and paying for it later. The annual percentage rate (APR) of interest for borrowing money on credit can be as high as 35 per cent. This means that for every pound borrowed you must pay back 35 pence in interest each year.

With *hire purchase* the customer pays a deposit and then makes monthly repayments including interest. The customer does not get a discount (money off) when using hire purchase but the good can be returned with nothing more to pay once half the repayments have been made. The customer does not own the good until the last payment has been made.

20.8   Worked Examples

Example 20.1

Study the table carefully, then answer the questions which follow.

House purchase in selected regions of the United Kingdom

	London and Home Counties	West Midlands	North East	Belfast	United Kingdom (average)
Average price of property purchased	£45 398	£27 142	£24 392	£17 971	£34 257
Percentage of price lent to buyer by building society	59%	68%	69%	77%	64%
Average amount put down by buyer as deposit on property	£18 518	£8 829	£7 643	£4 216	£12 459
Average annual income of house buyers	£14 530	£11 116	£11 106	£9 942	£12 509

Source: Adapted from Nationwide Building Society Background Bulletin, November 1984

(a) What do we call a loan used for buying a house?   **(1 mark)**

(b) In which of the four regions shown is the percentage of the price lent to the buyer the highest?   **(1 mark)**

(c) Using the data, explain why it would seem easier to buy a house in Belfast than in London.   **(4 marks)**

(d) In what way does it help our understanding of this data, to be given the average figures for the United Kingdom?   **(2 marks)**

(e) Unemployment in London and the Home Counties is lower than in any of the other three regions shown on the table.

Explain how this may be responsible for the higher average income and for the higher price of houses in London and Home Counties.   **(6 marks)**

(f) (i) Explain the term 'standard of living'. **(2 marks)**
    (ii) To what extent does this data permit us to compare the standards of living in the four regions shown? **(4 marks)**

Solution 20.1

(a) A loan used to buy a house is called a mortgage.
(b) Belfast has the highest percentage of the price lent to the buyer at 77 per cent.
(c) It is easier to buy a house in Belfast than in London because houses are almost £28 000 cheaper in Northern Ireland.

    While average annual income is lower in Belfast than in London, house prices are less than two times annual salaries in Belfast compared with over three times annual salaries in London.

    Potential house buyers need a much lower deposit in Belfast than in London and building societies are prepared to lend a higher percentage of the house price.
(d) The inclusion of data for the UK average allows a comparison of a particular region with the rest of the nation.
(e) Low unemployment suggests a large demand for workers in London and the home counties. If workers are in demand then incomes will tend to be higher than the national average.

    If an area has a large number of people in employment earning a good income then the demand for houses will be high. House prices will tend to rise. Since workers are earning a good wage they will be able to afford to pay more for their house.
(f) (i) The standard of living refers to the amount of goods and services consumed each year by the average household.
    (ii) The data do mention average income and prices and could be used to calculate the relative standard of living of house owners in the four regions.

    However, the information given in the data is limited. For example, the prices of other goods such as food are not mentioned. The data tell us nothing about the amount of leisure time people have or the amount of consumer durables they own. You could not use the information to give an accurate measure of the UK standard of living.

Example 20.2

Study the photograph on the next page of a traffic jam in the summer in central London.
(a) Give two reasons why the traffic in the photograph is at a standstill. **(2 marks)**
(b) State and explain two costs of the traffic jam met:

    (i) only by the private motorist; **(3 marks)**
    (ii) by society as a whole. **(3 marks)**

(c) Give an alternative type of transport which would have avoided the traffic jam for:

    (i) a holidaymaker on the way to Devon; **(1 mark)**
    (ii) a businessman on the way home from work. **(1 mark)**

(d) Why are the alternative methods of transport given in your answer to (c) not used more? **(4 marks)**

Solution 20.2

(a) The traffic in the photograph is at a standstill because the roads in a city are narrow and cannot cope with the flood of rush hour vehicles.

(b) (i) The private motorist uses a large amount of petrol while stuck in a traffic jam. The motorist is also wasting time which could have been used for work or leisure.

    (ii) Society is faced with an increase in the amount of noise and pollution caused by the jam. Each car is turning out toxic exhaust fumes into a confined space.

       Pedestrians and local residents have to breathe these fumes. Buildings become dirty from continued exposure to pollution.

(c) (i) A holidaymaker could have avoided the traffic jam by using a train to make the journey to Devon for his holiday.

    (ii) A businessman on his way home from work could have used the underground to avoid the traffic jam.

(d) Travellers are reluctant to use public transport systems because they are less convenient than using their own cars. Few travellers live close to a railway or underground station. Trains run to a fixed schedule which may not suit the individual needs of the passenger. There is a limited railway network which may not have a station near the destination of the traveller. Finally, travellers with heavy or bulky luggage find it inconvenient to travel by train.

Example 20.3

Study the table here which shows the percentage of men and women taking part in a particular leisure activity at least once a month.

Activity	Males	Females
Going out for a drink	64%	46%
DIY	51%	24%
Reading books	50%	61%
Keep fit	11%	5%
Squash	4%	1%
Spectating at a sports event	11%	5%

Source: Adapted from *Social Trends*, HMSO, 1986

(a) Which is the most popular leisure activity for (i) men and (ii) women?
    (2 marks)
(b) From the table, rank from most popular to least popular the leisure activities of women. **(2 marks)**
(c) Explain the term leisure activity. **(2 marks)**
(d) To what extent do the data permit us to compare the leisure activities of men and women? **(4 marks)**
(a) What are the total economic costs of reading a book? **(5 marks)**

Solution 20.3

(a) (i) Going out for a drink (64 per cent).
    (ii) Reading books (61 per cent).

(b) First, reading books, 61 per cent; second, going out for a drink, 46 per cent; third, DIY, 24 per cent; fourth equal, keep fit and spectating, 11 per cent; sixth, squash, 4 per cent.

(c) Leisure is the time when someone is not working, at school or doing housework. A leisure activity is a particular use made of leisure time, for example watching television.

(d) The data are incomplete and show only a small number of leisure activities. For example, pastimes such as needlework and watching television are not included.

    The data do not say how much leisure time men and women have. The majority of women still perform unpaid housework and this may involve working longer hours than those in work. Those women specialising in housework may have less leisure time than men in paid employment.

(e) There are two main sources for obtaining a book. If the book is bought from a bookseller then the cost of the book (less its second-hand value) must be included.

    If the book is borrowed from the library then some allowance must be made for the wear and tear on the book from one reading.

    Libraries are expensive to run. Part of the administrative costs of the library must be included in the calculation.

    It is also important to include some measure of the leisure time involved in reading. A worker could have spent an hour used reading a book to work overtime. The total cost of reading a book includes this lost overtime.

233

Example 20.4

Study this photograph of a hypermarket (a large self-service shop of 50 000 square feet or more) outside Caerphilly, Wales.

(a) Use the photograph to describe three economic features of the hypermarket.
   (3 marks)
(b) Why do some consumers drive miles to shop at a hypermarket?   **(3 marks)**
(c) What can consumers do if they find when they get home that a good they have bought from the hypermarket is faulty?   **(4 marks)**
(d) Explain briefly three types of insurance the hypermarket owner is likely to have.
   (6 marks)

Solution 20.4

(a) A hypermarket covers a large area and has its own car park and petrol station on the site. The hypermarket is on the edge of the town but the photograph shows the site has good road links.
(b) A hypermarket has an excellent choice of goods under one roof. Prices are very low. Many shoppers are prepared to drive miles to do a whole week's shopping under one roof. Parking is easy and usually free.
(c) The Sale of Goods Act states that goods sold must be undamaged. The Act states that a customer sold faulty goods is entitled to a replacement or a refund. Providing a consumer has kept the receipt, the hypermarket is obliged either to change the damaged item for a new one or to return the customer's money.
(d) The hypermarket owner is likely to have insured the buildings and contents against the risk of fire. If a fire occurs the insurance company will replace damaged goods and pay for the building to be repaired. The insurance

company will also pay the hypermarket's rates and rent while repairs are carried out.

By law, the hypermarket must have public-liability insurance. This means that if any member of the general public is injured while shopping then the hypermarket is able to meet any claim for damages from its insurance policy.

By law the hypermarket must have employers' liability insurance. This means the hypermarket is covered if any worker injures themselves while working for the company.

20.9 Questions

1 Why do councils provide rented accommodation?
2 A dispute over rent between a private landlord and a tenant is settled by ....
3 A loan given by a bank or building society to enable the purchase of a house is called ....
4 List three costs involved in moving house.
5 How does an estate agent earn his living?
6 List two fixed and two variable costs involved in renting a house.
7 Give two types of public transport.
8 Explain the difference between the standing and running costs involved in owning a car.
9 Third-party car insurance covers:
   A damage to the driver's car, only
   B damage to other people, only
   C damage to other people and their property, only
   D damage to the driver's car and other people
10 What is meant by the term indemnity?
11 What is the difference between national insurance and liability insurance?
12 What is the opportunity cost of leisure time?
13 A chain store is:
   A a unit shop
   B a shop containing many separate branches under one roof
   C a hypermarket
   D one of many branches owned by the same firm
14 State two reasons why firms advertise their products.
15 Explain the difference between informative and persuasive advertising.
16 Which organisation tests a variety of products and publishes its results in a monthly magazine called *Which?*
17 What is a personal budget?
18 An advertisement for credit includes the statement 'APR = 22 per cent'. What does this mean?
19 Until payment has been made in full, goods on hire purchase belong to ....

20.10 Answers

1 Council houses are homes provided by the local authority for people who cannot afford to buy their own property.
2 A government rent officer or the rent tribunal.
3 A mortgage.
4 See section 20.1(c).
5 By charging the seller of the house commission.
6 The fixed costs of renting a house must be paid out even if the house is vacant. These include rates, rent and insurance payments. The variable costs of renting a

house are only paid out when the house is occupied. These include electricity, gas and telephone bills.

7 Any two of trains, buses, and tubes.

8 See section 20.2(a).

9 C

10 Indemnity means being put back to the same financial position as before an accident.

11 National insurance is a compulsory scheme for all workers, run by the government which covers the risk of unemployment and provides a pension. Liability insurance is offered by insurance companies and is not always compulsory. Liability insurance gives cover for accidental damage to other people and their property.

12 See section 20.4.

13 D

14 Any two of: to increase sales; to increase profits; to create consumer loyalty; to create a brand image; to make demand for the good more price inelastic.

15 See section 20.5(b).

16 The Consumers' Association.

17 See section 20.7(a).

18 The annual interest rate is 22 per cent. For every pound borrowed you must pay 22 pence in interest each year.

19 The seller or the hire purchase company.

21 Coursework

21.1 Coursework Aims

Coursework refers to one or more pieces of original written work done by the student and makes up at least twenty per cent of the final mark for internal (school-based) students taking GCSE. Coursework is an excellent opportunity to show the examiner your enthusiasm and interest in the subject.

21.2 Choosing a Coursework Topic

Each examining board has its own approach to coursework. Some allow a completely free choice of assignment while others ask you to select from a fixed menu of topics. Make sure you have read any regulations and advice issued by your board. The address of each examining group can be found in the Acknowledgements section at the front of the book, on pages xi–xiii.

Make sure you involve your teacher when you choose and plan your assignment. Here are some points to think about yourself:

(i) Choose a topic which interests you and which allows you to demonstrate what you know, understand and can do.
(ii) Make a list of questions raised by the topic. Then select one key question about your topic.
(iii) Turn your question into a *hypotheses*, i.e. a statement that can be proved or disproved by your assignment. For example, the question 'Why are some workers paid more than others?' can be turned into various hypotheses for testing:

(1) Wages depend on qualifications.
(2) Wages are related to trade unions.
(3) Women earn less than men.

21.3 Collecting Information

Collect information about your topic which you can use to prove or disprove your hypothesis. There are methods you can use:

(i) Using *primary sources* involves doing your own interviews, surveys and questionnaires.
(ii) Using *secondary sources* involves looking at books, newspapers, magazines, government statistics, and maps.

21.4 Analysing Information

Analysis involves looking through the information you have collected and deciding its significance to your topic. You should use writing, graphs, diagrams and tables to present a well-thought-out argument.

Draw conclusions based on the information you have collected. In particular, your analysis should show whether the information collected supports your hypothesis or not.

21.5 Presenting Coursework

The final report should state what you set out to do, how you did it and what conclusions you have made. Your teacher will advise you on how to present each item of coursework. You might think about including:

(i) a front cover containing the following information as shown in Fig. 21.1;

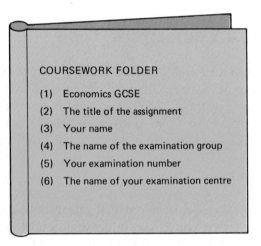

Figure 21.1 A coursework front cover

(ii) a contents page listing the title of each section, as for example in Fig. 21.2.

CONTENTS

Section	Page
Acknowledgements	1
Introduction	2
Methodology	3
1 Title	4
2 Title	6
3 Title	8
4 Title	11
Conclusion	12
Sources	13

— 1 —

Figure 21.2 A coursework contents page

Remember that the acknowledgements section should state the amount of help you have received from teachers, parents, and others in writing the assignment.

The introduction explains the aim and purpose of the assignment.

The section on methodology states the method you have used to write this item of coursework.

The section on sources gives a list of the books, articles, etc you have used in writing your assignment.

There is nothing to prevent you using tapes or video recordings as part or all of your finished assignment.

21.6 Good Practice

The examiner will be trying to give you marks for good practice. You should try to:
  (i) Be original and include primary data.
 (ii) Include carefully selected photographs and diagrams from magazines and newspapers.
(iii) Make sure your material is relevant.
 (iv) Present material in a logical manner.
  (v) Apply simple economic concepts such as scarcity and opportunity cost.
 (vi) Distinguish between well-thought-out arguments and mere statements of opinion.
(vii) Highlight key points.
(viii) Put material you are quoting in inverted commas, and give the source of your quote.
 (ix) Offer solutions to particular economic problems.
  (x) Explain how far your answer supports your hypothesis.

21.7 Bad Practice

The examiner will not be able to give you any marks for:
  (i) untidy and disorganised material;
 (ii) waffle and needless repetition of points;
(iii) vague and confused conclusions;
 (iv) statements of opinion;
  (v) copying out large passages from books, magazines, etc;
 (vi) scrapbook collections of irrelevant pictures from magazines and newspapers;
(vii) unlabelled diagrams;
(viii) exceeding the number of words allowed for each assignment.

Index

Ordinary shares 53
Organisation for Economic
    Co-operation and
    Development (OECD) 195
Organisation of Petroleum
    Exporting Countries (OPEC)
    195
Output method 108
Outputs 108
Overdraft 116
Over-manning 46, 98
Overtime ban 98, 102

Partnerships 49, 51–52
Payee 116
Pension funds 132
Pensions 91, 107
Perfect competition 41, 46
Petroleum revenue 141
Picketing 99, 101, 103
Piece rate 93
Planned economy 11
Population 15–21, 108, 220
    natural increase in 19–21, 221
Population pyramids 16, 22–23
Preference share 53
Premium 227
Price, equilibrium 78–80
Prices and incomes policy 163,
    156, 186–187
Primary sector 170
Primary sources 237
Principle of comparative
    advantage 192
Private costs 29, 35
Private limited companies 49
Private sector 12, 48
Privatisation 50, 56
Producer good 7–8, 197
Productivity 27, 102, 190, 211,
    220, 223
Profit 5, 136, 151
Prospectus 50–51
Protectionism 176, 192–194, 198
Public corporation 12, 50, 55
Public good 153, 158–159
Public limited companies 50
Public sector 48
Public sector borrowing
    requirement (PSBR) 143

Quotas 163, 176, 193–194, 199

Rates 141, 150–151
Rationalisation 41
Real national income 108
Real wages 88
Redundancy 44
Regional development grant 61
Regional policy 61, 156
Regional problem 57, 61, 69
Regional unemployment 168
Rent 5, 91, 226

Reserve assets 117
Resources 5
    allocation of 6, 11–12
Restrictive practices 98
Retail price index (RPI) 112,
    131, 136–137, 178, 184, 186,
    191
Retailing 54, 183, 234
Revision technique 2
Rights issue 131, 136–137
Running costs 227

Salaries 88
Savings 53, 105, 110
Scarcity 5, 9
Seasonal unemployment 168,
    171
Secondary sources 237
Securities 143
Securities and Investment Board
    (SIB) 131
Self-employment 91
Services 9
Share issues 130
Share prices, changes in 131
Shares 51, 138
    types of 131
Shortages 11
Single capacity 135
Slump 154
Social costs 29, 32, 35–36, 57,
    221
Social Security benefits 111
Social services 92
Sole trader 49, 51–52
Special drawing rights (SDR)
    195
Specialisation 27, 30
Speculator 131
Stag 131
Stages of production 40
Standard of living 25, 91,
    108–109, 111–112, 160, 170,
    188, 223, 231
Standing costs 227
Standing order 116, 121
Stock exchange 130–132, 134
Stock exchange automated
    quotation (SEAQ) 131
Stock exchange council 131
Stock value 94, 96
Stocks 52
Strikes 98, 101–103
Structural unemployment 168,
    174–175
Subsidies 74, 79, 108
Substitute 71, 77–78
Sunrise firms 192
Supply 72–73, 81, 86
    curve shifts 72, 77, 81
    factors influencing 72
    movement along 72, 84
Surpluses 200

Take-over 40, 45, 136
Tariffs 193
Taxation 23, 92–96, 105,
    141–143, 158–159, 180
    burden 145
    direct 142, 144, 152
    indirect 74, 108, 111, 142,
        144, 152
Technological
    unemployment 168
Tertiary sector 170
Time rate 93
Total cost 28, 34
Total revenue 29, 33–34
Trade cycle 155
Trade unions 97–103, 139
Trades Union Congress (TUC)
    98, 102
Trading bloc 202
Transfer payments 107, 110,
    158
Transport network 31, 39, 227, 232
Treasury 147
Treasury bills 143

Unearned incomes 107
Unemployment 103, 147, 149,
    154, 166–169, 231
    policies 168
    rate 171–172
    types of 168, 171–175
Unit cost 42–43
Unit trusts 132
Utility 71

Valued added tax (VAT) 82,
    108, 141, 144
Variable costs 28, 32, 34, 36,
    235
Velocity of circulation 182
Visible trade 204, 207, 209

Wage drift 89, 93
Wages 5, 88, 91, 98–99
Wages spiral 180
Wants 5
Wealth 87, 89–90, 94–95
Wealth distribution 89
Weight gaining industries 60
Weight losing industries 60, 62
Weightings 178–179, 184, 186
Withdrawals 105–106, 110
Work to rule 98, 102
Working population 166, 170,
    173
World Bank (IBRD) 195

Yield 136
Youth Training System (YTS)
    168, 174–175

242